ARCHETYPES OF THE OCCULT

Stephen James Wakefield

First Published 2021. Copyright S. J. Wakefield

To our own little holy trinity - Ralph, Edward & Edgar

CONTENTS

Title Page	2
Dedication	4
Foreword	8
MICROCOSM	12
I: Blood	14
II: Sex	70
III: Death	131
MACROCOSM	206
IV: Correspondences	208
V: Symbols	270
VI: Abyss	339
Bibliography	381
Books By This Author	388
Books By This Author	390

FOREWORD

There are Archetypes (those images and ideas, often linked to Jungian psychoanalysis, that are said to derive from a 'collective unconscious') and there are archetypes (images and ideas that serves as perfect examples of a given thing or are the original model of that thing from which all else are but variations of). The two are interlinked and are often seen as interchangeable, but they are nonetheless different notions, certainly when it comes to their application.

The concept of the 'archetypal' does bring us well within the sphere of Carl Jung, who will frequently be acknowledged in this work, but it also unites us with certain theories of Plato and, when it comes to unifying notions within philosophy, mythology, religion and occultism, a panoply of thinkers and practitioners from across the centuries.

Archetypes in this more general form are a useful tool for the human mind because they are singular and cohesive representations of emotions, events and entities; they allow us to comprehend and communicate on a given subject without having to account for every variation that may have arisen, as we refer and cogitate instead on its 'archetypal form'.

Not to rely on this might offer hope of a more insightful, nuanced understanding because we would only be considering the specific form in question – but this approach would be overwhelming and impossible to maintain, as we cannot afford such focus to every fundamental in our lives. Archetypes are the sum-total of a given thing, the golden mean by which individual reflections are perceived, experienced and considered, and they are central to our understandings in both esoteric and exoteric spheres. They also evoke instinctual responses, emotions and memories that would otherwise, likely, remain dormant.

For the sake of this study, the archetypes are those recurrent and ubiquitous elements of thought and faith as they apply to the various guises of all matters spiritual. We may not choose to consider them as emanating from a collective unconscious – we may not, in fact, even consider them as 'universal' – but they will be seen to result from fundamental responses to the human condition, regardless any specific creed, country or context.

On the microcosmic scale, that directly relating to human existence, we will consider the ideas connected to blood, sex and death, which equate to the cornerstones of gestation and birth as well as the state of being and its ultimate dissolution, which in turn raises questions of the nature of life and reality, the issue of duration and the subject of the soul or spirit, particularly in terms of any destination it may be leaving for as it departs the material, mundane level.

On the macrocosmic scale, that pertaining to any reality that is 'supernatural' or at least beyond the perception of mortal man or woman, we will look at correspondences (the links and patterns seen between diverse elements that are applied to heighten one's awareness and energies) and symbols (the somewhat more spiritual domain where images communicate to parts of the human being that are sub- or supra-conscious).

Finally, moving beyond the constraints of perception and known reality, we will reflect on the concept of and responses to the 'abyss', that which lies beyond the threshold, the domain of what we might term 'chaos', that great and often terrifying unknown.

It will be seen that many of the same themes and ideas recur when we consider these various forms of human thought and their communication; this might simply reflect a common frame of reference through which the world and the cosmos is experienced, but it is understandable why many have glimpsed a greater truth, and a single unity, between and betwixt these recurrent archetypes. True, such a belief cannot be empirically proven and appears to speak more of wishful thinking and faith than any provable 'reality', but in the realm of myth, faith and magic this is not the barrier to thought that it might prove to be elsewhere.

Such a truth and/or unity is an influential focus for thought, faith and creativity because it speaks to the imagination as well as to the deepest needs and fears of most, if not all, of us – and offers a degree of hope towards an overarching and profound meaning to existence that belies our day-to-day understanding. More than that, it offers a sense of belonging that we all share with one another and the cosmos, and the vision of some form of return to our source.

Even where this is all rejected, reflection on the archetypes of the occult, where they might derive from and how they impact on us – as well as the manifold, colourful responses to them – can tell us a great deal about ourselves, not least those aspects that we believe to exist and just occasionally feel to be active, but which remain compellingly out of our reach. Any truth we can learn from the archetypes is indeed priceless, because it is a truth which relates to who and what we are in the deepest and most profound sense, offering answers to the otherwise unanswerable questions that humanity has forever carried within itself.

MICROCOSM

I: BLOOD

Blood is life. There is little doubt that this is the case, given what we are without its precious, indeed life-giving properties. In fact, such a statement appears so factually obvious that we can read or hear it with very little thought, meaning that we rarely consider the wonder that blood is, or its true meaning to us, even when we are confronted with such a truism.

Blood supplies oxygen to the tissues of the body; it supplies nutrients and removes waste from our system; it regulates our temperature, where possible retards its own escape through coagulation and fights foreign matter, maintaining our health with tireless efforts that are hardly ever witnessed and rarely considered by the majority.

However, as with the fang of the hungry vampire on a willing victim's neck, we need only scratch the surface for blood's true import on us, our history, beliefs and existence itself to be recognised. Understandings of and relationships with blood therefore find expression in early art, mythology and ritual, just as they are the focus of certain magical pursuits, psychological analyses and scientific works, ensuring that both the reality and the symbolism of blood present us with a fascinating glimpse into the drives, hopes and fears of essentially all civilizations since the very earliest.

Of course, if we put ourselves in the place of a 'primitive' being some thousands of years ago who has not had his/her imagination stunted by the finer biological points, it is perfectly understandable how and why blood would take on such a mantle as to be something of a power in and of itself, likewise how blood might come to be used in rituals to speak to gods, enhance abilities and powers, or expose us to uncanny dangers. After all, if a man bleeds then he weakens, and if he loses a sufficient quantity then he expires – thus blood is by observation a vital essence, a house of the character and perhaps the soul. Blood *is* life.

Chronicles of Norwegian hunters drinking the blood of the bear or the East African Maasai imbibing that of the lion are far from shocking in this light, given that the vitality of the animal could be seen to reside in its blood and with that vitality something of each creature's especial qualities. A successful hunt would frequently be the difference between survival and death, therefore any attempt to ensure success by taking on the character of a beast renowned for its hunting abilities would be perfectly reasonable. Certainly, it could be seen to be foolish to reject such a powerful weapon in one's arsenal.

It might be more of a challenge for a modern Western mind to counter, but the same can be said when considering tribes such as the head-hunters of Sulawesi in Indonesia – and elsewhere – who would drink the blood and eat the brains of a victim in order to energise the body and make it stronger. Likewise, specific body parts might be consumed in order to grant singular abilities. It was known for these tribes to also mount heads as a form of prestige, and so here, too, the taking of life is acknowledged as a profound act, and the imbibing of another's 'essence' is a far from casual activity to undertake.

An important point is that any similar use of blood would result from a considerable respect for the life it represents, and the very beliefs in the potency of blood would result in a carefully observed ritual element to avoid any negative repercussions. The fact that certain groups such as the North American Indians would avoid tasting blood at all due to their belief that the soul of its bearer resides there adds further weight to this, suggesting that no such practise is undertaken lightly, and even where we encounter sacrifice in these environments it is performed with reverence for the life being expiated, and for the forces that are believed to be being tapped.

Even within the sacred and liminal space of ritual, wholly focussed on faith and religious observance and devoid of such primary needs as a successful hunt for nourishment, blood retains a prominent and singular place. This can be glimpsed in its use by the Aboriginal peoples of Central and Western Australia, whereupon the young might be anointed with the blood of those deemed to be wiser, blood might be daubed on individuals' bodies before the performance of sacred dances, or used as a solvent when attaching bird feathers to bodies.

Robert Lawlor (b.1938 C.E.) has sited that the latter usage of blood is due to the connection it is seen to make between the wearer of the blood-glued feathers and the Dreamtime, the very foundation of Aboriginal religion and law from which all knowledge emanates. As such, blood is charged with a power (both spiritually and biologically) that enhances perception, awakens the subconscious, and charges a ceremony and its participants. Blood is thus a thing of some magic, a catalyst for life and change that should only be tapped with due reverence.

With this in mind, it is no surprise that blood can also be seen to be a dangerous commodity, a potential bringer of ill-fortune and even death that has frequently been treated as taboo by various tribes and cultures. As already noted, American Indians would avoid tasting blood due to the life essence it contains, and they are far from the only group that would actively avoid contact due to the potential consequences that might be incurred.

Dark blood has perhaps most frequently been thought to be an unclean substance, as opposed to the bright red blood that would be seen as life-giving; for instance, there is a Chinese belief that dark blood would bring unhappiness and ill-health to any person that made contact with it. Given this and broader approaches to gender and spirituality, it is perhaps unsurprising that menstrual blood in particular has been feared by numerous peoples as a bringer of sadness, infirmity and decay.

At times women have been caged during menstruation to avoid their making contact with other people – though in some cultures avoiding the gaze of such a woman might be deemed sufficient, for others removing the threat entirely would be a more acceptable option. Again, this can be seen within certain Aboriginal tribes of Australia, where menstruating women would be barred from walking on paths or touching items that men might also use. Here blood is a contaminant, and must be untouched and ideally unseen at all costs.

The Golden Bough' of James Frazer (1854 – 1941 C.E.) notes several approaches to girls when they reach puberty, including that of the Tlingit or Kolosh Indians of Alaska, which saw the girl isolated in a small hut that had but one air-hole, for the duration of up to a year – further to this, she would be expected to wear a hat of such form that she would not offend the sun and pollute the sky, nor meet the gaze of another upon whom she would bestow ill-fortune. Frazer also notes the Guaranis of Southern Brazil who would sew the girl up in a form of hammock for two to three days where she would undergo a fast before a matron would release her, cut her hair and instruct a further fast from red meat until such time as her hair had grown long enough to cover her ears.

The blood of childbirth is still more of a danger, and we again find instances in the work of Frazer that highlight this – notably how certain South African tribes believed that should a stillborn baby be hidden to avert fear and mistrust, the place where the blood had settled would nonetheless become apparent as no rain would dare to fall, and the land would effectively be blighted. There was no hiding from the truth when blood was spilled.

and cruel-looking claws, and have eyes that continually weep blood. At other times they are noted as having wings, or appearing as intimidating huntresses carrying torches, sickles and scourges.

Their rage would be unmerciful, particularly in the case of one who had killed a parent – most notable when a son had committed matricide. Indeed, they were protectors of the bloodline that would haunt a wrong-doer until the cosmic scales had been balanced, which usually meant the drawing of further blood in the name of the fallen, and it is telling that a later name given to them, Eumenides, denoted goddesses of a more even and calm temperament so that the mention of the Erinyes would not invoke them in their hellish guise.

This later name ties into the story of Orestes, who killed his mother Clytemnestra after she had murdered his father. Orestes was pursued for over a year by the Erinyes, who would not be pacified by his attempts to make amends for his crime and cleanse his blood of the curse he had wrought upon himself. In desperation Orestes pleaded for protection in a temple of Apollo, and a resulting trial saw the gods vote against his punishment.

The Erinyes were incensed by this and threatened to shed blood upon the earth to make it barren and likewise make man sterile so as to kill off humanity – but they were eventually appeased through sacrifices that would be made to them at a sanctuary in Athens. The name Eumenides was thenceforth adopted, though this change in character perhaps speaks more of a patriarchal society binding the energies and maternal protection that the Erinyes embodied.

Sacrifice of blood was therefore a powerful tool for those who would seek to appease gods, spirits and other supernatural entities, though in some early rites it might be milk, wine or honey that was offered as a representation of blood. At other times only blood would suffice, such as in ancient Mesopotamia where an animal would be slain and then food and drink given to the gods to ensure their continued protection, or in the Homeric legend where Agamemnon was to sacrifice his daughter Iphigensia in order to win the favour of Artemis and grant victory to the Greeks in the Trojan War.

The sacrifice of entire households of staff and retainers is a well-known aspect of early Egyptian funerary practise that was also applied by the Mongols and Mesoamericans among others, with the intention of securing continued service in the afterlife and the maintaining of status in the eyes of the gods. On what is perhaps a more palatable scale, certain citizens of the Roman Empire would bury the remains of sacrificed dogs, horses and cattle alongside pots and other goods under properties and, later, a feast be enjoyed, to offer obeisance and seek protection for the home.

In all of these cases blood was an essential and 'activating' aspect of the ritual, energising the omnipresent channel between god and man and bringing the two closer together through the giving and taking of life, and more fundamentally through the blood that not only symbolised but gave and took that life.

Rituals frequently served the purpose of veneration, notably in the instance of Attis, consort of his mother Cybele who represented the cycle of nature and its fruits through his self-mutilation, death and re-birth. James Frazer stated that Emperor Claudius (10 B.C.E.- 54 C.E) introduced rituals for Attis into Rome, seeing a pine tree felled annually on 22nd March and taken to the sanctuary of Cybele, where it was bound as a corpse, wreathed in violets and treated as a god.

On the third day of such treatment, a high priest was said to draw blood from his arms and present them in offering, before lower-ranking priests followed his lead while dancing which ultimately led to a feverish state of ecstasy. Blood would be strewn about the altar and the tree, which Frazer took to show at once a state of mourning for Attis, and an offering of blood which would give him sufficient strength to achieve resurrection.

Also cited is a ceremony whereby an initiate would be baptised into the order and crowned with gold, before a descent into a small pit which was enclosed by a grating overhead. A bull, garlanded with flowers, would then be escorted to the grating and stabbed to death with a consecrated spear. By bathing in the blood of the animal the initiate was cleansed and purified, a re-birth of sorts taking place that would see the initiate met with awe and veneration by his cohort upon leaving the pit. A compelling image that for many would encapsulate the worst of the pagan excesses, it was most exhaustively described in poem form as an attack on pagan faith by the Christian Prudentius, around the 4th century C.E.

Nonetheless, this ceremony – commonly called the Taurobolium – certainly did occur to an extent as described with the aim of purifying an individual for a period of twenty years, and was developed from an earlier form (with the first known enactment dating to 134 C.E.) where a bull was sacrificed and its flesh shared by those present. It should be noted that the Taurobolium that the rites became were not exclusively the privilege of a male fellowship; regardless of gender or public standing, the purification by blood was a transformative experience that was open to all.

The reason that this rite gained the level of notoriety that it did is likely due to its serving as a symbol of paganism to both the last remaining pagans as they fought repression, and the Christian oppressors determined to stamp out such primitive beliefs and behaviours. Depending on the audience at hand it stood as a powerful statement of pagan faith that might unite in its wake, and a retrogressive abomination that had no place in the modern world of the later Roman Empire.

The development of faith is particularly striking here, as the earlier form of worship to Attis had already undergone change to better suit the mores of the Roman Empire, in that the sacrificed bull's testicles would be removed for a blessing ceremony where previously the priests of Attis would have followed their god's example and self-castrated – a step too far for the Romans, just as the sacrificial rites would later offend the Christians.

Blood could also be applied in numerous ways to gain supernatural vision, through all manner of divinatory practices. Certain Shamanic initiations involved purification through the blood of a goat (reminiscent of the Taurobolium), but the blood of a ram or a sheep could also be used for augury: grain would be scattered before the beast which was then cut, its blood then sprinkled on the grain; if the animal fed of the grain then the omens were good, while the grain being rejected suggested dire portents that must be contested with.

The Chinese thought of semen and the milk of mothers to be forms of blood, and believed that a woman's chastity could be tested by observation of her blood when placed in water. The chosen girl's cheek would be pricked and the resulting blood dropped into a container of water, where it would only show as red and mix with the latter liquid if the girl was indeed pure and chaste.

Sources depicting Celtic rites describe the ritual slaughter of animals and the eating of flesh so that a greater level of consciousness might be attained and potential revelations might be experienced in dreams, though it cannot be said that this was a common occurrence. It has also been recorded that certain Indian priests ritually tasted the blood from a slain goat's throat in order to establish a form of communion with Kali and gain visions of the future.

As we have seen, ancient Greece and Rome bear much more documented evidence of similar beliefs, such as that described by Pliny where a storm of what appeared to be blood rain was interpreted as a sign of great pestilence to come, and the temple of Apollo at Argos saw the monthly slaughter of a lamb so that a chosen woman might imbibe its blood and seek visions from the gods.

Plutarch (c. 46 – c.119 C.E.) listed many reasons that were had for the shedding of blood in the name of augury, including those who desired news on which force would be victorious in a battle, those who wished to know if it was fortuitous for them to make a certain journey or marry. All human needs were addressed, just as they were when a 'haruspex' priest browsed the entrails – particularly the liver – of a beast slain exactly for that purpose, but here as elsewhere there were also efforts to find a sign as to whether or not the sacrifice itself had been met with approval or disdain by the gods; the letting of blood was a serious business that could not be performed lightly or without just cause.

Still more dangerous was the application of blood in rites of necromancy, which in itself was frequently deemed to be an act of the darkest and least controllable magic. The most widely-read example of this is to be found in Homer's *'Odyssey'*, where the witch Circe instructs Odysseus to dig a pit that should be filled with offerings of honey, milk and sweet wine but also the blood of a male and female sheep that have been sacrificed, over which the shades, the restless souls of the dead, gather to enjoy a rare moment of vitality through which they can be seen and heard by the living.

Similar acts in a still more eldritch vein were described in the Roman figure of Erichto, a legendary witch most prominent in Lucan's *'Pharsalia'*. Here she is a grotesque figure who frequents places of death such as graveyards, sites of battle and places of execution. Her magic largely centres on the use of the bodies that she finds, and Lucan relished describing the revels of the witch as she drew eyeballs from dead sockets with her bare hand and ravages corpses as much for personal pleasure as for practical need.

When she is sought out by one Sextus Pompeius to discover the outcome of a battle she locates an ideal corpse, cleans its insides and fills the body with a potion of warm blood among other noxious ingredients, and successfully summons a spirit to animate the corpse and give word on the battle. Sextus Pompeius therefore achieves his desire and is given an answer, but it is appropriately enigmatic for knowledge obtained though the damned art of necromancy.

Erichto enjoyed something of an opportunity to redress the balance so badly set against her by Lucan when she later appeared in Goethe's *'Faust'*, but as a clear literary reflection of various fears, not least the wayward and despicable type of personality that would engage with blood and sacrifice in the name of magic, the earlier portrayal is perhaps the most informative.

Offerings

Given the variety of ways in which blood was appropriated within a ritual context, it is no surprise that it was believed to be especially effective where the favour of a god or gods was required. The aim may be to win favour and thus fecundity or good fortune, or the appeasing of deities who had already been aggrieved and therefore were inflicting hardships upon a chosen people – regardless the context and the focus of the ritual, blood was often a common ingredient as it was unrivalled in its sheer potency. Little else contained the inherent magical principle of life to such an extent, and nothing else captured the attention of a deity or otherworldly spirit so readily.

After all, it had long been noted that blood could quench thirst and re-energise the weak and starving (as any nourishment well might), just as it was seen to quench the thirst of the earth whenever blood was spilled upon it, given how the liquid would soon have disappeared into its depths. This, together with the awe and respect bestowed to blood through its life-containing essence, ensured that blood offerings (and, by extension, offerings of flesh and of life itself) were a fundamental aspect of faith across nations for thousands of years.

Glimpses of this perceived association between blood or sacrifice and the health of the earth and its fruits are manifold, not least in the myth of Osiris who died and was then resurrected in the form of earthly fecundity, notably as the sustaining waters of the Nile and as profuse crops of corn. Persephone experienced a similar 'descent' into the Underworld only to return to the living world annually with a gift of new life, and the growth of fresh crops.

Blood could connect man with his gods, in seeking wisdom, wealth, health or good fortune. It could entreat for a profitable hunt or war, just as it could seek to avert disaster by placating the gods or the spirits who were vengeful or malicious. It could also be used on a regular basis to ensure the ongoing means of a village, town or city, including the return of crops, the end of extreme weather and the banishing of illness. In short, blood was the key to an audience with the macrocosm, an almost universally-lauded substance vital to the work of shaman, priest and magician alike.

The use of outright sacrifice, then, can be seen as something of a foregone conclusion. There could be no 'creation' or any form of dramatic shift in being or environment without a catalyst, and it was usually held that the powers or spiritual energy being requested must be met with an offering that was of proportionate meaning or value – therefore a life would often be the sole means of redress.

Animal sacrifice was certainly a meaningful offering, as domestic animals were vital to the existence of tribes and cultures in terms of food as well as labour, while wild animals could serve as food and yet also be seen as profound and uncanny beings that would only be offered in sacrifice exactly because of their exalted status, a belief that can be seen in most of the major civilizations from ancient Egypt onward.

Animal remains have been found in large number at Egyptian burial sites, which is unsurprising given the level of domestication that they practised. Sheep and goats are notable examples, though at some sites the remains of somewhat more 'exotic' creatures like hippopotami suggest a ritual element in addition to daily work, farming and sustenance.

Herodotus (c.484 – c.425 B.C.E.) gives a later Greek insight into the animal sacrifices of Egypt, such as the ox's that would be offered to Epaphos (after a careful inspection by a priest who checked that the mouth and tongue of the beast were clean, the hairs of the tail grew appropriately and that 'no single black hair' grew anywhere on the body).

So chosen and approved, the throat of the animal would be cut and the head removed; the head would be taken to a market as it was deemed unsuitable for use, while the body would have its lower entrails removed, also the legs and the remaining part of the loin and neck. The cavity in the body would be filled with spices, loaves, honey and figs and then saturated in oil before the entire parcel of goods was burnt, while the onlookers prepared for a feast by beating themselves in mourning.

Thus the male ox was fit for sacrificing, though a penalty of death would befall one who offered a candidate that did not bear the seal of approval from the priest. Further to that, females of the species were sacrosanct and to be shown reverence as they were sacred to Isis, who was often depicted bearing the horns of the cow.

Herodotus notes that animal sacrifice in later Dynastic Egypt was largely restricted to domestic animals like sheep and cattle, an approach reflected in Europe at the close of the Copper

Age (at around 3000 B.C.E.) where again, the remains buried at sacred sites largely consisted of sheep, cattle and swine.

Herodotus also notes that the Scythians (nomads of possible Iranian origin who established a culture along the Pontic Steppe which stretches from the Black Sea to the Caspian Sea) likewise offered livestock, but that special ritual was connected to the slaying of a horse – a practise that may extend to parts of Europe in the Iron Age, if findings are thus interpreted.

Like the ox of the Egyptians, the purity of the animal to be sacrificed was of immense importance to the ancient Greek. We have already noted the usual proceedings in this form of ritual, where the beast was paraded garlanded with flowers and the like before its throat was slit at the altar and the blood was collected. Various animals might be employed depending on the deity in question or simply the circumstances of the gathered worshippers, but they usually consisted of livestock. Sheep were the most frequent recipient of the honour that was sacrifice, but bulls, cows, goats, pigs and even poultry could be utilised.

A similar approach was exercised by the ancient Romans, likewise similar animals chosen. Again as with the Greeks, an important aspect of the ritual was that the creature was heralded and well-treated as the sacrifice approached, as it was necessary to offer a willing, if not happy, victim. The ritual was therefore a peaceful one, where the calmness of the animal – even at the point of slaughter – was prized and seen as an effective offering to the gods.

Associations between the deity and its chosen offering were notable here; where underworld figures were the aim of veneration or plea, a dark and often fecund (pregnant) animal would be used in order to instil energy and life in the realm of death. Conversely, the glorious white realm of the outer heaven would demand the sacrifice of a white beast, such as a cow – and ideally one that was infertile.

The festivals including an animal sacrifice were numerous, though one of the most widely-sited is the 'October Horse' which saw offerings to Mars annually on October 15th, as military and farming activities drew to an end for another year. This particular event took place during a horse-racing meet; indeed, it was the right-hand horse of the winning chariot that was ultimately driven through with a spear, its head (with a competition between groups to win the favour of displaying it) and tail (taken to the 'Regia' or 'Royal house' where it consecrated the sacred hearth) both being removed.

Other festivals included the 'Hecatombe' (of Greek origin, under the auspices of Apollo) where a hundred oxen would be slain; 'Ambervalia' where an ox, a pig and sheep were lead across the land before slaughter in order to ensure protection and profundity of the crops; 'Lupercalia' which saw a goat or a dog sacrificed and skinned, before youths wore the skin as a girdle and lashed any young women they met, either to encourage fertility or offer obeisance to an unknown wolf deity.

Crops would also flourish following the 'Thesmorphia' which was celebrated only by women, who prepared for it by abstaining from sex for nine days before the ritual commenced. Swine would be thrown into pits believed to contain poisonous snakes, then their flesh reclaimed some three days later by 'antlerai' or 'Drawers' and placed on the sacred altar. To appropriate some of this flesh and sow it with new seed would result in an abundance of one's crops by the time of the next harvest.

Women, too, were the celebrants at the 'Orgia' or 'Bacchanalia' which was the night-revel in the name of Bacchus by his female followers. During the ceremony a bull was torn apart by the women, and its raw flesh devoured as a sign of obeisance and dedication to the god of the vine, vegetation, fertility, and madness.

Some of these rituals may appear to draw us some way from the study of blood in ritual, though of course blood was a component even where it was the offering of the life and/or the body of the deceased that was believed to be the focus of any divine response. Blood was a central aspect in many of these assorted rites, and was used as a catalyst for the heightening in emotion – and, as with the 'Bacchanalia' mounting ecstasy – of the congregation, as well as in establishing an active link between those present and their god through the unique qualities that blood contained.

This is perhaps more apparent in the associated rites of 'Blót' or 'blood sacrifice' that were common within Norse Paganism and later Germanic religions which focussed on gods, various spirits and even ancestors, and exclusively offered blood, both of animals and prisoners-of-war, to those entities as a form of worship and as a means to vitalise those taking part.

Blóts were not restricted to seasonal events, but the more notable of them were linked to the cyclical changes of nature. The year was divided between Winter, which began at the middle or end of October, and Summer, which began at the middle or end of April, but Blóts marked an 'autumn sacrifice' ('Haust Blót') as well as the height of Summer ('Sigrblót') and Winter ('Yule'). Various lesser festivals took place for the home and local townships that were specific to the region and the people involved.

The usual ritual saw a sacrifice take place, after which the meat of the offering was butchered and cooked while some of the blood was ceremonially sprinkled on the statues of gods (similar to the rites of the ancient Mesopotamians), on the interior and exterior walls of buildings and on those who had gathered for this event, as well as for the subsequent drinking of mead that was met with a blessing. These events could take place in all manner of 'Ve' or 'sacred spaces', including an indoor or outdoor 'Hörgr' (altar) or a 'Lund' (grove).

Horses were a particular staple of the recorded Blóts, including the 'Völsi Blót' which saw the penis of a stallion cut from the animal during the Autumn and then housed in a coffin with linen and leeks by the lady of the house, who would later retrieve it and pass it to those who had gathered at her home. A prayer would be offered as each person held the member, and with that the plea that the sacrifice be accepted and welcomed. Swine were also a common choice, though accounts describe the use of dogs, hens and cattle in other rites.

To modern eyes, human sacrifice appears to be of an altogether more serious nature than the offering of a cow, a hen or a horse, and it is true that in some circumstances the blood of a man, woman or child may have been chosen in order to prove a level of need or dedication, or to create a more powerful magical impact. However, to believe that a human life was offered only when animals were seen to have failed or to fall short in terms of importance is to both underestimate the reverence afforded to many animals, and overestimate the worth that might be placed on human life!

There is evidence suggesting that human sacrifice dates back to the prehistory of Neolithic man, though such evidence is hardly extensive, and so remains open to interpretation. The Mesopotamians and Egyptians certainly did offer human lives, though as we have already seen this largely took the form of 'retainer sacrifices' where the staff of important households were slain – likely by poison to ensure that ever-important calm and apparent willingness – alongside the remains of their master or mistress, for future service.

Human sacrifice in China pre-dates 2000 B.C.E. and again suggests the ubiquitous desires for protection (80 skulls of teenage girls found buried beneath the eastern wall of the fortress city of Shimao) and service in afterlife (with servants and concubines regularly slain following the death of a notable male). Efforts to stop such practices by the likes of Ximen Bao of Wei (445 – 396 B.C.E.) and Duke Xian of Qin (381 – 338 B.C.E.) were turning points in Chinese culture, but were not wholly successful.

Child sacrifice was a popular pastime of the Phoenicians and Carthaginians, or so writers including Philo, Tertullian and Plutarch would have us believe. Where Plutarch offered a degree of kindness by noting that the children so offered were already dead by the time of the rituals, Diodorus Siculus (91 B.C.E. – c.30 B.C.E.) described a statue of Cronos that was purposefully cast so as to drop live children from his arms and into a ceremonial fire.

The Old Testament paints a similarly gruesome picture in its attack on the followers of Moloch, such as in Jeremiah 32:35: 'And they built the high places of Baal, which are in the valley of the son of Hinnom, to cause their sons and their daughters to pass through the fire unto Molech which I commanded them not, neither came it into my mind, that they should do this abomination, to cause Judah to sin.' The problem had in accepting these accounts is that the Greek, Roman and early Christian writers were not unbiased where peoples like the Phoenicians were concerned therefore we can only look to archaeological evidence which fails to substantiate or deny the accusations.

This is equally true of the dramatic and horrifying images painted by Diadorus, Strabo and Caesar in describing the Druids who, they said, exercised the rite of human sacrifice on a huge scale. Slaves would be thrown onto the funeral pyres of their master, while pagan gods demanded sacrifice via hanging, beating, drowning or immolation, and the singular construct of the Wicker Man claimed the lives of many living souls at once through ritual fire. As W. Winwood Reade notes in his *'Mysteries of the Druids'* (1861): 'From these same blood-thirsty Phoenicians who had taught the Israelites to sin, the Druids learnt to pollute their altars with human blood, and to assert that nothing was so pleasing to God as the murder of a man.'

A criminal, a prisoner or just possibly a martyr would be

decked in oak leaves and led to a sacred space, where he would sing the 'Song of Death'; the assembled bards would chant as the priest stabbed his victim in the back. Reade continues: 'With mournful music on his (the victim's) lips he would fall weltering in blood, and in the throes of death. The diviners would draw round, and would calmly augur from his struggles. After which, fresh oak-leaves would be cast upon the blood-polluted altar, and a death feast would be held near the corpse of the sacrificed.'

Similar rites did exist, but in exactly what form and on what scale cannot be adjudged today. As is so often the case when considering subsumed faiths, we have been left with the colourful accounts of outsiders, rather than evidence direct from the source. Ignorance and fear therefore fuel great distortions of truth as well as outright lies, just as propaganda neatly exposes the horrors of the 'primitive' culture that has been overwhelmed and liberated from its evils by those of a higher and more civilized nature. The truth is somewhere within the records, at least in part, but we cannot make any sound conclusions on the basis of Caesar, or W. Winwood Reade.

This being acknowledged, the archaeological evidence does indicate child sacrifice within Phoenician culture, but only on a scale comparable to the likes of the early Minoans at Knossos, where the bones of apparently butchered youths were unearthed. The latter remains suggest a potential link between ritual and the mythical Minotaur, to whom seven young men and seven maidens were sent every one, seven or nine years; selected by lot, the fourteen offerings would enter the labyrinth – the lair of the Minotaur – unarmed and meet their fate either by being lost in the maze and wasting away, or by being consumed by the half-man, half-bull as he searched his chthonic bailiwick.

Much of the extant evidence for human sacrifice within Greek culture is to be found in the realm of myth and legend, and it is interesting to note examples that may well chronicle in symbolic form the gradual abandonment of such practices – for instance, Tantalus is said to have been condemned to Tartarus (prison of the Titans and place of torment) due to the sacrifice he made of his son Pelops, while the life of Iphigeneia was saved when Artemis swapped her form for that of a deer that could be sacrificed in her place.

The Romans, too, were keen to explain any incident of human sacrifice as a relic of a more barbaric past – a necessary point to make when so much time was spent attacking other cultures for the evils perpetrated in the name of faith. It was often cited that with Roman civility had come the adoption of symbolism within rites, so that where human life might once have been offered there were later offerings of straw figures or puppets.

This development was reflected somewhat in the use of the term 'sacrificium', which became increasingly associated with the Christian Eucharist as opposed to actual blood offerings. The ritual taking of a life became something of a taboo in Roman culture, more the stuff of primitives and the basest of magic than any form of genuine worship.

The Romans, however, did actively engage in and somewhat revel in vivisepulture, and felt able to practise this without hypocrisy because in their eyes such events did not constitute a ritual sacrifice. As such, Vestal Virgins who were believed to be impure could be buried alive, so too genetic oddities like hermaphrodites, as well as offerings made when the protection of the gods was required at times of threat from war.

Pliny stated that human sacrifice was outlawed in 97 B.C.E. and other writers stringently defended Romans against the act well before that date, but where there was seen to be the justification for a clean offering, the citizens usually found a means to enact a suitable ritual and dispatch a necessary victim.

Away from the Mediterranean, the Guanches who were early inhabitants of the Canary Islands off the coast of North Africa were known to throw youths from the cliffs of Tenerife, and other remains have been found that suggest other forms of ritual slaughter, while the Vikings were known to run their ships over prisoners to stain and anoint the ship with their blood so as to pay homage to the gods of the sea. It seems that the youth and purity of children was a particular boon where a sacrifice was required, just as the relative insignificance of the life of a prisoner or enemy was a useful tool when a blessing was needed.

The aforementioned Blóts of the Germanic peoples gradually lessened in their appeal, but as late as 1087 C.E. a nine-day festival was held in the vicinity of Uppsala in Sweden where, it was said, nine males of all species including human men were sacrificed and their remains hung in a sacred grove. Within India, too, the utility of human sacrifice was being justified as late as the 11th century, where country or peace was in peril – and the practise was found to be sufficiently efficacious on a more local level for such sacrifices to be not infrequent occurrences throughout the Middle Ages.

Indeed, lives were claimed in rites for the likes of Shakti and Kali well into the 19th century alongside more symbolic offerings; such 'pagan' rites were difficult to eradicate given how long they had been exercised, the profound links that the rites had with generations of stories, myths and beliefs – and the continuing reverence that the substance of blood and, with it, life and spirit engendered.

In the United States of America, the people of the 'Mississipian Culture' of 800 – 1600 C.E. are believed to have practised human sacrifice in the form of the familiar 'retainer' sacrifices where servants and slaves would be killed to join their owner in the grave. Mass burials have been found which certainly suggest this, including men, women and children that were slaughtered in various ways such as strangulation (before careful arrangement of the bodies) and through violent attack, which did not occur without signs of struggle (before the bodies were effectively strewn randomly into the tomb). It is possible that still others were not quite deceased when they were interred.

The Natchez, the last such Mississipian culture, continued to practise such human sacrifice into the 18th century, with similar retainer burials alongside the bodies of rulers and those of noble standing, though these rites were usually performed with great solemnity and dignity befitting the likes of the 'Chief', and great reverence was afforded to those that would be laying down their lives to join him in the grave.

Of course, no account of ritual human sacrifice is complete without mention of the Pre-Columbian faiths of the Americas, as no known culture anywhere else in the world has heralded blood and sacrifice with the same degree of honour as that known to the likes of the Aztecs and the Incas.

For these peoples, blood represented wholly understandable (and familiar) concepts, such as brotherhood and kinship, as well as the bloodline that might be corrupted, cursed or afforded with regal qualities. Blood was in some schemas the stuff of creation (with the gods of the Maya mixing their blood with maize and making a paste that ultimately gave form to man) and it was a powerful token, in reality and symbolism, as the life-force.

The depictions of ritual in this part of the globe frequently focus on what appears to be an obsession with blood and the taking of life, though this undermines the religions that were at the heart of all ritual operations. However starkly these rites compare with the mores of the 21st century, they (like many others we have noted in this study) were an integral part of religion and therefore with everyday as well as extraordinary events, exactly because of the profound respect that was given to 'life' and the blood that gave such life.

This largely relates to the aforementioned creation story,

which instilled within these cultures a sense of 'blood-debt' that must be paid to the gods who had given of themselves to form man. The Mayan *'Popol Vuh'* or *'Council Book'* tells of the gods extinguishing several races of men who failed to sufficiently honour them with prayer and blood offerings, which more than adequately underlines the importance of blood in the maintaining of cosmic equilibrium and ensuring not just the favour of the gods, but the very survival of life as it was known.

Bloodletting was therefore a common ritual act throughout Mesoamerica, from pieces of obsidian or bone that were used to cut the skin, likewise the use of the serrated barbs of a stingray or the spines of the Maguey plant, to prisoners being exsanguinated so that their blood could be used in sacred temples, to tools being placed with bodies during funerary rites. Blood was vital to the beating heart that was the city and its people, just as crucial on a broader and symbolic scale as it was to the individual's own body.

Autosacrifice, essentially the letting of one's own blood, was exceedingly common, and the Aztecs linked this rite with sacrifice in the story of Quetzalcoatl the feathered serpent god who stole bones from the Underworld and cast blood drawn from his penis in order to generate a new race of men. Mayan men would follow suit and draw blood from their penis, while the women would usually draw it from their ear or their tongue. Dropped onto paper that was then burned, the act of veneration and thanks would drift up as smoke to departed ancestors.

Slaves and children might be purchased specifically so that they could be offered as sacrificial victims, but they were so slaughtered because the gods demanded it – and it was believed that the victim of sacrifice automatically passed to an afterlife exactly due to the nature of their demise. Sacrifice was not a punishment, it was in many ways an honour, a necessary act that bestowed worth to the life given and helped to maintain payment of the debt owed to the gods, if not going so far as to save the world from destruction at their vengeful hands.

One of the best-known examples of the use of sacrifice is the 'ballgame' which was an ancient and widespread pursuit that took place across Pre-Hispanic Mexico and Central America for thousands of years. Usually played with a rubber ball, the games took place in a 'ballcourt' (effectively an alley between buildings) and consisted of two opposing teams made up of two or three players.

The rules varied (including one form of the game that saw the players use something akin to hockey sticks and a smaller ball) but the usual form of the ballgame saw the players strike the ball with their upper arms and thighs with points scored if set markers at either end of the court were reached. The meaning and interpretation of the game varied too, as the ballgame could be played for recreation, while also serving as a symbolic representation of the cosmos, as the re-enactment of a battle or as that of the passage from life, to death, to rebirth.

Sacrifice was not included in every form of the game, but where it was celebrated it could see prisoners-of-war bound in such a way as to actually be the ball that was played with, or the victors decapitating their less-fortunate opponents before adding the skulls, as trophies, to specially-constructed racks that sat next to the 'ballcourt'. Where the game was a means to resolve a dispute between cities – a manner of avoiding outright war – the losing team/city's ruler would be beheaded to mark a suitable conclusion.

Among other rituals of sacrifice, the Aztecs most frequently made human offerings at 'Veintena' or agricultural festivals, such as when the heart of a victim was removed with the use of a flint before the body was flayed. Indeed, flayed skin was a powerful ritual tool that might be worn by someone impersonating 'Xipe Totec' ('Our Lord the Flayed One'), such as when a woman had her skin removed during a harvest rite and then donned by another who became as the ripening crop of corn – as the old skin disintegrated, the new life was seen to emerge from within. Warriors, too, might wear the skin of their defeated opponents for up to twenty days before casting it away, making tours, collecting moneys and performing mock battles all the while.

There is no debate that the Pre-Columbian cultures engaged in blood and human sacrifice given all of this information, but there remains doubt as to the extent of the described acts. Estimates relating to the Aztecs, perhaps the most active in this area, range from 20,000 a year to 250,000 a year, while elsewhere it is suggested that at one event alone, a re-consecration of the Great Pyramid in Tenochtitlan, some 80,400 prisoners were slaughtered.

The truth is unlikely to be revealed, not least due to the limited archaeological data and the atypical commentaries that spoke about the Aztecs, Incas and Mayans by those who 'discovered' the lands in the 15th and 16th centuries rather than texts detailing the beliefs and psychology of the peoples from within those civilizations. However, the centrality of such rites was rarely so prominent as in Mesoamerica, where the *'Popol Vuh'* made clear its value, its power and potency at all levels of creation: "Sacrifice yet again, even do it to yourselves! Let's see it! At heart, that's the dance we really want from you," the lords said now.'

Such concepts would be anathema to the 'civilised' religions like Christianity and Judaism, though even in the 16th and 17th centuries there were still occasional animal offerings made in the name of various Saints, for example with the ritual slaughter of oxen for St. Benyo at Gwynedd, Wales, in 1589. Even today, some rural communities as can be found in Greece, Armenia and elsewhere offer animal sacrifices within Christian ritual, though admittedly these groups are somewhat aloof from the orthodox faith and are not regarded positively by others within the Church.

The predominant understanding of blood sacrifice, though, resulted from clear messages within Scripture, not least Leviticus 17:11: 'For the life of the flesh is in the blood: and I have given it you upon the altar to make an atonement for your souls: for it is the blood that maketh an atonement for the soul.' Blood was still life, just as it was still seen to contain something of the psychic self of the bearer, and sacrifice was fundamental to salvation and one's relationship with God – but individual sacrifice would become of an increasingly symbolic nature, once the Son of God had laid down his own life for the sake of humanity.

For some Christians, illness or acts of penance would come to be interpreted as a form of sacrifice that united them with Christ on a more profound level, a point which is apparent when we consider the number of martyrs and Saints that followed in his footsteps and suffered for their Lord. Blood itself, however, was something of a taboo even by the time of Christ due to the numerous Scriptural warnings against its use, such as in Genesis 9:4 where Noah and his sons are stopped from eating meat with blood still in it.

Similar messages are also given in Leviticus and in the New Testament, for instance Acts 15:20: 'But that we write unto them, that they abstain from pollutions of idols, and from fornication, and from things strangled, and from blood' – an ordination that would underpin the majority of Jehovah's Witnesses in their rejection of blood transfusions, even where such a procedure would be potentially life-saving.

Ritual sacrifice had all-but ceased among the Jewish tribes since the destruction of the Second Temple in 70 C.E., and came to be seen as a pagan mode of worship that had been surpassed (by the majority, at least). Blood needed to be purged from meats before consumption, and covered after the slaughter of an animal exactly because the blood contained something of the soul within it; to cleanse the meat of blood was therefore necessary, not for the benefit of the animal but for the man or woman who might be overcome with animal passions if unclean meat was tasted.

In addition to representing atavistic and backward beliefs, blood also became associated with magic and sorcery as in 2 Chronicles 33:6: 'And he caused his children to pass through the fire in the valley of the son of Hinnom: also he observed times, and used enchantments, and used witchcraft, and dealt with a familiar spirit, and with wizards: he wrought much evil in the sight of the Lord, to provoke him to anger.'

It was believed that evil spirits were attracted by freshly-spilled blood, and it is noted in Exodus and Leviticus that incense should be burnt to cleanse the air and drive those malefic entities from the scene of ritual, even at a point in time where sacrifice was an act that might be ordained by God himself.

Of course, after the death and resurrection of Christ, the God of the New Testament held much more stringent views on bloodletting and burnt offerings, but even in the Old Testament (notably the Pentateuch that forms the Jewish Torah) we find the example of Abraham preparing to offer up his son as a sacrifice, only for an angel to proffer a ram that could be used in his stead.

That story may be another example whereby older forms of practise (human sacrifice) are remembered as having given way to a more acceptable means of veneration (animal sacrifice), but the move away from physical offerings rapidly progressed from this point on and the utilisation of blood rites was seen to be diametrically opposed to the tenets of the Christian faith – the stuff of devil-worship and black magic.

It is interesting, however, that even today the diversity of the faith allows for contrary views on blood, and where the Protestant will sip the wine of the Eucharist and experience Christ symbolically and as a spiritual presence, the Roman Catholics, those of the Eastern Orthodox tradition and others taste the actual blood of Christ, transformed from the wine through the Eucharistic rites. Christ is in these circumstances a physical presence as well as a spiritual one, an immediate and energising force that is not dissimilar in nature to those tapped in the much earlier rites that we have seen in ancient civilizations.

Consumption of blood is certainly prohibited in Islam, with the Qu'ran stating: 'Forbidden to you are: dead meat, blood, the flesh of swine, and that on which has been invoked the name of other than Allah' (sura Al-Ma'ida 5:3). Blood in general is unclean, and so – as we have seen in various other cultures – the shedding of blood through menstruation or childbirth necessitates ritual cleansing, and the slaughter of animals for food is carried out in such a way that the carcass is exsanguinated before the meat is touched.

For Muslims, though, animal sacrifice is an acceptable practise. Eid al-Adha or 'Festival of Sacrifice' sees Muslims make a sacrifice as Ibrahim/Abraham once did, before dividing the meat of the animal (cow, sheep, goat or camel) into three parts – one for he who has performed the sacrifice, one for that man's relatives, and one for the poor. This act is part of the annual Hajj (pilgrimage), and those who are not actively travelling perform a simplified version of the sacrifice to observe the ancient custom.

Estimates for how many animals are slaughtered on an annual basis are varied, not least as they are affected by broader economic circumstances, but it is said that nearly a million animals are taken from Saudi Arabia for the Hajj sacrifice in Mecca alone. The Qu'ran makes clear, however, that the offering being made is not one of blood, but of remembrance of Ibrahim and reverence for Allah: 'It is neither their meat nor their blood that reaches Allah. It is your piety that reaches Him.' (22:37)

It is also the sacrifice and not the blood that is relevant in the 'aqiqa' ritual which ideally takes place during the first week of a child's life. Two goats are ritually slaughtered and their meat is distributed among the poor, but the act of sacrifice is believed to unite the child with the faith of Islam and protect it from evil in the process.

Far more restrictive to any taking of life are the likes of Buddhism, some Hindu castes and Jainism, where non-violence is the code and all forms of meat offerings and sacrifice are forbidden. This is not the case with other forms of Hindu such as Shaktism, which utilises texts like the *'Devi Mahatmya'* and *'Kalika Purana'* in a faith that worships various forms of the Devi (Goddess) including Durga, Lakshmi and Kali.

Rural sacrifices are a common act among rural villages, with goats and other animals decapitated and the blood offered to the Goddess by being smeared around the vicinity of the temple. Likewise goats, fowl or other native creatures like water buffalo are slaughtered in the name of the Goddess in parts of Nepal and Assam – but elsewhere these practices have either been banned (as with the Nepalese Gadhimai festival that saw huge numbers of annual sacrifices before prohibition in 2005) or ritualised symbolically so as to avoid the taking of a life. Vegetable or sweet dishes can now be served to Kali as an appropriate substitute for a slain goat.

The Dharmic religions have therefore not fully extricated animal sacrifice from their practices, likely due to the gravity, immediacy and energy that blood rites continue to offer. For all the global and cultural changes experienced across the last thousands of years, the shedding of blood as a purifier of evil or disease, as the mark of a male's coming of age or as the highest form of offering for a god – or goddess – that either spilled their own blood to give peoples existence, or shed the blood of others to protect those peoples, retains an intense religious appeal that is not easily discarded or replaced.

Even today, blood speaks of existence on a cosmic level, the life of the individual, one's link with the past and one's nature, character and very soul. Its importance in a biological sense has hardly diminished, thus it would be difficult to see its symbolic meaning reduced following such a history of contemplation and worship. On a ritual level blood connects us with the macrocosm and the gods just as it connects us with our brother and sister, and such an innate connection cannot easily be disregarded in spite of our loftiest rationalisations and mores.

Bloodlust

Despite multifarious variations and many nuances dependent on place and time, the throughline that saw blood rites descend from the heart of myth, worldview and faith into the darker and more sinister veins of religious and mystical practise is nonetheless clear. The worship of blood and its use in ritual became inextricably linked with the dark arts, with magic, madness and depravity – an outdated and shameful mode of worship that could only be the domain of the 'other', the wayward souls and the outcasts.

In turn, the blood rites that these malefic figures practised were believed to work because the blood attracted the spirits and entities that craved life the most – denizens of the underworld or the dense woodland that had never known true existence, and spirits, monsters and demons that yearned for the death and destruction that blood represented. Nightmares fuelled folklore that fuelled nightmare in return, and a bizarre cornucopia of blood-suckers was born.

Thus stories spread telling of the Greek Lamias that entranced with beauty before revealing the grotesque truth to a terrified male victim and draining him of life, if they were not occupied eating children. The Lamias descended from a Libyan queen that was dedicated to endlessly avenge the death of her children at the hands of the goddess Hera, and would also strike terror as the 'empusas' or 'children of Hecate' that would kill a man after entrancing him with their unearthly wiles.

The 'striges' or 'screech owls' of Rome were believed to descend on children at night, tearing them apart so as to imbibe their blood. Their origins lie with the dreaded Harpies of Greek lore that had originally served symbolically as pestilential winds but now bore the face of a woman and the body of a fierce bird with oversized claws. As Virgil (70 – 19 B.C.E.) put it: 'Bird-bodied, girl-faced things they are; abominable their droppings, their hands are talons, their faces haggard with hunger insatiable.'

In Europe we find stories of the 'baobhan sith' of Scotland that would, like the creatures just noted, beguile a man with a beautiful and familiar form as a prelude to drinking dry his body and soul, while even fairies would suck the blood of cows while their owners slept or, worse still, the blood of humans if water was not left out for them overnight.

These figures and many more besides, including the aforementioned Erinyes, largely echoed the stories of Lilith, Adam's first wife, the 'terror by night' of Psalm 91. Lilith copulated with demons after being rejected by her husband, and she and her offspring revelled in blood-lust thereafter, seducing and exsanguinating men or claiming the lives and the life-blood of newborn babies and their mothers. Lilith had been created of mud and filth and yet had the impertinence to demand equality with Adam, therefore her debauchery, crimes and eternal evil were hardly surprising within the frame of reference of successive patriarchal cultures.

We have written accounts of the vampire and the werewolf elsewhere (*Black Arts: Journeys on the Left-Hand Path*), but the fears and repressions that they represented – the wild and untamed, the liberated being in a state of abandon, desire, animal lust and raw sexuality – are intrinsic to the wider schema of folklore and legend that built around the letting, consumption and use of blood. In a context whereupon sacrifice was a pagan act and the offering of blood a clarion call to the Devil and his ilk, all that had gone before was suppressed and bound together into stories of supernatural horrors and humanity at its most depraved.

Given the popularity of the fairer sex in these stories, as those more likely to be corrupted, or those with malice or evil at their heart, the close ties between blood and the developed witchcraft of the 16th and 17th centuries is hardly surprising, but the numerous ways in which the application of blood highlighted their inhumanity is striking.

It was said that blood would be fed to the familiar of a witch as an incitement to act before it was sent on one of its nasty errands. Among many examples is the 1566 trial of Agnes Waterhouse, where it was said that she 'gave him (a drop of her blood) at all times when he did anything for her, by pricking her hand or face and putting the blood to his mouth, which he sucked.'

The sexual component of such an act was also frequently apparent, whether as a reflection of the witch's perversion or – more likely – the knowledge that, in confession, something titillating would be more readily accepted and the torture just might cease. The latter was potentially the case with the account given by Ann Asher in Suffolk, England, in 1645: '…she felt a thing like a small cat come over her legs once or twice, and that it scratched her mightily. After that she felt two things like butterflies in her secret parts, with itchings, dancings, and sucking.'

Pacts with the Devil tended to be signed in blood, no doubt harking back to the most atavistic belief of sympathetic magic in that by giving another party a sample of one's blood, a permanent connection was established, and the fate of the blood reflected the fate of the signatory. The idea and mention of pacts became increasingly popular through the centuries of the 'witch craze' and were seen to have a foundation in Isaiah 28:15: 'We have entered into a league with death; we have made a covenant with hell.'

Such a pact, and the willingness of a witch to submit to and work with demons, was the fundamental sin that many accusations and trials focused on – after all, a curse may be belittled as nonsense or simply not succeed due to all manner of trivialities, but the crime of heresy had already been committed with the intent to harm, and the act of turning away from God.

Witches' grease, the substance that would be smeared about the body so that a witch could magically make the journey to the Sabbat through transvection or some form of bodily metamorphosis, contained numerous distasteful ingredients of which the blood of the lapwing or bat were but two recommended options. Eating the brain of a cat or boiling the bones of murdered babies to obtain the fat were further possibilities, allowing the witch to fly to the infamous event or fall into a stupor and envision him- or herself so doing, depending on the case at hand.

Sacrifice of both animals and humans, especially children, were apparently popular at the Sabbats, though this was more towards a spirit of total degradation than mere blood-letting, as the French judge Pierre de l'Ancre (1553 – 1661 C.E.) explained: 'Here behold the guests of the Assembly, having each one a demon beside her, and know that at this banquet are served no other meats than carrion, and the flesh of those that have been hanged, and the hearts of children not baptized, and other unclean animals strange to the custom and usage of Christian people.'

Of course, where the witch was most likely feared was in her guise as a magical assailant, and it was well-known (if not a foregone conclusion) that her potions and spells regularly required blood. Poisons were the most common product to inflict harm through 'magic' and the potential ingredients were endless, and mostly unpleasant – nail clippings, the fat from babies, semen, menstrual blood and the blood of all manner of creatures from toads and cats to men and women were noted as highly potent, alongside toxic plants and foodstuffs.

Love philtres were no exception to this; rather, they were more likely to involve the use of blood due to the intense connection that was being sought between two parties. One manuscript (the *'Zekerboni'*) suggests that a powder must be made from the womb of a swallow, the liver of a sparrow, the heart of a dove and the kidney of a hare, before being mixed with a sizeable amount of blood from the person making the philtre and again reduced to powder. To imbibe a quantity of this powder is to be left in thrall to the one that has produced it, with 'marvellous success.'

However, just as blood was the making of a witch in terms of pacts and potions, it could also result in a witch's undoing. It was commonly thought that to 'score above the breath' or cut the face of a witch so that it became bloody nullified any power being exerted through magic and release any victim.

As such we find, among others, the confession of one John Davis at the Warwick assizes in 1867, who stated that the assault he was charged with was defence against a witch – convinced that he was being haunted as a result of a certain neighbour's spell, he entered her home and made a gash on her cheek, stating as she bled before him 'There, you old witch, I can do anything with you now!"

Witches in England were commonly 'pricked' to draw blood so as to draw their familiar to them in the hope of suckling, revealing her malefic secrets in no uncertain terms. Further to this, blood could be used to draw the witch him- or herself to the scene of a crime, by filling a witch bottle made of glass or iron with hair, blood and urine along with the likes of nail parings and other excreta of the afflicted; as the contents boiled on the hearth at midnight, the blood of the guilty witch would likewise boil and force an appearance in the hope of some relief. If the bottle exploded, it was believed that the witch had expired.

It should also be noted that one of the justifications for the burning of witches, where that form of execution was deemed fit, was that the unearthly powers were thought to pass to any progeny in the blood, and that only fire could nullify this. Thus, we once more find a connection with the most instinctive and primitive of responses not just to misfortune, but also the means by which such misfortune is inflicted, and in turn how it might be overcome.

There are various reasons why the revelries of witches so closely matched those rumoured of heretics like the Knights Templar, the pagans and a number of ancient civilizations. The ritual use of blood represented the animal in man, the ecstasies of debauch and the excesses of the flesh. Blood had become a thing of symbol within a ritual context, so any use of it within a ceremony was branded as a backward step, a degradation that suggested one's turning away from God.

The bloodlust of the dark goddess, the vampire and the werewolf were united with the drives of the witch or sorcerer and their magical acts because the choice was being made to subvert the will of God and shed another's or one's own blood in order to activate powers and communiqués that were sourced in the lower realms. The use of blood, then, was an unclean act in itself, but so much more nefarious within this occult context.

Sacrifice and blood rites were certainly apparent in the developed concept of the Black Mass, where we can perhaps find the greatest hyperbole in relation to both 'magic' and the use of blood within ritual, as in Rollo Ahmed's *'The Black Art'* (1936):

'The ordinary participants, inflamed with drugs and drink, maddened with blood and sadistic excitement, would certainly have had no thought but of expressing their lowest and filthiest impulses, and of wallowing in a mad phantasmagoria of sexual lust.' Of course, there is truth in this account, not least due to the efficacy of blood within ritual as a means of heightening the senses and raising one's consciousness, and one's abilities.

The act of sorcery certainly relied on this heightening of self and senses, and so blood was even more integral to the associated rites of its magic. Sacrifice and blood were, as before, a powerful offering of life-force to the god or entity in question, but within sorcery they also served to arouse certain qualities of the person performing the ritual, energising the environment and empowering the individual. The related dangers were therefore not simply related to the taking of a life or the challenging of the powers being summoned – they also involved the strength of will and sanity of the practitioner.

Pacts with the Devil were forged in this sphere, too, though whereas the witch was usually approached and seduced by the lure of the unholy, the sorcerer was the one that did the seeking, himself composing a pact in blood and eagerly offering his signature in order to seal the deal and be granted the pleasure, knowledge and power that he so craved.

The blood of sacrifice, though, was most commonly to be found within the rites and instructions of grimoires. The '*Arbatel*' speaks of a magic rod or wand with the form of a snake that can be bent to form an Ouroboros and used as a protective circle; this needed to be stained in the blood of a lamb. The protective 'Seal of Solomon' that would ensure safety in goetic magic was also to be drawn with the blood of a 'black cock that has never engendered', on virgin parchment – which itself was to be produced by strangling a kid, to ensure the purity of the materials so used.

It should be noted that the white-handled ritual knife that would play an important role within the rites would have been, at the time of its own creation, 'steeped in the blood of the mole' or a gosling, depending on which Solomonic text the sorcerer was using. A similar, black-handled knife would have been 'extinguished in the blood of a cat.'

More practically, among the charms that might necessitate the use of blood, the magic 'SATOR' square that repeats that word five times and reads the same in any direction could be activated by using the blood of a pigeon – worth securing, as it could protect a person from, among other misfortunes, pestilence and sorcery, and no witch could bear to remain near it.

Pliny reported beliefs that to mix the blood of birds and consume the 'snake' that this produced would enable the partaker to understand the speech of birds thereafter, while Agrippa espoused the virtues of menstrual blood that can kill bees, dull blades, rust iron and make dogs mad. It apparently also has a profound effect on the fortunes of farmers, as a menstruating woman can walk though fields of corn by night and banish all pests, or walk it at sunrise to wither the corn and spoil the harvest (lore that echoes some of the earliest beliefs we have considered).

Systems of correspondence are ubiquitous within magic, and so the type of animal to be sacrificed – and the character of the blood so used – was frequently charted within grimoires and other magical tracts. As ancient religion had once offered a goat to Bacchus, a dog to Diana or Hecate and a goose to Isis to acknowledge the cosmic link between forms of beast and the deity being honoured, so too sorcery utilised a careful understanding of blood that reflected the operation being practised, particularly where an animal's traits united it with a heavenly body and the associated qualities that could be tapped through it. A white dove is therefore suggested as veneration for Venus, while the Sun would require the blood of the cock and Saturn that of a black goat.

Where charging someone's blood was the focus of the magic, it was logical that obeisance would be given to Mars, as a successful operation would result in corresponding qualities such as power, fury, strength and uncontrollability that would be very useful if a competition, a feud or an outright battle was being entered into. The rites of Mars would utilise suitable substances and be performed at appropriate environments where the desired qualities might be more readily tapped, namely places of former battles, likewise places of slaughter and execution.

Blood, as well as attracting demons, spirits, the witch's familiar, and the spirit of the dead or damned, was a desirable substance to elementals and even the man-made homunculus that was fed on human blood for 40 weeks inside a glass vessel that would be placed deep within a quantity of horse dung. The little boy that emerged thereafter required careful care but was perfectly proportioned and not without magical qualities of his own.

The use of blood was clearly a prominent factor in the magic of sorcery, and whether we judge sorcerers as foolish or unbalanced individuals, so too their magic as inconsequential, the stuff of divine will or the rites of devil-worship, we are nonetheless left with a set of beliefs and rites that sought to force changes on the world and on others, communicate with otherworldly beings to gain knowledge and wisdom and afflict and kill as well as benefit those around them.

The entire process of a ritual, from the making of tools to the observance of fasting or sexual abstinence revolved around the developing will and energies of the sorcerer, with the intent of altering the level of consciousness and piercing a veil that would mean the exceeding of normal human awareness and ability.

Blood rites, with or without slaughter as an aspect of the

actual ritual, were particularly charged features of the ceremonies in question exactly because the taking of a life was an act of immense significance, and the blood a bearer of character, energy and life itself. Indeed, few if any acts could compare with the impact on a ritual, a congregation and certainly not the sorcerer/priest himself as the sacrifice of another. As a result of this, the blood of sacrifice frequently served as a climax to a given ritual so as to epitomise and release the pent-up energies and will that had been built through fasting, abstinence, suffumigation and single-minded obsession with this one pursuit.

Sacrifice can be understood as a purifier, as seen when the ancient Jewish tribes chased the scapegoat from their settlement or the blood of the witch was spilled to nullify her malicious spells, and it can also be seen to be an act of purification here – within sorcery, powers were supposedly sought for benevolent and God-fearing reasons and so no life was taken through malice or with evil intent. Cornelius Agrippa (1486 – 1535 C.E.) notes that purity is a vital characteristic of the practitioner, and that in releasing the blood of a sacrifice, the sins and vices of the individual performing the rite are similarly dissipated, resulting in a cleansed mode of being that is necessary when performing such dangerous magics.

However, the use of blood was – and continues to be – predominantly concerned with the raising of the self beyond the normal limits and a heightening of consciousness, which bestows powers and abilities on humanity that, for, many, are anathema and diabolic. Aleister Crowley (1875 – 1947 C.E.) espoused quite elegantly on the place and importance of blood within ritual 'magick', though even at his most pleasing his thoughts were unlikely to appease his own, or the broader opponents of sorcery.

Crowley acknowledges the importance of blood in his *'Magick in Theory and Practise'* (1929), stating that to release blood is to liberate the energies of the creature. He does also note that a great magician need not take a life to make a successful sacrifice but can offer up some of his own blood, though he does go on to make jest about the most potent sacrifice of all being that of an intelligent child, so any hope of balance is as ever lost to a casual or hostile reader!

Interestingly, Crowley does espouse the importance of a daily Eucharist to a magician, stating that it is a central form of 'sustenance' which replaces the physical with the spiritual, enhancing one's being and its abilities. The ritual in question, however, need not utilise physical substances but can be of a symbolic nature.

Where there is agreement between myth, faiths, and magic in all their guises is that blood is unique in both nature and power. How it is personified, the extent to which it is propounded and the ways in which it is, or is not, practically applied vary greatly, but the unchanging wisdom holds that blood is a profound substance that is to be respected on religious, spiritual and magical levels as much as it must be on a mundane, worldly level: 'For the life of the flesh *is* in the blood.'

One final occult sphere in which we encounter the rumination over and practical use of blood is that of alchemy, where the beliefs, rites and very language are at once that of symbol as much as of any potential act.

Gerhard Dorn, one of the pupils of the famous Paracelsus, espoused the use of human blood in the latter alchemical process, stating that it would infuse the solution with life-force, while Arnald of Villanova (c.1240 – c.1311 C.E.) penned a tract that discussed the distillation of human blood, here being 'good red blood', from the healthiest of men (with perfectly balanced humours, supposedly) aged between 25 and 30 years – though the blood-letting should only be performed in April or May.

Others were dubious, however, as to the suitability of blood in what was ultimately a purer, often spiritual process. Roger Bacon (c.1219 – c.1292 C.E.) saw no place for the substance in his Hermetic works, just as he failed to see the worth of other Hermetic staples of the time like egg shells and excrement. Later, Thomas Vaughan (1621 – 1666 C.E.) lambasted the 'sluttish broilers' who worked with the assumption that blood was the First Cause, noting that man – and therefore man's blood – had not always been existent and so was a product in itself, and not a progenitor.

Richardus Anglicus perhaps summed up this feeling rather succinctly in his work *'Correctorium alchymiae'* when he said that 'Whatsoever a man soweth that also shall he reap. Therefore if he soweth filth, he shall find filth.' Blood was thus a common symbol within the Great Work, rather than a practical ingredient – as such we see the Pelican among the ubiquitous characters of Hermetic texts, tearing its breast to feed its young with its own lifeblood, reflecting the sacrifice that Christ made on the cross.

Nicolas Flamel (c.1330 – 1418 C.E.) in his *'Philosophical Summary'* wrote that the 'blood of the pure bird hatched in the egg of the alembic is a universal panacea by any other words.' The red tincture of the philosopher's stone can be therefore be described as being that of the pelican's offering, or dragon's blood, and we see mention of the 'blood of the metals' that is a result of the alchemical process. Indeed, the resulting liquid at various stages in the process could be compared to blood depending on the text, resulting in a veritable labyrinth of meaning that juxtaposes reality with allegory, something which alchemy always excelled at.

Sacrifice held a key role in Hermeticism, just as it did in religion, magic and mysticism, not least due to the concept that to re-create in a higher and purer form, one first had to face a form of death and deconstruction. In this light, the sacrifice is a symbolic one focussing on the individual who is seeking a higher truth, wisdom or some form of spiritual insight or epiphany. There is no doubt that this 'giving up' of oneself may not be without pain, but this form of sacrifice tends to be willing, if not eager, and the sacrificial 'victim' has offered themselves up with a view to personal expansion.

This is self-sacrifice, and Carl Jung (1875 – 1961 C.E.) certainly recognised the importance of such an act if individuals were to truly know and understand themselves and live healthy lives from a psychological perspective, which most definitely resonates with the more spiritual forms of alchemy. For Jung, the slaying of the dragon in Hero myths, the slaying of the bull within the story of Mithras and the 'Night Sea Journey' of Jonah and others all represent the conclusion of one state of being – a shedding of psychic skin that takes the individual through the depths of the unconscious – to another.

The philosopher's stone, then, is the triumphing of the higher being over the primitive drives, the success of one's ego over unnecessary and regressive psychological trends – and the blood sacrifice of old that has been ritualised, mythologized and demonised becomes something even more profound and meaningful precisely because it is here symbolic, and an act performed as a result of one's free will.

It might be argued that the ability to choose self-sacrifice despite the allure of atavistic drives, for physical acts and wholly literal expressions of worship, is itself a first step towards personal salvation; the key to transcendence is present within us, and will not be gained by offering another in our place. The symbols of myth, ancient religion, magic and alchemy all speak of central truths, but the shedding of blood and the practical giving of life is here seen to miss the point – humanity need not appease gods or pledge bloody allegiances in order to transcend its mode of being; rather, each individual must confront the self, and the pain that this leads to, in order to sacrifice that which is outmoded and attain the higher truth of the total, balanced being.

Modern Rites

Though ritualised blood-letting gradually became an archaic practise for many, the importance and inherent power of blood continued to hold sway in various quarters all the same. One notable area in which blood played a rather unique part was within cruentation, a method of investigation in murder cases that was practised in Germany of the medieval period and later Eastern Europe, and through those countries, colonial North America, until the 18th century.

Cruentation was employed when a murder trial was faltering and substantial new evidence was required. The alleged murderer would be taken to the body of the deceased and, should the body's wounds begin to bleed, the guilt was said to have been proved (though a speedy confession might also be given to either avoid such a confrontation, or at least to draw the uncomfortable meeting to a close).

Doubts about the validity of this method were aired from as early as the 15th century and even where it was used, the results of cruentation were not always taken as fact, but it was nonetheless used as a means of trial for some hundreds of years, suggesting an especial belief in the qualities or character of blood, likewise a degree of 'sympathetic relationship' between a criminal and his crime.

On a more mundane level, blood has continued to feature as an ingredient in many dishes worldwide, and though most examples of this are simple uses of animals common in a particular area and/or the tastes of a locality (soup made from goose blood in Sweden, rice boiled in goat's blood in Colombia and numerous varieties of blood-sausage in the United Kingdom, France, Hungary and Nepal and several other countries), there are other forms of blood-as-food that do connect us with some of the beliefs and rituals that we have already considered.

For instance, snake's blood is for some a potent aphrodisiac in China and Vietnam, while the latter country also sees blood soup (the raw blood of an animal) as a satisfying dish, though this is less widely imbibed now than it was due to concerns for potential disease that might be passed to the soup-drinker. The practise of drinking the blood of cattle has also been widely documented within accounts of the African Maasai, often after rituals that demarcate rites of passage like childbirth.

Clinical vampirism and 'Renfield's syndrome' are an extreme psychological variant of the consumption of blood, especially interesting as where popular culture has adopted these mental aberrations for novels, films and television, there is very little empirical evidence to suggest them as a reality. They are also not recognised officially within psychological studies, with cases linked to them instead ascribed to various other mental conditions such as schizophrenia and paraphilia (formerly sexual perversion).

Criminal cases thus do arise like that of Peter Kürten (1883 – 1931 C.E.), 'The Vampire of Dusseldorf' who brutally murdered a number of people and was known to have tried to drink the blood of some of them. The sexual and sadistic elements of 'vampirism' therefore can be identified, but the actual drinking of blood was more of an afterthought or an act born of the moment, rather than a raison d'être, even if that was what the media and the wider population singled out from the horrors that he perpetrated.

It is likely, then, that just as apparent cases of 'vampirism' have a deeper-seated psychological cause, the concept of this kind of 'living vampire' and 'Renfield's syndrome' are self-fulfilling myths – the macabre images of the vampire and blood-drinking lend themselves toward certain mental conditions, which see the perpetrator taking on what they believe to be a suitable guise, with suitable traits, to match the image that they hold of themselves.

Where the modern day certainly does exhibit continued blood rites and sacrifice is within Voodoo, Umbanda and other varieties of religion that have a foundation in African beliefs, so too the more magically-focussed Obeah. Their mention here is not only due to their relevance to the 21st century rather than history, but because the likes of Voodoo have received much the same treatment as 'vampirism' in that they have been mythologized by popular culture to such an extent that the truth has been distorted beyond any reason, which is unfortunate given the vibrancy, immediacy and potency that these faiths and their rituals demonstrate.

The stereotype held by Westerners was founded early on, markedly with stories that were told about Haiti, its Voodoo and Obeahmen by the likes of Sir Spencer St. John (1825 – 1910 C.E.) and William Seabrook (1884 – 1945 C.E) with a focus placed on cannibalism, child sacrifice and the more nefarious forms of magic like curses and necromancy.

It is true that the African diasporas saw a rich intermingling of folk religion with Western rites and beliefs, but the 'horrors' so described in numerous books can frequently be seen, in another light, as 'primitive' rites seen through the eyes of a shocked, 'civilised' man, or as magical acts that were only those being practised throughout Europe and the Americas due to the common popularity of grimoires like the *'Petit Albert'* and the *'Dragon Rouge'* that had largely been disseminated through French culture.

This is not to say that these beliefs did not result in acts that had largely been found to be anathema in terms of religion and morality across much of the globe, but similar acts were being performed in many other cultures before, during and after the formation of Haiti and the rise in popularity of Hoodoo in America – and these acts were not fundamental rites within those movements, but variations and excesses of them that were not exclusive to those of African descent.

For the sake of this study, Voodoo is a fascinating subject because it links so much that we have already seen with the modern day, combining ancient African beliefs with the inherited rituals and scripture of Catholicism. As such a 'service' might contain what are essentially pagan and Catholic rites, with preparations and accoutrements that can be found as staples of magic within the Solomonic works or the magnum opus of Cornelius Agrippa, *'The Three Books of Occult Philosophy.'*

Sacrifice is a mainstay, with offerings a key aspect of the relationship between the people and their deities. Offerings are made to the various loa or powers with the intention of welcoming the appropriate entity into a ritual space and strengthening it, therefore the offerings that are made need to suit the taste of that loa and be of suitable potency.

Blood is, as ever, an especially powerful offering and can be made in the form of chickens, bulls, goats and other creatures, though there is required to be a link that suggests the suitability of the beast to a loa, such as white-coated animals for the powers of water (Agwé) and black-coated animals for those of death (the Ghede). As with some of the earlier rituals and, notably, the magical arts as described in the grimoires, a sacrifice in this context is a fundamental aspect of a ceremony that is a culmination of sometimes exhaustive preparation (possibly including a period of sexual abstinence and fasting), alongside the ubiquitous ritual elements of music, dancing and chanting – the sacrifice is a liberation of pent-up energy toward a strongly-willed and focussed end.

The animal to be sacrificed is commonly given food and water before the moment of slaughter, as it is believed that in accepting the nourishment the beast is showing its willing participation in the act to come. Further still, once the animal has tasted of the proffered meal, the loa is believed to own it, resulting in great affection being offered to the animal as a being that is now sacred; this, along with the believed possession of the individual that is to make the sacrifice by the loa suggests an all-pervading spiritual power that encompasses the liminal space of the ritual as the sacrifice approaches, and is eventually made.

There are examples of the likes of chickens and goats being mutilated before the moment of sacrifice (organs and testicles removed), so too examples of the blood of the animal being tasted by an officiate, but the offering remains a gift to, and the property of, the *loa* and will be placed appropriately within the space to ensure that this is clear. Dismemberment of the carcass similar to what we have seen in older rites would here be avoided, as the remains of the sacrifice are imbued with an energy that, at this point, may well prove hazardous if unleashed.

The syncretistic religions of Brazil have much in common with Voodoo, and blood rites are apparent here also, including 'Candomblé' where an initiate of the spiritual rites is ritually depilated before having her head anointed with water that bears traces of blood from every sacrifice that has been performed at the site. The 'ôrunkó', a later ceremony where the initiate receives the name of her personal 'Orisha' or spirit, sees the sacrifice of roosters, goats and birds before the sacred stones of the Orishas are carefully bathed in the resulting blood.

Similar echoes of ancient sacrificial rites and medieval sorcery occur within Macumba (where that term is pejoratively used to insinuate black magic) and Umbanda (another syncretistic Afro-Brazilian religion combining African faith with Roman Catholicism and Spiritism). Rites similar to those described above can be found alongside familiar methods for mixing love spells and protective goods, utilising blood as an ingredient, just as they would have been found in centuries past across the globe.

The Santeria of Cuba also continues to see the application of animal sacrifice, but as in all cases the number of such acts has lessened through the years – though it is worth noting that both a 1993 ruling by the American Supreme Court and a 2009 Texan ruling defended the freedom of religious expression, here including the right to perform animal sacrifice, where such acts were a fundamental rite within the religion.

Aside from the copious links that we can find between these religions, with their continued observance of blood rites, and the sacrificial rituals we have described in ancient Egypt, Greece and the Roman Empire, the key similarity to grasp is the reverence afforded to blood and sacrifice, the power that they are believed to bestow and unleash – and the immediacy of the worshipped deity or power at the moment when blood is spilled.

These rituals do not trivialise life, rather they worship it as the greatest source of energy available, and they use blood in order to bring the spirits and gods into direct contact with a given congregation. It is here that we see something of the way of life that we mentioned in relation to the ancient Mesopotamians, where faith *is* life – a constant aspect of existence that defines all understanding and demands awe and respect due to its inextricable presence.

Blood rites thus continue to hold a powerful allure within many faiths, even where religion, culture and law have made efforts to suppress their practise. Sacrifices that might run into the hundreds or, reportedly, the thousands were being made upon the death of a monarch in Western Africa well into the 19th century while, in the same region and at the same time, the 'Leopard Men' were slaughtering and cannibalising their victims in order to enhance their strength and vitality (with similar 'Lion Men' active in Tanganyika which is part of modern-day of Tanzania).

In India, where human sacrifice has long been illegal, the taking of life and use of blood within ritual nonetheless continued, whether in the efforts of black magic to cast afflictions and seek treasure, or as offerings to goddesses as aspects of death like Kali and Shakti – instances of which have been reported more than once in the 21st century.

The Pawnee Indians of Central America maintained the use of sacrifice into the 19th century, with the annual 'Morning Star' ceremony involving the use of a female offering. A captive of either sex could also be kept in a state of comfort for some time before a sacrificial ceremony whereby they would be bound to a cross and observe solemn dance, before their head would be cleft by a tomahawk and the blood cast over newly-sown seed, and potentially their flesh being cut into pieces so that the blood could be used to propagate a wider expanse of 'new life.'

New cults have also utilised the rite of sacrifice to enforce the intent and impact of their beliefs. Aztec-inspired blood rites were adopted in a Mexican cult based in Nuevo Leon, which saw up to a dozen murders, and on occasion the imbibing of human blood, in 1963. More recently still, The 'New Light of God' in Panama's El Terrón made human offerings in 2020 as a form of punishment for those held to have not sufficiently repented their transgressions. Alongside the sacrifice of a goat, children, their pregnant mother and a neighbour were beaten and beheaded, while other potential victims managed to escape various tortures that were intended to be a prelude to their sacrifice.

Of course, the ability to spill blood or take a life can stir passions that are altogether removed from any degree (palatable or not) of religious meaning, and there are countless examples of those who have practised blood rites that appear to be based on irreligious motivations, to achieve ends that are wholly more personal and frequently more sadistic, just as those that occurred in El Terrón. Among other equally disturbing cases of the 21st century, child trafficking from Africa for sacrifice and magical 'bushmeat' has been reported in the United Kingdom, while black magic has been linked to the assault and ritual murder of several children that occurred in Brazil between 1989 and 1993, and the murder of a Catholic nun in Sondrio, Italy in 2000.

Regardless the opinion of outsiders, some instances of blood rite and sacrifice can be defended as part of an established spiritual belief – but the cases just mentioned are drastically removed from any semblance of defence, and speak more of perversion, sadism and mental aberration than even the most apparently blood-thirsty spiritualities.

It is a fundamental point that human sacrifice, even in 21st century life, does not automatically demarcate subversion, insanity or diabolism. Just as it is difficult for many to begin to comprehend the world of the ancient Mesopotamian, the Aztec or the American Indian, it is nigh on impossible to appreciate from outside a faith, the spiritual relevance that blood and/or the taking of a life can have within a ritual context – and that statement is not intended to champion human sacrifice, it simply notes the starkly opposing views between those within the 'liminality' of a given faith or ritual, and those outside of it.

Blood itself is as divisive a substance and a symbol as many others within the spheres of religion, magic, and much else of a wholly less spiritual concern. Some of the earliest conceptions involving blood were based on the blood covenant or bond that united a tribe or tribes through kinship, just as blood was seen to link humanity with its ancestors and afford a spiritual foundation for man on which to base his existence and understanding of the world – but that same concept has also led to the idea of racial superiority and subsequent genocide. As it unites, so too it divides!

What can be acknowledged as a throughline from our most

distant forebears to ourselves, aside from the dissentions arising from our various frames of reference, is the continued potency and meaning associated with blood and any connected rite of sacrifice. They have long had a profound impact on us spiritually, psychologically and sociologically, both as realities and as symbols, and will continue to for centuries to come if only due to the depth, breadth and profundity of relationship that has been maintained. In whatever light we consider it, and on whichever level, the blood most definitely is the life.

II: SEX

If the blood is the life, then the sexual impulse may well be the most powerful instinct that drives that life forward. For all the ruminations on its higher meaning, its place within human existence, the effects of its excess and its absence, the condition of the human being is frequently – some might say constantly – at the mercy of attractions, obsessions and desires both to procreate and/or sate a taste for physical pleasure. Sex is a ubiquitous factor of the human condition, whether or not it is actively engaged in.

Within faith and occultism, just as within broader, exoteric understandings, sex can be seen as nothing more than a carnal pursuit, or the epitome of being alive; a vice of the needy and the materialistic, or an attempt to raise the self beyond its immediate limitations; a sin that distances man and woman from any opportunity of 'purity', or the very purest expression of faith and love between both individuals and their idea of any creative force or god.

As with much else common to this study, sex is a fundamental ingredient in the make-up of life (a connection that all living beings share if only due to the act that led to their generation) that has been utilised in manifold ways in the realm of the spiritual and magical, and used as a means of defining the relative 'good' and 'evil' among peoples through a basis of moral or religious mores.

The manifestation of the sexual impulse, as well as the form of its practise, have frequently served as handy weapons exactly because it is of such a nature as to reveal the core, or 'heart's desire' of a person or group and so is a rather neat way to highlight differences in philosophy, standing and character; indeed, the idea as well as the reality of the sexual act runs through esotericism and mysticism as much as it does through practically all other spheres of thought and expression, often as fixatedly by those opposed to it as those in thrall to it.

Sex is, then, all manner of things to all manner of people, and is both blessing and curse depending on the views at hand, not least because it can be seen as the instigating act that led to all of existence, and its relentless perpetuation through the countless men and women that followed that initial cosmic act of union.

Generation

According to the various creation stories extant within myth and religion, there are a number of ways by which existence came into being. For instance, ex nihilo stories recount creation through the imagining, breath, word or indeed secretion of a singular entity – as such we have the Heliopolitan Atum, a self-generated god who created air (Shu) and moisture (Shu's sister, Tefnut) through an act of masturbation, with the offspring of their eventual coupling demarcating the earth (Geb) and the sky (Nut).

In a similar vein, the Persian Gayomart was a giant First Man who emanated light and, upon his death, gave his component parts to create the physical world, notably his soul which became the gold in the earth, and his semen which fell to the ground and became rhubarb shrubs from which sprang the first human couple.

Elsewhere, stories tell of the earth itself as the universal 'Genetrix', with Hesiod's *'Theogony'* sharing the Olympian myth whereby Ouranos or Uranus nightly mates with Gaia, the earth, and creates the first beings the Titans, the Cyclopes and the giant Hekatonkheires. Such a hierogamy between a 'Sky-God' and an 'Earth Mother' can be found in the myths of Oceania, Africa and the Americas, and are a common interpretation of the cosmic copulation of the heavens and the earth toward the instigating of life.

These are all 'world parent' tales, but where the story of Gayomart suggests an animistic understanding of the world and its various forms, the likes of the *'Theogony'* relies on what is essentially a single entity being divided into two – sky and earth – and then producing new life by the unions that result, most often in a form of sexual act. These are particularly pertinent stories in that such life-giving is understood to have been impossible while the entity is a single unit; only through the division of the one into two does creation of new life become a potential, if not inevitable, act.

Studies throughout the last century frequently cited instances whereby civilizations strove to re-enact this cosmic union; the 'hieros gamos' or 'sacred marriage' was practised by the Sumerians, Babylonians, Phoenicians and Mesoamericans among others, though not necessarily with the inclusion of ritual sex that so many scholars previously focused on.

There are stories of Sumerian Kings mating with the High Priestesses of Inanna (later Ishtar) among other sexual rites to promote strength and fertility, just as James Frazer noted the ritual defloration of unwed girls in Babylonia. Herodotus gives detailed accounts of this type, explaining that all women would, at least once in their lives, stay at the Temple of Aphrodite (Ishtar) until a man had paid her for her sexual services.

To an extent these stores are salacious and exaggerations of the truth, but there is no doubt that forms of 'sacred prostitution' did exist, with references to the Temples at points denoting them as 'taverns', suggesting the role of Ishtar as a form of Madam looking after her women, but this does not necessarily mean that this form of prostitution was anathema.

In the story of Gilgamesh, Enkidu on his deathbed refers to the natural place of the whore as being the tavern, the crossroads and the city walls – they are thus the outsiders, the wayward ones within society; however, Hammurabi's Code of Laws (c.1754 B.C.E) went to especial lengths to distinguish the special rights and high standing that these priestesses should be afforded, including powers over land and finances that no other woman at the time would have had any means to exercise. The Temples may have been seen in a derogatory light by some, but they were protected by the goddess they embodied and by law, and so a considerable importance must have been placed on the 'hieros gamos'.

Aztec sexual rites are difficult to authenticate given the lack of primary sources, but there is some evidence attesting to similar sacred prostitution, and there was certainly an understanding of the role of sex and sensuality in existence by the culture, with Xochiquetzal worshipped as a protector of prostitutes and the makers of luxuries, and Xochipili a patron of homosexual prostitution. The Inca also acknowledged the place of male prostitution, with boys occasionally dressed as girls and ritual sex performed on holy days.

On a somewhat more mundane level, though certainly no less profound in meaning, human marriage has been seen as a symbolic enactment of the cosmic union. Mircea Eliade (1907 – 1986 C.E.) noted the rites of the Omahas, whose village was separated into two halves (Heaven and Earth), with one party from each side making up a couple and effectively repeating the original hieros gamos.

As such, marriage and indeed sex were powerful re-enactments of the initial movements that begat all of existence, and could be used to maintain stability but also ensure victories, wealth, the fecundity of the land and the fertility of a people. The May King and Queen are a clear example of this, though the nature of the 'union' could be symbolic (with those of Germany, the Ukraine and elsewhere in Europe rolling over the ground to mimic copulation upon the earth) or wholly more practical (with orgiastic gatherings to recreate the chaos of primordial existence and release vital energies in a form of 're-setting' of creation), depending on the culture and the time in question.

What is apparent regardless the form that these rites took is that *being* was seen as a result of creation, which naturally suggested a union of two forces –one bearing the seed, and another which received and gestated the new life that was produced. On a microcosmic level man and woman appeared intentionally constructed to honour that union by repeating it, and where ritual could magnify and make sacred that act, the resulting appreciation of the creator gods and the energies that might be tapped would be immeasurable.

If nothing else, sex was – as it still is – an everyday instinct to most that required some form of acknowledgement, even where it was not a central concern of a religion or the basis of a fundamental ritual. Whether or not the faiths and understandings of a culture incorporated the idea of creation from a cosmic union, concerns regarding the fecundity of the land, re-generation, beauty, the male and female energies, virility and fertility, as well as simple lust, ensured that a rather vast panoply of gods were venerated in the name of generation, across all civilizations and eras.

Ancient Egypt offers deities that rather neatly sum up the central (and frequently recurring) forms that fertility was worshipped in. One of the earliest such figures was Min, whose Pre-dynastic representation was a horizontal line with a disk at its centre, a form likened by some to an image of lightning; later portrayed at points as a human figure holding his phallus in his hand, he was somewhat unsurprisingly linked to male sexual potency.

A broader range of beliefs were afforded to Isis (motherhood, wisdom and fertility) and her mate Osiris, who she helped to reassemble following his murder and dismemberment at the hands of Set. Osiris was himself a god of the afterlife, not least due to his resurrection from the depths, as well as of vegetation and the fertility of the Nile – which his missing phallus endowed with annual surges that covered and 'fed' the ground and its crops.

From just these three figures, much can be found represented which is common among worldwide gods linked to modes of fecundity and generation, whether that be interpreted in terms that are distinctly environmental (the nourishing waters, womb-like earth and the seed-carrying wind) the union of man and woman in marriage, the product of that union, or the act of sex that is a nonetheless potent union of opposites, as we have already seen.

Among countless others, the waters were associated with the Egyptian Sobek, the crocodile-headed god of the river, fertility and warfare; likewise, the Iranian Anahit (the Old Persian Anahita) who was linked with healing alongside the life-giving waters, and the Aboriginal Australian 'Rainbow Serpent' that was worshipped as god of water and rain alongside prominence as a creator god (with destructive qualities implicit).

The earth and vegetation had Osiris in Egypt, alongside Sopdet who was a goddess of the soil at flood as well as a guide to deceased pharaohs through the chthonic depths of the underworld. The Greek Demeter was the goddess of the harvest and agriculture, while the Incan Mama Sara was a goddess of grain, with unusual growths at times being dressed in her image as recognition of her presence.

Marriage was the sacred bailiwick of the Indian Parvati, goddess of marital happiness and dedication toward a spouse, while childbirth was under the purview of the Roman Juno, the Norse goddess Frigg and a number of Chinese deities including Chén Jìnggū and Bixiāo Niángniáng. The Native North American Iroquois have worshipped Atahensic, who is a goddess of childbirth as well as a sky goddess that represents affairs associated with the feminine principle; having fallen from the sky, she was saved from the waters by a giant turtle and went on to give birth to the Earth Mother.

Fertility is represented by a suitably fruitful multitude of deities, including the Indian lunar goddess Chandra (linked to plants and vegetation), Manasa (goddess of snakes, fertility and prosperity) and Yogmāya (a benevolent aspect of Durga also known as Vindhyavasini). The Greeks had the infamous figures of Dionysus, god of the grape, wine and festivity, and Pan, who made flocks fertile (with the annual Roman Lupercalia seeing two young men clothed in naught but a girdle of animal skin and running round the boundary of the old city in the name of Pan and striking anyone they met, with the ability to cure any woman so struck of infertility or barrenness).

The Japanese Ainu (or Ezu) people worshipped Shinda as bestower of fertility, while the Hawaiians focussed their rites on Haumea, who was herself the mother of various other deities and had a similar link to the act of childbirth. The Aztecs venerated the plumed serpent Quetzalcoatl (who also served as god of wind, water and chocolate) and Chimalma, the mother of Quetzalcoatl who represented life, death and re-birth. The Voodoo 'Guédé' are a notable family of loa who also represent the connected energies of life and death, highlighting the close relationship between the vitality of existence and the passage of that vitality to another form or plain.

Sex itself, whether interpreted in terms of gender or the actual act of coupling, is no less popular a focus of worship. One fascinating deity is the Pilipino Lakapati, who is a hermaphroditic figure that represents fertility in perfect order, the 'consummated' union of opposites that separate gods and goddesses, being of but one gender, perhaps fail to establish; under the auspices of Lakapati the catch of fish is abundant but not excessive, the seeds are successfully sown and the waters that nourish life from that seed are in perfect measure.

The Taíno (Pre-Columbian natives) bore allegiance to Atabey, the goddess of earth and water who represented and blessed female fertility, alongside Yúcahlu, a god of creation, sky, the harvest and male fertility. The Chinese paid obeisance to Jiutian Xuannü, a goddess of fertility, sex, war and longevity, while the aboriginal Wunambal people of North-western Australia have Ungud, a snake god of earth, water, rain – and the giver of erections to the Shaman.

Indeed, the male member and prodigious erections are a common representation of creative energy – a point which is certainly pertinent to this study. The Romans in particular were keen and ardent venerators of the phallus, with the likes of Immus (god of sexual intercourse), Fascinus (both a deity that embodied the penis and protective amulets and effigies that were made in the form of such a member) and Priapus among the proud and somewhat outstanding figures to be worshipped.

Priapus is an especially prominent god of the phallus who was venerated by early Greek colonists through to Italy of the 3rd century B.C.E. Bearing a huge and permanent erection, he was a god that protected fruits, plants, livestock, and male genitalia. At different points he was considered to be the son of Dionysus and Pan, but suffered the fate of being impotent in spite of his endowment due to a curse placed on him by the goddess Hera.

There is certainly something of the pornographic about representations of Priapus, but worship of him was largely of a serious nature, not least as a protector of livestock (with stories of him living in exile as a shepherd following the onset of his curse and fall from divinity). A different focus of the deity was vaunted much more recently by the St. Priapus Church that was founded in the 1980's; still active today in North America and Canada, the largely homosexual adherents worship the phallus as creative force, engage in ritual masturbation and consider the imbibing of semen to be a sacred act.

Alongside the aforementioned gods, Ancient Greece and Rome also noted the existence of satyrs (to the Greeks men with the ears and tail of a horse, to the Romans men with the horns, ears, tail and legs of a goat) that were drunken and licentious dwellers of the woodland, as well as fauns and the female nymphs who peopled the natural world and beguiled the living with their supernatural and haunting beauty.

Regardless the extent that any form of myth, story-telling or faith were woven into the fabric of the concepts behind these beings, it is apparent that attraction, lust and a keen sexual appetite were vented in Greek and Roman lore, both as a reflection of cultural mores and an outlet for widely-held passions. The natural world was resplendent with creative energy – the very act of existing was the result of cosmic union – therefore the life of men and women must feature similar expressions embodying desire, union and pleasure.

This could be the case even where sex was not perceived as a positive act; indeed, Gnostics like Carpocrates (died 138 C.E) considered it a duty of humanity to sin, as God have given that instinct so that sin would be committed, and salvation duly sought. However, sex was mainly embraced as a form of worship rather than a necessary evil, and the practise of 'orgia' in Ancient Greece was a common means of attaining higher plains through ecstatic means.

It is possible that orgiastic rites stretched back to the deities like Cybele for whom, as we saw in our consideration of blood rites, priests castrated themselves in remembrance of such an act by Attis. Orgies nonetheless became associated with the Mystery schools, where a variety of approaches were taken to effectively pierce the veil of reality and lift the self to a point of direct communion with the god or goddess in question.

Dionysus was a somewhat infamous, if not legendary, recipient of such veneration who was heralded with torch-lit processions by masked congregants, the use of intoxicants, invocations of spirits, wild dance, general debauchery and animal sacrifice. The goal was 'enthusiasmos' or 'ekstasis', a state by which the god himself would fill them, be one with them, and grant a state of being , power and wisdom otherwise beyond the ken of mortal men and women.

This heightening of the senses to a point of abandon is apparent in the Orphic Hymns to Dionysus, one example of which (XLV) reads as follows: 'Liknitan Bacchus (Dionysos), bearer of the vine, thee I invoke to bless these rites divine: Florid and gay, of nymphs the blossom bright, and of fair Venus (Aphrodite), Goddess of delight, 'Tis thine mad footsteps with mad nymphs to beat, dancing thro' groves with lightly leaping feet: From Jove's (Zeus') high counsels nurst by Proserpine (Persephone), and born the dread of all the pow'rs divine: Come, blessed pow'r, regard thy suppliant's voice, propitious come, and in these rites rejoice.'

The Dionysian rites were commonly seen as exclusive to women, though other similar ecstatic forms of worship were seen equally, or exclusively, to men. Regardless the following, the Roman senate came to view orgia – or as they came to be known within the Roman Empire, 'Bacchanalia' – as a subversive element within society and made efforts to ban them in 186 C.E.

Livy (59 B.C.E. – 19 C.E.) was one supporter of such an approach, and it is his questionable accounts of the worship of the 'Carnival' that became the most widely-known to the Western world, with sex, blood and murder a commonly cited factor among any, be they men, women, children and all classes and stations in life, who joined the revels. That said, as popular as Livy's attack on the Bacchanalia were and to some remain, the laws that attempted to control them under the threat of execution were more likely created as a means of overriding division and dissent at a time of strife in the Empire.

The rites, then, were forced to change and become, at least on the surface, more palatable and less frenzied, but they did not disappear altogether. One key development following the enforced changes was the relative merging of identities between Dionysus and Bacchus (as well as the god Liber, who enjoyed a Roman following as patron of viniculture, fertility and freedom close to 200 years B.C.E).

Other, similar male gods of fertility, excess and wilderness would later become synonymous with one another, including the Celtic horned god Cernunnos, Pan and even the English Herne the Hunter, first documented in Shakespeare's *The Merry Wives of Windsor* (1597) and just possibly a creation of the Elizabethan master that gained mythical status thereafter. The individual identity of the gods and deities thus diminished somewhat, but as an archetype of the untamed, the rut and the power of creation, they united and continued to impact on consciousness, culture and worship.

One English embodiment of this are the Agapemonites, who were founded in the 1840's by the Rev. Henry James Prince. Prince had early on gained quite a following for his lively and passionate sermons, but was eventually banned from preaching in his own church due to scandalous rumours that began to circulate that directly involved him and his wayward activities.

Relocating to Brighton, Prince declared himself to be free of sin and also immortal, promising a similar feat for those who followed him, as well as a sexual freedom that was divinely-ordained by such inspirational scripture as the 'Song of Songs.'

Bolstering his following and his coffers, Prince purchased a 200-acre estate in Somerset that came to be known as the 'Agapemone' or 'Abode of Love', and his followers became known as the 'Agapemonites', a term linking them to the divine love called agapē by the Greeks, and 'agapae' or 'love-feasts' practised by early Christians.

Religious rites diminished in number over time, but ritual acts were far from absent at the Agapemone where Prince (now 'the Beloved One' lived with his wife and a number of his loyal congregation, all of whom were female). The 'Great Manifestation' followed, which saw Prince seduce a young orphan of 16 years (one Zoë Patterson) and claim her to be a 'Bride of the Lamb.' This union, as with all of those that Prince had enjoyed, was meant to be a mystical one, and so when a pregnancy followed – not the first to occur at the Agapemone – it was deemed to be the work of Satan.

Prince died in 1899, which was something of a shock given his self-declared immortality, but some followers remained, and others arrived, to worship at the feet of his successor. The Agapemonites existed even beyond the death of that successor (another immortal), only disappearing toward the close of the 1950's, which suggests that even the idea of sexual freedom and religious sanction to 'sin', however disappointing for many in reality, could have a profound hold on the imaginations and desires of a number of people.

More in-keeping with the archetype of the untamed and wild god was the resurgence of poetry, prose and 'worship' of Pan that arose during the latter-stages of the Victorian era. Romantic poets like Shelley and Keats waxed lyrical over the beauty and power of the wild in place of what was for some a stifling urban existence, which could be seen in the very landscapes as much as through the idea of any horned god and the associated beings that inhabited them.

To city-dwellers, the country was both a profound and terrifying commodity as the simplicity of life offered comfort and balm, while the ruggedness and lack of rule and restriction was overwhelming – particularly to a prurient Victorian sensibility. The 'god of the woods' was thus a genuinely numinous being in that he appealed to a primitive aspect of humanity while striking fear as a symbol of liberation, just as had been so alluring to the revellers of the Bacchanalia in Rome.

For a period of time, Pan in particular took centre stage as a symbol of virility and release, an ideal focal point as the shackles of Victorian mores were gradually dropped and the likes of Freud revealed the latent sexual condition that underpinned much of common thought, deed and of course 'neurosis.' As Somerset Maugham remarked: 'God went out...and Pan came in.'

Among other instances, Hector Monro (a.k.a. Saki; 1870 – 1916 C.E.) penned a short story about Pan, and odes or 'hymns' to Pan vividly explained the divine ecstasy that the god could engender when venerated without restraint – notably in the works of Victor Neuberg and, later, his teacher Aleister Crowley, where homosexual overtones actually suggest an attempt to reclaim the orgia of the Mysteries, and a union between man or woman and the god of the rut:

> 'Thrust the sword through the galling fetter,
> All-devourer, all-begetter;
> Give me the sign of the Open Eye,
> And the token erect of thorny thigh,
> And the word of madness and mystery,
> O Pan! Io Pan!'

The horrors of World War One would seemingly negate this optimistic yearning for and conjoining with nature, but the allure and meaning of the horned god, like the other fertility deities before and after him, would not be fully forgotten. Numerous civilizations had sought to understand, embrace and honour the concept of generation and with it the sexual act, and the need to explore that ubiquitous facet of the human condition would not be overcome; rather, from the death and stagnation of war, salvation would wholly rely on the abilities of the world and its people to strive for better, to hope for better – and to generate new life as an expression of that striving and hope.

Degradation

Other forms of faith would approach sex in an entirely different manner, and while the 'typical' Christian view is far from the only such example, the history of sex and carnality is nonetheless a fascinating one when considered through a historical Christian perspective.

As we have already seen, the new faith was in part the cause of sweeping changes within the Roman Empire, with various rites seen as more overtly pagan becoming anathema in favour of the Christian message of redemption and salvation, and a positive understanding of sex subsumed along with the more excessive orgia and ecstatic rituals that had been practised before.

The seduction of Eve and the subsequent Fall of humanity in the garden of Eden made clear that temptation was the fundamental sin, and acquiescing to one's base desires was the stuff of evil – accepting the wisdom of the serpent was a turn away from the glories of God toward wholly material pleasures that would stifle any thought or hope of transcending the limits of the flesh.

Certainly, among the consequences of the Fall was the loss of the angelic language previously known to Adam and the widespread corruption of Nature, both of which further distanced humanity from its creator and effectively enthroned humankind as rulers of a base and bestial world. Though some (notably more mystical) theological schemas would espouse a more affirmative understanding of sex as an innate attempt to recreate the unity of being which man had sprung from, the most widely-held view of the carnal act was as a product of folly and vice.

St. Paul shows a degree of understanding – if only to acknowledge the inevitable – when he writes '...it is good for a man not to touch a woman. Nevertheless, to avoid fornication, let every man have his own wife.' Augustine of Hippo (354 – 430 C.E.) may have had this in mind when he stated that the begetting of a child was no sin, but the act of copulation was not without evil; he certainly did not approve of sex for its own sake, namely between those who were not wed, those of older age than was sensible for child-bearing and those for whom the act of love-making was the result of desire, rather than practicality.

Indeed, Augustine notes that desire is akin to 'a whirlpool', 'chains' and 'a seething cauldron' in his *'Confessions'* (written between 397 and 400 C.E.) though this may result from what had, it seems, been a sexual profligacy in his youth and the subsequent guilt that he felt for what he perceived to be his own spiritual weakness. Martin Luther (1483 – 1546 C.E.) would have no such compunction, with the devout Protestant reformer echoing the more strident of Hippo's works and stating clearly that *no* 'marital duty' took place without sin.

As such the desires of the physical man and woman must be suppressed by anyone that wished to develop spiritually. Among the groups who based their interpretations of Christianity on this point were the Shakers, or the 'United Society of Believers in Christ's Second Coming', who were founded by former Quakers before being bolstered by one Ann Lee (1736 – 1784 C.E.), from England, in the mid-1700's.

The Shakers were so known because of the ecstatic manifestations of their worship, but it was Ann Lee that would make the movement distinct from all others when she experienced an epiphany that revealed to her that the act of sexual intercourse was the root of all evil in creation; a married woman, she was clearly a strong exponent of her faith and a compelling speaker of it, as her husband not only accepted this belief, but became one of her followers in England before a move to America beckoned.

The Shakers lived together, with men and women in separate apartments. Marriage was discouraged as a source of 'lustful gratification' though married couples were able to join, as long as they joined their brethren in the celibate lifestyle. Sobriety and hard work were cornerstones, along with plain, simple dress and frugal living.

Where there was a trace of excess, perhaps as a result of the energies repressed through sexual abstinence, was in the dancing that gave them their informal name. Marches were common, and part of the standard ritual was dancing (with men and women in separate groups), where one participant might engage in Dervish-like spinning and an acute spiritual event experienced.

For Ann Lee and her disciples, God was both male and female, thus both genders had intrinsically equal rights and standing in society. Somewhat more contentious was the belief that Ann Lee was herself the second incarnation of Christ, a point which will no doubt have played a part in the sometimes vociferous and violent mobs that greeted the Shakers when marching. Mrs. Lee was often a target of this violence, the wearing nature of which will have been a contributing factor to her relatively early demise at the age of 48.

The Shakers enjoyed a sizeable following through the end of the 18th and 19th centuries, but the membership declined thereafter – a result that may have been linked to the ascetic lifestyle of the Society, but was certainly reflective of a group who required a constant stream of new members from outside, as none would be conceived and brought into their midst from within.

More extreme attitudes and beliefs are apparent where copulation with spirit partners, rather than human mates, is considered. The Mysteries certainly acknowledged the role of spirits and deities as a means of wisdom and insight, and shamanism the world over sees shamans assisted and inspired by 'spirit spouses', the finding of whom and union with can be an intrinsic stage in their initiation into the role.

More than a 'spirit guide', the spouse is the spiritual half of an intense partnership that can be symbolic, but can include love or even sexual gratification. Rituals are enacted to maintain and heighten the connection between shaman and mate, with unions made through trance states or dreams, and so the spouse is as present and as vital as a human mate would be, with the vital added element of knowledge and power on the spiritual plain which is where the shaman performs much of the work of healing, fertility and protection.

However, where sex is a sin and union between men and women is something of a curse, any idea of relations with a spirit is nothing less than an act of great evil, and quite literally the stuff of nightmares. In this context, we are in the domain of malefic spirits, hellish creatures like the Lamia and the Striges and the seductive wiles of the likes of Lilith, the first wife of Adam who had laid with demons to sate her desires, so noted in Isaiah 34:14: 'The wild beasts of the desert shall also meet with the wild beasts of the island, and the satyr shall cry to his fellow; the screech owl also shall rest there, and find for herself a place of rest.'

In this light, nightmares were frequently interpreted as a ministration of diabolic entities, where the tormented mind of sleep and the body pressed into the bed as though a great weight be upon it would be interpreted as the invisible presence of a demon or spirit squatting on its prone victim (an image vividly brought to life by painter Henry Fusili in his aptly titled 1781 oil work *'The Nightmare'*).

The repression of desire and the subsequent neuroses that might develop as a result, according to Freud and the psychoanalytical movement, would be an understandable root of sexual imagery in dreams and a guilt-complex/resistance that would result in a traumatic sleeping experience – indeed, the deeper-rooted the desires and the greater the conflict within the psyche, the more vivid and overwhelming the experience would likely be, hence the common feeling of helplessness that accompanies such events.

Of course, the fact these nightmares might result, at least in part, with no small degree of pleasure at the sating of wayward or suppressed lusts only add to their profundity for the man or woman experiencing them, as they are being forced to confront a part of their hidden self that is an uncomfortable if not torturous occurrence, particularly where the presence of sexual desires is directly opposed to the faith that is potentially their raison d'être. The result is an accusation that some 'other' is causing the nightmares, as they cannot be the product of a devout and pious mind.

The Jewish mystical work the *'Zohar'* notes that the erotic dreams of men are those created by the succubus, and where there is eroticism and allure we are frequently told that an outside agent must be at work, not least where we find historic outbreaks of manic behaviour and sexual 'nightmare' in nunneries – indeed, the repression of sexual energy and desire into a wholly spiritual relationship with Christ or with God seems to have made an ideal melting-pot from which this kind of dream could emerge and run riot, leading to apparent possessions, the citing of demonic pacts and eventual tortures and executions.

One well-known example of this occurred in Auxonne, France

of 1660, when a dashing young Priest (Father Nouvelet) began to appear in the erotic dreams of a number of Sisters under his care. The cause of such a disturbance was clearly the result of witchcraft, and so witches were ultimately brought to justice for the crime (receiving a relatively light sentence of banishment, only to be torn apart by the baying mob that waited for them outside the court).

The Father administered his own cure for the diabolism that had been summoned, exorcising the nuns by lying prostrate with them in bed and performing ceremonies at the altar while they took up erotic postures nearby. The Mother Superior, it should be noted, aired her objections to what began to look like something decidedly unbecoming for her charges, but was subsequently accused of witchcraft and lesbian desires herself.

Nuns' however, were but the tip of the iceberg when it came to these subconscious bacchanals. Men might be the victim of a succubus or witchcraft (often the act of a woman), but women were wholly more susceptible to sexual urges and of giving in to those urges, as they were the weaker sex, and no more equipped to fight animal desires than Eve had been.

Robert Burton's *'Anatomy of Melancholy'* (1621) states that nightmares of this sort can be removed through the act of marriage, an approach that is also said to have worked in certain cases of haunting, including those involving poltergeist activity. Marriage to the Church or to Christ was clearly no substitute for a woman so in thrall to her base needs, and this is no surprise when we also consider the works of Paracelsus, where we learn that demons are created by menstrual flux – not only are women more prone to the wiles of the spirits and demons, but they are responsible for their materialisation in the first place!

Sexual repression can be rather easily identified in the beliefs and actions of the prurient inquisitors of the time, but the addition of that to the heightened desires of religious celibates (if not all red-blooded men and women), so too the hysteria created by accusation upon accusation, incarceration and torture, it would be somewhat inevitable that every conceivable perversion and abomination that can be imagined would feature, whether through fear, lie, mental breakdown...and possibly the occasional truth. Sex was sin, but it is so inherent an aspect of human nature that it served to inform the 'good' and the 'wicked' in equal measure, and with it horrors on both sides of any judgement.

The concern for the evil of sex frequently harked back to the time of the Creation, and where Eve was not the centre of spiritual indignation, it was Lilith and the demons that were created from the mating of angels with, again, those weak-willed women. The *'Book of Enoch'* tells of fallen angels overtaken by desire for human women and coupling with them: '(they) began to go in unto them and defile themselves with them', while the pseudepigraphical *'Testament of Solomon'* from the early centuries C.E. has Asmodeus declare himself to be 'born of angel's seed by the daughter of men.'

Genesis echoes this (6:4) with 'The sons of God came unto the daughters of men, and they bore children to them' and, despite atypical Scholastic debate over the literal truth of these charges, the Church Fathers largely continued to connect sex with sin, if not evil itself. Demons were therefore the progeny of degeneracy and through that were desirous to bestir further degenerate acts.

As such, Augustine's *'De Civitate Dei'* or *'City of God'* from the 5th century C.E. describes devils as 'desiring and acting carnally with them' and Thomas Aquinas ruminated on the detail at some length in his *'Summa Theologiae'* (1485). These ideas were assented and given further credence by the likes of Pope Innocent VIII (1432 – 1492 C.E.) who was a keen supporter of the investigation of witchcraft, and works such as the infamous '*Malleus Maleficarum.*'

The concern of a Pope is not surprising given the frequency with which this form of devilry found ideal breeding grounds within houses of God. The Malleus tells of a Bishop Sylvanus who appeared to copulate with a nun, only for this to be revealed as a lie when the good Bishop denied the heinous charge. His rank and faith were of suitable standing for his proclamations to be accepted, and the predator was revealed to be nothing more than an incubus.

Similarly, Alphonsus de Spina wrote in 1467 of nuns waking from sleep to find their bodies and bedding in such a state as though they had laid with a man; where no man on the premises would or could act in such a way and the thought of any masturbatory act could safely be rejected due to the piety of the nuns in question, the only logical conclusion was infernal agency – after all, if the devil would stoop so low as to try to tempt St. Margaret of Cortona from the holy path by singing her filthy and bawdy ditties, then the seduction of sleeping nuns would be as nothing to him.

Of course, these activities were not restricted to nunneries. Jean Bodin's 1580 work '*Demonomanie*' mentions cases where girls as young as 6 years old were tempted to intercourse by demons, while Francesco Guazzo details several cases in his '*Compendium Maleficarum*' (1608) including that of a beautiful girl from the Moray Firth in Scotland who rejected a number of marriage proposals from nobles, only to fall prey to the advances of an incubus.

The girl admitted to her parents that a striking and handsome stranger was her paramour, a young man who appeared and vanished without explanation between his trysts with her. When a servant later declared that this young man was with the girl, the house was secured and the parents, along with servants and a Priest entered her room to find her in the embrace of a 'horrible monster whose appearance was terrible beyond human imagination.'

The Priest maintained his composure and recited the Gospel of John, which caused the demon to cry out, set fire to the furniture in the room and flee (taking the roof with him). The girl later gave birth to a monster as a result of this incident and '...lest it should be seen and bring disgrace upon her family, the midwives lit a huge fire and quickly burned it.'

Whether the recipient of a demon's affections were seen as victim or aggressor, the sin in these instances was that of bestiality, as the partner was perceived to be no more and no better than an animal. This understanding perhaps resulted from and in turn led to stories of the Devil mating with women in the form of a dog, a cat, deer or fowl among other creatures; Henri Boguet's *'An Examen of Witches'* from 1590 offers notable examples of this, including that of a convent in Cologne, 1566, where a dog was found lifting up the robes of the resident nuns to abuse them.

The succubus is rather less prominent than her 'male' counterpart, a fact which is most frequently ascribed to the aforementioned weak will of women, alongside their relative lasciviousness in comparison to the temperate, morally-courageous and spiritually strong men.

That said, female spirits did appear at points to tempt and distract several men of no little religious bearing, including St. Hippolytus (d. 236 C.E.) who on one occasion threw a chasuble at a nude woman in his presence only to find the corpse of a crone before him, and St. Anthony of Egypt (251 – 356 C.E.) who was challenged to sin by the devil in the form of a beautiful woman.

Guazzo confirms less holy targets of these predators, including one young man who actually had a succubus found for him by his parents so that he could lie with her, only for him to discover that penetration was far from pleasurable '...as if he had entered an icy cavern.' With this in mind, the popular record of the man who was executed in Bologna, Italy, in 1468 for running a brothel staffed entirely by succubi becomes a truly bizarre and compelling story, not least for the questions it raises about the true allure of the 'night-hag' to the general Italian male.

Albertus Magnus (1206 – 1280 C.E.) went so far as to state that there were '...places in which a man can scarcely sleep at night without a succubus accosting him,' which suggests a scale of persecution on a par with the victims of incubi, though the usual understanding is that women are by far more likely to be targeted – and claimed – by the charms of demons and spirits of this form. This is because such beings were said to attack those with the weakest wills, with a view to degrading them through engaging in any manner of vice, of which sex was a foremost and especially popular choice.

Certainly any form of perceived depravity, including the taking of drugs and criminal behaviour, could be said to lead to the same end of sin and therefore estrangement from God, but sex was a firm favourite for demons and inquisitors, just as with men and women, because the desires that fuelled it were in no short supply, and the sating of those desires required very little beyond a willing partner to successfully induce.

A further reason for demons choosing the sexual aspect of humanity extends beyond it being an easy target due to a common weakness of the flesh, as some writers and theologians believed that the goal of these nocturnal trysts was the forging of new life among beings that themselves had no means to procreate. Caesarius of Heisterbach was one proponent of this belief, stating that devils collected the semen from men in the form of a succubus, in order to plant it within the womb of a willing female when in the form of an incubus.

The Franciscan Ludovico Maria Sinistrari (1622 – 1701 C.E.) explained in greater detail, noting that the devil takes on the mantle of a human corpse, or fashions a body from various corpses before selecting 'robust' men and women to perform this infernal generation. The semen that is collected is suitably '...abundant, thick, rich in spirits' and the female bodies that are chosen to house this seed are similarly vital in nature. Sinistrari adds that the orgasms attained through intercourse with a demon are more pleasurable than those experienced with a mortal partner, which is perhaps an inadvertent, early link between what would later be termed 'psycho-sexual energy' and supernatural activity.

Where there is a product of this act, it is invariably grotesque (as in the case of the girl in the Moray Firth), with mentions of a child that fed only on blood, a tapeworm, a baby with a wolf's head and a snake's tail, among other delights. There are the whispers of a more serious and disturbing point here, in that any unexpected child, or any baby seen to have a physical defect, might be heralded as a result of supernatural involvement such as witchcraft or, indeed, the work of an incubus.

Other forms of demons that are inextricably linked with sexual urges and repressions include the ubiquitous vampire (bearing associations of all manner of sexual 'deviance' including necrophagism – eating of the dead, necrosadism – murder in order to copulate, and necrophilia – pleasure from relations with the dead) and werewolf. Both are manifestations of suppressed atavistic desires, and the fear of/acquiescing to the abandon of lustful excess, and are on this level different manifestations of the same drives and fears that fuelled the concept of the incubus and succubus.

These malefic figures would not succeed in their aims, however, without the participation of a mortal in uniting with them, and away from the torment of the nightmare and its ignorant victims, the obvious party to consider in this concept of sex and sin were witches, thus we find almost universal ideas pertaining to their rites, works and revelries that consistently link them to every variation of sexual desire and, indeed, sexual act.

Of course, though men were accused alongside women in crimes of witchcraft, it is largely the women who gained the notoriety and appeared to be the prominent aggressors in these instances. We are brought once more to the simple and widely-accepted fact of the time that women were more susceptible to sin, with St. Jerome stating that woman is 'the gate of the Devil', and the medieval grimoire '*The Sworn Book of Honorius*' making clear that in magic, woman is a risk that is too profound to be worth taking: '...be penitent...forbearing all female enticements...for it is better to live with a bear or a lion in its den than to live with a woman.'

After all, if a woman was more likely to be tempted by the Devil and his like, it was more likely that a woman would be the tempter toward further excesses and depravities – one need only consider the shameful image of the witch, clutching the phallic-broom between her legs in the hope of transportation to a place of vice and physical pleasures, to understand the threat that women might pose.

There are therefore a number of ways in which both the reality and the developed myth of the witch and witchcraft were associated with sex, not least of which are the examples of their magic focused on carnal relations – whether with the aim of abundance or prohibition – between couples, a desiring individual and their unrequited love, or perhaps complete strangers.

'Love potions' are a notable and widespread work of witchcraft that often employed ingredients that had associations with sex and fertility, frequently because of similarities in shape or being connected with animals that were believed to be virile and sexually profligate. For instance, lizards might be used as their shape was similar to that of a phallus, while the Greeks baked phallic-shaped loaves to achieve the same ends; conversely, beans might be used due to their resemblance to the form of female genitalia.

Partridges or fish were employed due to their apparent fecundity and perceived promiscuity, while mandrake (that which appeared to grow in the form of a human and said to shriek as it was torn from the ground) was said to offer potency, as was the oyster. Less palatable but integral to the magical workings were the bodily excreta of the person desiring to force an outcome and/or that of the individual that was the target – blood, sweat, nail parings, hair (including pubic hair) and ordure were all used at various times, energising the final concoction with the human will that would direct the spell.

Such mixtures were common across civilizations, with no little effect ascribed to them; it was said that the Roman poet Lucretius (b. 94 B.C.E.) was driven to suicide in a bout of sexual frenzy following the taking of a love potion, an incident that may well not have happened in truth, but the story of which tells us something of the use and the infamy of these intoxicating philtres. A more direct approach might be had with the power of the 'evil eye', which would overpower and warp another's will when employed successfully.

Elsewhere, a cake baked with menstrual blood would ensure the fidelity of a partner and cause that mate's impotence with any woman but his own, and men would add semen to the mix when hoping to attract and bewitch a desired party. At one time, even the act of consuming human flesh in a ritual context was said to revive the attractions of a lover.

In Brazil, the making of 'witches' coffee' is a continuing magical rite to instil the powerful attraction of another; typically consisting of coffee, a generous amount of sugar and menstrual blood or the result of coffee being passed through the undergarments of a woman, the hearty beverage has to be imbibed at breakfast and dinner while a spell is cast for it to have a suitable effect on the lucky recipient.

Away from this devil's banquet, the Greeks and Romans were

keen adherents of 'binding' spells to attract and deny attentions, with dolls in human form pierced and contorted and tablets engraved with incantations and buried with the dead as different means of realising their wishes – though the idea of 'binding' someone to love seems a somewhat more sinister and macabre activity even than binding someone to suffer, it was an approved method of 'winning' a heart all the same.

The causing of estrangement in a couple and making a man impotent or a woman barren were also possible through the efforts of a knowing witch, with bindings again being utilised (such as a knot being tied or a lock secured during a wedding and the secured goods hidden or cast into an expanse of water in order to create a barrier to any act of consummation).

Where a man's inability to perform his conjugal rites was desired, it might even be possible for a witch to use magic to remove his member entirely – an act which, it might be argued, is more myth than truth, but which nonetheless strikes a suitably Freudian link between men, rejection of the mother, fear of castration and the projection of that fear onto the archetypal image of the witch!

The epitome of the relationship between the witch and sex is, again, where legend and folklore more blatantly blends with any semblance of reality, namely in accounts of the Witches' Sabbat and the associated orgiastic rites that were said to take place there. That obsession of clergy, inquisitor and the common man and woman with sex again comes to the fore, with an opportunity found and indeed used to conjure images of every possible perversion and peccadillo imaginable.

Orgy was only one stage in the purported Sabbat (following the osculum infame – the kissing of the Devil's behind – a recital of one's sins, then feast and wild dancing) but it certainly garnered some of the most intense scrutiny and attention by writers, critics and those confessing alike. One 18th century engraving of a Sabbat taking place on the Brocken in the Harz

Mountains, Germany, offers a neat summation of the supposed revelries, with a joyous procession taking place amid a number of smiling demons, witches and demons enjoying sexual dalliances, one in particular having her breast cupped and another, in the sky, with her legs up in the air and her skirt hitched up, having just enjoyed the attentions of a goat.

Pierre de' Lancre repeated the confession of 16 year old Jeanette d'Abadie to similar effect: '...she had seen every one mix incestuously and in violation of the laws of nature...she blamed herself for having been deflowered by Satan and carnally known 'an infinity of times' by one of her relations and others who condescended to go with her.'

Rarely were there any offspring from these revelries, though such was possible according to accounts when women coupled with the Devil himself; the result may be typically monstrous, or inhuman (reptiles and toads being mentioned) and they would likely be offered for sacrifice at the next Sabbat, or so the stories told.

The endowment and ability of the Devil was of course another important focus of these tales, though frequently the depictions were contradictory – as such, his member was at points described as 'immensely large' and only 'as long and thick as a finger'; it was scaled like a serpent and, again cited through a confession by Pierre de' Lancre, '... of two parts, half of iron, half of flesh, and similarly his testicles.'

In one final quote, de'Lancre offers the epitome of what any confession – and indeed any enacted Sabbat – was intended for, the apogee of blasphemy, sin and titillation, still concerning the Devil's member: '...at other times wholly of horn, and commonly forked like a serpent's tongue; he customarily performed both coitus and pederasty at once, while sometimes a third prong reached to his lover's mouth.'

The Scottish witch Isobel Gowdie (1632 – 1662 C.E.) offered her own testimony of the Devil's manhood in one spontaneous confession: 'His members are exceeding great and long; no man's members are so long or as big as they are...He is abler for us that way than any man can be, only he is heavy like a malt-sack; a huge nature, very cold, as ice.' Here a number of the stories do agree, in that the member and its ejaculate were ice cold yet burned with its touch, with a long-lasting effect on the mind and body that was, like the act itself, a thing of simultaneous pain and pleasure.

Aside from the no less prevalent element of sexual politics, these stories are remarkable in that they share much with accusations that had been previously aimed at heretics like the Cathars and the Knights Templar and would later be aimed at the figure of the Satanist. It should be noted that some kernels of truth may well be found within all such accusations, from the Cathars accepting of any sexual act that did not result in pregnancy, because the material world was itself sin and therefore no 'fall' could occur, to the Knights Templar potentially engaging in homosexual acts because they were an exclusively male group of warrior monks with natural urges and lusts.

The Sabbat, too, may well have occurred in forms similar to certain accounts we read, even if the scale and frequency of the gatherings be exaggerated beyond sense. With that in mind, the contentious accounts of the Devil's prowess and the size and appearance of his member may be due to the confessions and reports being entirely fictitious, or to the fact that different revelries might have been led by different figures posing as the Devil, with the very likely possibility that artificial phalli were employed to ensure an unnatural effect.

Witches have certainly plied their trade over the centuries when it has come to attraction, repulsion and curse, therefore the entire corpus of accounts cannot be rejected. However, what is apparent amidst the murky waters where reality, gossip, fantasy and perversion meet is that any 'enemy' was the target of the most salacious accusations, and the most despicable imaginings that their opponents could ascribe, and this was no less so with views and attitudes toward witchcraft as the centuries progressed.

This inextricable mix of fact and fiction is also apparent with the 20th century Satanism of Anton LaVey (1930 – 1997 C.E.) and other modern-day movements for whom sex is not perceived as sin, even if the opposition and oppression of these groups is not as vociferous nor as destructive today. The typical 'Black Mass' with a defrocked Priest and a prostitute as acolyte, a virgin spread-eagled on an altar, an upturned crucifix, a defiled host and sexual rites did gain something of a reality with LaVeyan Satanism, but this was as much for show as it was an act of blasphemy (after all, for many Satanists God does not exist, therefore there is no such act as blasphemy).

For LaVey and others after him, sex is a part of 'free love' that is the right of every man and woman, with the freedom of each individual being the core concern. Orgies, sadomasochism and any peccadillo or fetish can be enjoyed without fear of moral or spiritual reprisal, so long as those participating are there by consent and not by force. This is not to say that no wrongs have been perpetrated within these schemas, or that 'decadence' is the best/only approach to a rounded life...but the scale of myths and stories that repeatedly blur reality with fancy suggests that the place of sex in faith, magic and in everyday life has far from been resolved as we venture into the 21st century.

The sexual liberation that Satanism speaks of no doubt attracted as many adherents as it repelled opponents, those for whom overt physicality was as close to sin as an increasingly secular mindset can recognise, and in reality sex was and remains a viable means of stirring both fellowship and dissention because it is inherent, timeless and, whether we like the fact or not, fundamental to who and what we are.

Conjunction

Away from the extremes of biases that are stoked by the Fall of Adam and Eve, the heady Bacchanal, the orgies of the infernal Sabbat and the sex rites of Satanism, there is a broad canvas of symbolic interpretations of the sex act and union that lend themselves to a decidedly more mystical and, perhaps, nuanced understanding.

Here, the double-headed axe is the womb of woman cleft by the phallic member which serves as the handle, and the spade being driven into the earth to activate the generation of new life is an intrinsically sexual and yet spiritual act. The practical applications of magic are still apparent, such as with the use of shells (resembling the vulva and thus bestowing fecundity when worn as a necklace), but the associations are often decidedly more numinous in character (as with the pearl, which is perceived as a foetus in the womb of the oyster's shell that mirrors the spark of God that resides at the very core of each man and woman).

This is clear with the 'Sephirothic Tree' or 'Tree of Life' of Jewish mysticism, found within the Cabbala. Kether the crown sits at the top of this tree, serving as the highest point that can be interpreted from the distance of the material plain, representing the supernal unity of creation from which the dual principles of male and female emanate.

These principles exist in a form of dynamic tension alike the Yin and Yang of Taoism, serving as opposing yet complimentary forces that are of the same origin which are compelled to seek a return to that original state of union and godhood, and thus interact on all levels of existence – the return to a condition of completion requires the male and female to approach, understand and embrace the various manifestations of active and passive energies that are latent within themselves, much as Jung espoused the importance of each man and woman recognising the anima or animus that is the subconscious of the mind.

The second sephira is the male Chokmah, the phallic line or creative impulse that penetrates the third sephira of Binah that is the womb of fecundity and the great, primordial water; thus wisdom and spirit meet, merge and create understanding, from which further emanations and qualities in due course emerge. The division between active and passive is upheld by the opposing pillars of 'Joachin' or 'mercy' and 'Boaz' or 'severity', where we perceive the dualistic qualities of fire and water, consciousness and unconsciousness, the contained and the container – the plain of Form that is the archetypal feminine, led to a state of gestation through its interaction with the plain of Force that is the archetypal male.

The 'divine spark' that has been mentioned is held to be without gender because it is of Kether which, as creative force, is whole unto itself and therefore without dual principle; both aspects of the created dualism are thus intrinsic to existence, as each needs the other to gain genuine insight and wisdom.

It is an interesting point that the line of emanation from Kether to the material Malkuth or back through from 'earth' to 'crown' resembles a lightning strike that courses through all ten sephiroth on the Tree of Life. Not only do we see a distinct symbolic link between the glorious golden light of the creator with the divine sparks that are rooted within its creations, but we also find a common representation of light as life that connects with the dynamic phallic force and the effulgence of union and, with it, an epiphanic event or raising of consciousness that is described in various ancient texts and beliefs across the globe.

The mystical interpretation of numbers resonates with symbolism akin to that of the Tree of Life. I serves as the phallic creative energy of God or creator, from which is produced the

II that is the duality of opposing / attracted forces (while also suggesting the developed concept of the Devil as horned god and cosmic 'opponent').

III is the number that by its nature offers the potential and reality of generation, splitting the II and balancing them, potentially lifting them above their previous condition by uniting them. III, however, also connects those elements with the material world in that they symbolise the genitals, the very means of procreation.

IV is therefore the product of the union, which is both a physical and spiritual act. IV is form and physicality, a plateau of creation seen by the four points that make up the square and balance all from creator, through division and ultimate reunification (a key aspect of the Hermetic ideal).

It is worth noting that where we extend beyond the IV of form, we find the V of excess – a number associated with the senses and with sex for pleasure, because it follows on from the perfection of form; just how integral or needless this excess is held to be is a much-debated aspect of faith and mysticism, and it is arguable that V is the number of magic in that here man and woman move past natural abilities and indulge in pleasure and a desire for mastery over the world of form, through a will that is entirely human, rather than holy.

Three times V is XV, an exponential increase in physicality and of the sex act for pleasure, which makes that number a suitable place to find 'The Devil' in the traditional tarot deck. However, as with the tarot in general, no image is without various layers of symbolic meaning, thus the profound materiality that the card represents offers more than a crass rejection of sex as sin.

The card has links to the rutting Pan or horned god, not least through the obvious devil-image that usually dominates the scene. Associated with the ram of Capricorn which is itself ruled by the malign influence of Saturn, 'The Devil' of card XV is a sexual connection that is only of negative worth because it is borne of base instincts and nothing more – sex itself is no evil, nor the material world that offers its delights, but to limit oneself to the physical plain and the satisfaction of sense over spirit is to chain oneself to the domain of the flesh.

The Devil is temptation, the bastion of revelry and pleasure but only of the temporary sort. That said, the individual that acknowledges this limitation takes a vital step toward self-knowing and through that toward the knowledge of true enlightenment, therefore it can be said that both the Devil and the physical pleasures that he summates are necessary aspects of our being. There can be a liberation of body and senses, but this is not in itself an end – and it only serves as a form of hell (more similar to purgatory) for the man or woman who remains in thrall to the pleasures of the flesh without recognising all else there is to existence, to self and to soul.

Away from the obvious links with the Devil, the tarot offers copious forms of sexual symbolism, and it can be argued that within the schema of the cards the Fall of humanity, like the Devil, is a concept to be championed for its role within a broader cosmos, rather than perceived as a moment of tragedy and curse.

True, the gaining of wisdom led to a state of corporeality, but through knowledge of the flesh and of sex (and therefore of the union of opposites and procreation), Adam and Eve were granted a fecundity of life and a balancing of spiritual energies that they would otherwise have remained ignorant of. The Fall gave the means of spiritual liberation through sacred knowledge, and the tarot offers copious representations of that sacred knowledge, through all manner of correspondences but founded on the esoteric meaning of numbers, and the not-so-esoteric exploration of the sexual facet of humanity.

With no small degree of analogy to our previous glimpse at numbers, I of the tarot is the 'Juggler' or 'Magician' – Adam, capable of self-fecundity and the prime physical driver of creative energy, who finds his opposite in II, the 'High Priestess' or 'Female Pope', the female force of Eve. She is the nubile archetypal feminine that tames the creative force and gestates the resulting union of energy.

Card VI is 'The Lovers', the union of opposites in a distinctly more spiritual vein. A.E. Waite (1847 – 1952 C.E.) shows Adam and Eve before the Fall in his deck, though the Fall is nonetheless seen as an implicit consequence of the scene shown. The Lovers are the realisation of the attraction of opposites, and their ultimate conjoining as a microcosmic reflection of their creator – and the card denotes the ability of each individual to attain a higher mode of being through the unification of the opposing forces within.

Eliphas Levi (1810 – 1875 C.E.) spoke of love as being the meeting of '...void and plentitude...shaft and wound...' and the Lovers certainly offer a glimpse of the wholeness to which we aspire, both in our material life and the spiritual existence that was our origin. This neatly leads us to Aleister Crowley's 'Justice' card (VIII) which he named 'Adjustment', where his 'Woman Satisfied' holds aloft the sword and scales that he equates to the phallus and testicles; though the card speaks of equilibrium, its connection to the scales of Libra, ruled by Venus, nonetheless suggests a communion of sorts that can be linked back to the meeting of Lovers just two cards previous!

More blatant still is Crowley's card IX, 'Lust', which depicts the Whore of Babylon astride the beast of Revelation, which is emblazoned with the number '666'. As Revelation 17:6 describes this potent scene: 'And I saw the woman drunken with the blood of the saints, and with the blood of the martyrs of Jesus...'

The Whore is shown in a state of euphoria, with her senses completely overwhelmed – this is effectively sexual ecstasy, the 'divine drunkenness' (as Crowley himself put it) akin to the ancient rites of Bacchanalia, though it is notable that the

Whore still holds the reins as she rides...though she has been lifted and transformed, those same transformative energies have allowed her to tame the Beast.

More nuanced is card XXI, 'The World', where we often see a naked women draped in a veil – possibly Eve – serving as the great goddess or Nature, the female principle that, again, is the spirit descended to matter where it remains with longing until it can be duly energised and 'completed' by conjunction with the potent creative energy that will balance its innate character.

Of course, the suits of the minor arcana also represent variations on the theme of the male and female principle, with the Cups or Chalices the epitome of femininity and the means of gestation, and the Batons or Wands serving as the phallic energy that penetrates and stirs the waters of the Chalice.

Given the adaptation of gender and the sex act through Jewish mysticism, the esoteric lore of number and the tarot, it is hardly surprising that they received frequent adaptation within the art of alchemy, though – as with so much of the Hermetic corpus – the meanings behind each use of image and metaphor shifts like sand, depending on the author or the reader.

The use of sex as a symbol is something of a foregone conclusion when it comes to alchemy, given that the entire process (both physical and spiritual) relates to a series of separations and unifications of elements, towards the ultimate refinement that is variably the 'Philosopher's Stone', the 'elixir of life', 'gold' (which can be interpreted literally or symbolically) or itself a form of immortality: Calcination; Dissolution; Separation; Conjunction; Fermentation; Distillation; Coagulation.

Paracelsus (1493 – 1541 C.E.) stated that the 'Prima Materia' or 'first matter' from which the goal could be achieved was the mother of all elements and all created things, a unique product of God that had been corrupted supposedly, it would seem, by the Fall. Given that the goal in question was a stripping away of levels of consciousness toward a coaxing out of that ubiquitous inner divine spark, the essence of the Prima Materia may well be one and the same with the essence of the Philosopher's Stone.

The union of opposites is widely cited and illustrated among other complex and fantastic imagery, seen as the joining of the 'red man' and 'white woman' (the male sulphur, father of metals and the female mercury, mother of metals). The oft described 'Chemical Wedding' is the meeting and transition between states of the female principle, volatile and changeable, with the male seed sol, with the alchemical vessel of the marriage bed serving as the ideal environment for the former substances to effectively pass away, conjoin, and thus regenerate.

Alchemical texts speak of and depict incest, or in the case of 'The Book of Lambspring' (1556) of the father losing his son only to find him again and ultimately devour him (alike Saturn) before reposing in his chamber to 'sweat out' the new substance borne of the two elements. However the stages of the process were represented, the key was the continual meeting of opposing forces toward a purified unity and a higher nature than was previously held – whether as flawless gold, eternal life or spiritual epiphany.

As we have seen, some ancient beliefs centred on the idea of God as bisexual, and if humanity was deemed to have been created in the image of God, then humanity must have first existed as a bisexual being; indeed, there are early Jewish teachings whereby Adam and Eve exist as one before God cleaves them apart (with the phallic axe). The reunion of the dual aspects is thus an act which raises the individual to one of perfection, a salvaging and reclaiming of what has long been lost toward further reintegration with God, the original creative force.

A common figure in alchemical texts that exemplified the idealised state of integration was the hermaphrodite, the 'divine child' bearing both aspects in one body. Found in Greek myth as the child of Aphrodite and Hermes (and in turn of Venus and Mercury), Hermaphroditus was a beautiful young man who became conjoined with a nymph that beseeched the gods for them to never be parted. The resulting two-sexed being features in numerous mystical works as a representation of unity from opposition, which can be applied to all levels of human existence.

In one aspect of alchemy the hermaphrodite is mercurius, the universal agent that is philosophical mercury – the very stuff by which transformation is achieved – exactly because it consists of the dual aspects of male (sulphur) and female (argent vive/quicksilver). As it is noted in the *'Liber de arte chymia'* of Marilio Ficino in 1518:'Mercurius is all metals, male and female, and an hermaphroditic monster.'

In a more esoteric vein, this figure is the 'Rebis' or 'dual matter' that is a fundamental stage of the Hermetic magnum opus, the reconciliation of male and female and, by extension, of spirit with matter. Beyond duality and even beyond conjunction, the hermaphrodite was the meeting of the sun and moon, 'Red King' and 'White Queen', in a resplendent higher level of being and consciousness.

The androgynous figure of the hermaphrodite is applicable to the individual who is able to traverse the Sephirothic Tree and the spiritual development explored in the tarot – more directly, it can be glimpsed in the symbolism of Gemini, the twins who represent the procreative force and with that both creative and created nature.

C.G. Jung certainly appreciated the symbolism of alchemy, and in his own manner wove an intricate web through Hermeticism, myth, religion and the broader canvas of symbols inherent to humanity in his psychoanalytic works. Jung stated that all psychological phenomena equated to manifestations of energy, thus sexuality was an integral element even where it was not central to his understanding, as it had been with Freud.

The various explorations of duality, union and indeed the hermaphrodite of alchemy are vital to Jung's understanding of psychology, as these were all results of previous attempts by humankind to seek a wholeness that was absent in everyday life, a need to 'square the circle' and attain an integration of the self with a higher level of being (as in the case of the Cabbalist venturing through the various emanations of God, or the Gnostic seeking a more direct connection with the 'pneuma' or spark within).

For Jung, libido was symbolised as the sun, light, fire, sex, fertility and growth – which neatly unites it with everything we have considered from the creation myths of the ancients to the lightning-strike passages of soul to godhead – and while the libido was not the sole or central drive of humanity, to repress its expression and desire without acknowledgement was to force a regression of the self. Denying such desires or, worse still, anathematising libidinal urges altogether, would deform those urges into ever-greater perversions and lead to neurosis for the individual.

The balancing of opposites that would allow for harmony within (the awareness and acceptance of one's anima or animus) did not rely on either wallowing in or restraining from the sexual impulse, but did require a willingness to accept the self in its true light, which would include a sexual aspect. Libido is therefore accepted as a fundamental energy within men and women, but it is but one form of that energy; by overindulging in its wants is equal to denying them, essentially granting it a disproportionate prominence within the self, to the extent that no true balance can be achieved.

The idea of misspent energies and the meaning had for the individual was not unique to Jung, and can be seen in all manner of works such as the Mesopotamian epic of Gilgamesh (c. 2100 B.C.E.). Here, Gilgamesh is seen to be a great King and warrior whose people come to fear him because they interpret his now insatiable sexual appetite as a continued desire for conquest that might lead to disaster if left unchecked.

They pray for a worthy adversary and receive the giant Enkidu for their trouble, but Enkidu also suffers from a similar misuse of energy – before engaging in battle with Gilgamesh he spends a week in the company of a concubine, following which he is much diminished in strength, vitality, and even physical size! Ultimately the two men become firm friends, but they both appear to have found more suitable outlets for their passions and atavistic drives, with Enkidu showing less interest in sex and Gilgamesh going so far as to spurn the attentions of the goddess Ishtar.

Sex, then, has its place in many of these philosophies and spiritualities, but true wisdom comes from the equilibrium of spirit and matter. Excess and abstinence can be equally damaging depending on the individual, for whom the libidinal urge may be strong or latent, but for whom that urge nonetheless exists as one integral aspect of being. As in alchemy, sex is a dynamic framework through which the profound can be explored; by no means is sex nothing more than a sin, but nor is it an end in and of itself.

Transformation

There is also an ancient tradition within mysticism whereby sex is indeed a form of conjunction and the sex act is a profound ritual, though where the idea of misspent and excessive energy is fundamental to any degree of success. One beautiful representation of this can be seen in the Buddhist Yab-Yum, depicted as a male deity embracing a female partner to the point of interpenetration – the figure therefore represents a concept of primordial unity similar to that of Kether on the Tree of Life, a balance composed of compassion and insight in equal measure.

Chinese Taoism exemplifies this ideal in its fángzhōngshù or 'bedchamber arts' whereby rude health, vigour, longevity and heightening of consciousness can be obtained through ritualised sex that promotes the joining of energies. This form of practise was known during the Han dynasty (202 B.C.E. – 220 C.E.) and certainly held popular appeal throughout the Tang dynasty (618 – 907 C.E.), though the taboo that became associated with sex as a result of Confucianism all but erased it as a ritual form.

The lineage of such bedchamber arts was impressive to the extent of legend, notably with the story of the 'Yellow Emperor' Gongsun Xuanyuan (2717 – 2599 B.C.E.) who was said to have gained immortality through the ritual absorption of the 'vital fluid' from 1,200 women. Later forms of the ritual would emphasise the relative 'vampirism' that this tale suggests, though this is held to be a gradual corruption of what had been a more affirmative experience for both parties.

Indeed, the Yellow Emperor himself had a female advisor who confirmed with him ten notable signs of female satisfaction so as to enhance the pleasure of a union, which would see a greater production of 'ching' energy that could then heighten his 'chi'. This too sounds wholly one-sided, but it should be recognised that women were seen to have an essentially inexhaustible supply of their gestational powers and so no diminution would prove damaging.

As with the Yab-Yum, however, the pleasure of coupling and the benefits of a mystical union could be mutually rewarding, and it was not just men that were said to have gained spiritual insight and immortality through this Taoist approach to sex;

of course this is only just, given that both aspects of the dual principles of yin and yang are equally vital to any balancing of the dynamic cosmic energies, as the Taoist '*Book of Changes*' suggests: 'Male and female mix their essential forces and the ten thousand things arise.'

The sexual act itself is here one of pleasurable order, with a steady pace in a calm setting to ensure maximum duration for both partners. Through this the inherent energies are built in a measured way – and with measure being key to success, intoxicants like alcohol have no place within the ritual of sex, though use of meditation, prayer and suffumigation is acceptable and perhaps underlines the ceremonial aspect of the act.

Ultimately, the aim is the gradual raising of ching energy (which for men can be found in sperm and for women in menstrual blood) before its being conserved and effectively 'internalised' in order to feed the brain, and in turn invigorate both body and spirit. Similar rites can be found in other religions along with various esoteric teachings and beliefs associated with magic and sorcery.

As a natural act which is performed with care and control, lifting the physical consciousness and ultimately infusing the spirit, sex is a wholly appropriate mode of practise for those wishing to complement and fulfil the way of the Tao, not least because it utilises the physical manifestations of male and female toward an inner path of union – a dynamic perfectly symbolised by the Yab-Yum and of course the Yin-Yang, which denotes the interconnectedness of all forces and the potential transformations that are achievable through their various conjunctions.

Elsewhere, around the 4th century C.E., new esoteric works known as Tantras began to have prominence within Hinduism and Buddhism, espousing the place of mandalas and mantras within worship as a basis for meditation and the all-important raising of consciousness. Though in India this Tantrism would by some be associated with black magic due to its embracing of material existence as a means of attaining enlightenment, it certainly found a keen following within aboriginal Indian cults and Mystery schools, along with a long line of sages who understood physicality as a path to transformation, rather than as a barricade.

The term 'Tantra' is from the Sanskrit word 'Tan', 'to stretch', denoting a form of web or weaving, but in a broader Indian context is understood to describe any applicable framework within a text, technique or form of practise. As such, there are various forms of Tantra, of which sexual Tantra is but one – even if the Western world has lavished especial attention on that form over and above all others.

Indeed, even the term 'Tantra' has been cited as a 19th century creation by Western scholars who misunderstood and minimised the importance and following of the esoteric movement within the Indian faiths, not least as they offered a freedom of worship that frequently defied clear boundaries. The blinkered nature of the Western psyche perhaps makes itself known here, as the meeting of sacred with profane and lack of delineation is traditionally too chaotic for such a view, and the inclusion of sexual intercourse summons either schoolboy or prude among observers, rather than serious appreciation of the scholarly and the spiritual.

The effects and reach of Tantrism are far and wide, encompassing Hinduism, Buddhism, Jainism and Taoism and bleeding through into Western culture in a somewhat bowdlerised and yet striking manner, but for this study it is the role of sex within Tantra that is of primary importance, and to which we now turn.

The focus of this worship is most commonly Shiva and his consort Shakti, though again there is no prominent figure – both are equal in that they together represent the unity of balanced forces, and so both are equally important to the texts and rituals in question. It can even be noted that along with the prestige of sexual conjunction within Tantrism, the feminine principle (embodied by Shakti) is idolized above all else.

Heinrich Zimmer (1890 – 1943 C.E.) noted the proliferation of phallic imagery and form common to Indian symbolism where the concept of the creative energy and fertility is concerned (Shiva), but he also made clear the role of the 'Lotus' and the 'Earth Mother' that was Shakti. The act of creation necessitated the seed of the god, but without the nurturing gestation of the 'Womb of the Earth' that was his opposite, the created world would have been an impossibility, thus Shakti is the 'liberation' to the 'bondage' of Shiva.

Shiva, then, is the male figure of 'Purusha' or 'Pure Spirit' while Shakti is the woman of 'Prakriti' or 'Nature', but as with a lock and a key neither hold true meaning or achieve their potential without the other. Thus there may be negative connotations placed on modern interpretations of lines like 'I am Heaven, thou art Earth' as uttered by a husband in the *Brihadaranyaka Upanishad*', but the relationship is one of equilibrium and doting and does not entertain what are effectively petty power-plays.

As with the Yab-Yum, images of Shiva and Shakti at the point of conjunction are imbued with an intense passion that is borne of a connection beyond the physical, and so it should be as, alike Yin and Yang, Zeus and Gaia and others they are two-sides of the one coin, created in and of one another and so essentially one being that is finding rapture within itself. Even the greatest contentions of force and attitude between them emanate from one source, suggesting the various manifestations that emanate from the first two created sephiroth of the Tree of Life.

One striking story from the *'Shiva Purāna'* tells of Shiva appearing naked and holding his penis in one hand while performing lewd actions. Failing to recognise the deity, a group of sages who have been shocked by his appearance and manner cause Shiva's penis to drop off, but the member blazes 'like fire' and burns all that it touches between heaven and underworld until it is anointed with sacred water and placed in the 'mountain girl' in the form of the yoni or womb and, through ardent worship, finally loses its restless energy. Happiness and prosperity are regained, as the vital energies of Shiva have found an appropriate environment.

We can certainly see the parallel with the story of Osiris' member being cut off and fertilising the waters of the Nile, but more prominent here is the central symbolism of phallus meeting yoni , and through the resulting balance the focussing of the vital energies it contains so that fecundity and happiness reign in place of destruction and torment.

One form of Tantrism that fully embraces this symbolism and has its roots in the 1st millennium C.E. is that of the Hindu Kaula, the sects of which seek to actively break taboos in order to attain liberation from what are effectively social shackles. In this framework, an act is not itself impure or sinful (if such a term could be applied), and can only be deemed to lack purity if it is performed without due understanding or intent, thus freedom is a vitally important factor within faith and ritual.

Extremes of practise can result from this approach, and among certain sects this has included acts such as meditation being performed by an individual next to a rotting corpse, but these extremes are exactly that – and the predominant forms of worship that are encouraged are centred on oneself, one's body and the union of sex as a suitable means toward a wholly spiritual goal.

Development begins with a movement from the state of duality that is understood to be nirvikalpa samadhi or 'absorption into the spiritual heart', and fundamental practises involve coitus (sexual rites known as maithuna), Tantric body alchemy (which is the utility of the Shakti or spiritual energy) and the ultimate raising of consciousness beyond the self (atman) toward a level of oneness (siddhi) with the universal consciousness from which all of creation originated.

Sacrifice is a cornerstone of this Tantrism, though this usually takes the form of an internal offering and can be associated with essentially any ritual act evoking the higher consciousness that is the 'supreme reality' that is Shiva. Sacrifice can also relate to an external, material act, though the offerings are then of a symbolic nature rather than those explored in our study of blood rites – the intent and the act are the fundamental aspect of the offering, rather than the offering in and of itself, and so the attitude of the individual is the main component. The importance of freedom cannot be overstated within this mode of belief; the removing of the self and its limited perceptions away from the constraints of social mores and toward the true reality that lies beyond our blinkered consciousness.

'Tradition' is of profound significance here, in that it can be overturned to challenge one's own conditioned behaviours, alter one's frame of reference, and through that attain new levels of thought. As such ritual acts frequently include various antinomian elements, which can include the aforementioned contact with the dead, as well as the consuming of intoxicants and offerings to appropriate deities that would be forbidden within any other form of worship.

From this, and the potential taboo-breaking that is implicit, it is perhaps easy to see how associations between Tantrism, excess and magic can be made, but in truth this reconditioning of the conscious mind is based entirely on an acceptance and understanding of traditions and social mores exactly so that the rejection of them makes for such a powerful psychological and spiritual transition – crossing boundaries of experience has no meaning for someone who does not appreciate the place and worth of 'tradition', and so the religious intent behind the acts must be appreciated.

In spite of the freedom that the disciple experiences, a guru is nonetheless vital in the Kaula school as a being with greater awareness who can help to guide others and indeed harness the energies released so as to ensure harmony. For a disciple to 'join' with a guru is to be included within that guru's higher awareness, through the power of meditation, and become as one with that awareness/self (atman). Key to the success of this reflected and internally-disseminated wisdom is the balance and unity maintained within a group, thus the guru is doubly-important to the growth and the wellbeing of his initiates.

As noted, ritual can include recitations (mantras) which are the most common form of worship, along with visualisations of the goddess and the creation and contemplation of mandalas, all of which open the mind of the individual to the energies of the group self. However, the raising of consciousness does not here solely transform the self and the spirit but also the body and, by that token, the Panchamakara or 'Grand Ritual' of the five makara ('tantric substances') makes use of worldly essences to elicit the physical being as well as the spiritual: madya (alcohol), mamsa (meat), matsya (fish), mudra (gesture) and maithuna (sex, which is held to be the most important of the five) all have ritual use in the mystical pursuit of the ultimate reality.

In Tantric sex the couple becomes one unified consciousness, a microcosmic reflection of Shiva and Shakti in embrace. There is then an ultimate dissolution of all levels into one being, but without their attaining Bhairava illumination the ritual is not a mystical experience, but a purely physical act. Again, the intent and bearing of the participants is key to any form of spiritual outcome, as this is a ritual that glorifies the act of sexual intercourse as a means *towards* perfection; it does not promote sex purely for gratification, even if pleasure can and should be an integral aspect therein.

This is a physical combination of the female nature energy and the male spirit combining, and so initiates can evoke a suitable Tantric deity to enhance the energies and create the optimum environment and state of mind. Being a physical act that impacts profoundly on the body, such ritual acts can also involve the presence of a guru and observers, with a guru's guidance understood to be priceless. However, this is not always the case and Tantric sex can of course be a private act; the key is the ability of the participants, and whether or not they can alone tap the necessary levels of consciousness to achieve illumination.

Where Western minds can perhaps better perceive the mystical bent of Tantric sex is in the beliefs often attached to the matter of orgasm, and the bodily emissions that are produced: 'Shanta' is where the resulting emission is internalised to the benefit of the self, while 'Udita' is where the partner becomes the focus of the emission, and 'Santodita' is where these two forms are united.

Indeed, semen retention is noted as early as 4th century C.E, though in some movements (such as the Buddhist Kalachakra) this is the ability of a master, rather than all who might attempt it, as described by the '*Mahāyānasūtrālamkāra*' of Asaṅga (c.5th century B.C.E.): 'Supreme self-control is achieved in the reversal of sexual intercourse in the blissful Buddha-poise and the untrammelled vision of one's spouse.'

On a broader level, 'coitus reservatus' sees the male bring himself to the brink of orgasm and remain at that level of heightened passion and pleasure without ejaculation, which is believed to be retained by the male, a rite which is also seen in certain Taoist practices. Ejaculation is not completely verboten however, not least due to the control and mastery that is required but also because the central aim of the union does not necessarily rely upon it: rather, the focus of the ritual is the use of prana (psychic energy) to activate the gateways that are the chakras, the points of the body where the Logos infuses the physical form with 'divine life.'

Kaula belief depicts the divine feminine energy (Shakti) of the kundalini as rising through the chakras – a conception later adopted and disseminated through Hatha Yoga. Kundalini is the serpent coiled at the base of the spine; arousing this snake sees it awaken every chakra through the genitals, navel, heart, throat, between the eyes and finally at the crown of the head (Shiva), where a state of bliss is attained.

The 'Song of the Snake Charmer' is one depiction of this masterly act ("Dance, snake, dance!") where a siddha or sage, an 'accomplished one', makes efforts to control the mind and rouse the sleeping snake of the kundalini. Duly aroused, it passes like a zigzag of lightning ('Mahavayu') and blossoms at each chakra until it emerges as the lotus with a thousand petals at the head, and samadhi is reached. This is the will-force of the 'Serpent Fire', and it brings with it a unique aspect of self where that self is one with the ultimate reality.

As we have seen at a number of points, the image of light streaking through and activating as a potent symbol of heightened consciousness and enlightenment is a common one. The human body is here a mirror of the macrocosm, with five 'sheaths' or 'kosas' where the outward of the five is of physicality and the innermost is the light of divinity at the heart of man (alike the Gnostic pneuma we have mentioned within this study).

Elsewhere we find accounts of Zarathustra's expectant mother being radiant to the point of people fearing that a fire was breaking out, and Genghis Khan being born of a woman who was invested with life by a solar shaft penetrating the smoke hole of the tent that she was residing in. Light, then, is pure spirit and the seed of life, and so the connection of the semen virile with solar epiphany in the Vedic '*Brāhmanas*' and the image of light as the uncoiled kundalini serpent are entirely recognisable across continents.

Of course, in many forms of faith sex was not ascribed such a positive role. Even within Gnosticism, which could lend itself to a decadence that maintained a role for coitus (with the Phibianites, one notable movement, said to indulge in orgiastic rites, hold their hands up in prayer covered in bodily emissions and consume menstrual blood as the body of Christ), there were schools of thought which resulted in the other extreme of asceticism – and a rejection of intercourse as a propagation of the imperfect form of matter.

When we consider the tone of certain of the Nag Hammadi texts, such as 'Mingled am I...lead me out of the embracement of death' this attitude is understandable; with the pneuma of godhood so far removed from its source, union was a primary need of each and every man and woman, but it was union with the creator that was the goal, and with it the gradual restoration of all that was 'of God' back to God. The countless sparks of the sacred that lay 'trapped' within the mortal shell could not be helped, but would certainly be hindered, by sex and reproduction, and so carnality had no place within a spiritual life.

However, though the overriding concept of the Christian faith is one where sex is essentially sin and the source of a collective guilt, there have been significant exceptions to that understanding over the centuries who did not always have to overextend their exegetic abilities to any great extent in order to defend their stance through scripture – after all, the First Epistle of John 3:9 clearly states: 'Whosoever is born of God doth not commit sin; for his seed remaineth in him; and he cannot sin, because he is born of God.'

More compelling and decidedly more enigmatic is the apocryphal *'Song of Songs'* or *'Song of Solomon'* which is rather unique within the Hebrew canon for its lack of content regarding commandment and covenant – subjects which dominate other books. It instead creates an image akin to that of the Yab-Yum or the conjoining of Shiva and Shakti, with a man and woman bestowing love upon one another and clearly celebrating the sexual act.

The book has been interpreted both literally and metaphorically, and there are numerous examples that suggest either approach as sound. 'Let him kiss me with the kisses of his mouth; for thy love *is* better than wine' (1:2) and 'A bundle of myrrh *is* my wellbeloved unto me; he shall lie all night betwixt my breasts' (1:13-14) can be read as explorations of physical love but also lend themselves to a mystical relationship with God, though other passages are more difficult to see in the latter light: 'Thy lips, O *my* spouse, drop *as* the honeycomb: honey and milk *are* under thy tongue; and the smell of thy garments *is* like the smell of Lebanon.'

However the text is read, though, the singular power of the '*Song of Songs*' is the intensely mystical aspect of the relationship being described. If we consider it to be a purely physical affair then it is remarkable as an almost Tantric rendering of sexual intercourse, while if we see the players as a follower and his/her creator, then we are given a unique understanding of the Christian faith where the two are committed to one another to the point of unity, equals who truly are of the same 'spark' and who ultimately remain with each other until they can again, eventually, conjoin.

One such group with a decidedly more literal application of this sentiment was the Adamites, who had a following through the 14th – 16th centuries C.E. For them nudity was no taboo, and 'free love' was a positive act. Worshipping underground alike the adherents of the ancient Mystery schools, they ritualised sex as a form of worship as they strove to recreate and exist within a long-lost paradisiacal state. They may have been a minority in terms of their ethos, but they exemplified a significant attempt to balance the physical drives and desires of humanity with a faith in God that frequently denied those passions altogether – though not in the *'Song of Songs'*!

Activation

The energies and perceived heightening of consciousness espoused by Tantric sex and even, possibly, within the *'Song of Songs'* can found in numerous forms of wider spiritual beliefs, magic and supernatural phenomena, and actually links all three in the form of 'Shunamitism' which takes its name from the Shunammite virgin Abishag with whom it was said the aged and weakening King David gained vitality and vigour by merely sleeping next to her.

Sex can actually be seen to diminish the forces at play here as it actualises and 'earths' them, and the belief in a magical osmosis of youth and strength usually relied on a state of virginity, but sex was nonetheless a concern as it was the burgeoning passions of the chosen youth, in all its forms, that made them a suitable candidate for Shunamitism and its singular form of vampirism.

Among other keen adherents was the Emperor Barbarossa who had young boys lie on his stomach and genitals to take on their 'emanations' so that he might be invigorated, and a certain following in London and Paris in the 18th century where it was possible to visit an establishment and pay for a magical bath and the opportunity to sleep between two virgin girls (a sizeable deposit being lost along with any girls' virginity).

Sympneumata is a similar practise, developed by one Laurence Oliphant (1829 – 88 C.E.) and his wife, which again had two individuals lying together sans coitus, though at a maintained peak of sexual excitement, in order to transmit or receive healing energies. Based in Haifa, Palestine, the couple were proud exponents of their method and published a work on it subtitled '*Evolutionary Forces Now Active in Man*', though the focus of their efforts was decidedly religious, with Mrs. Oliphant seeing it as a holy work when she took to bed with an especially dirty man so as to offer him spiritual succour.

Another application for the sexual energies sees an individual observe a certain party and slowly begin to mirror their breathing before achieving a form of 'astral link' through a contracting of the anus (and corresponding chakra). The initiator then raises his or her own breathing to that akin to sexual excitement, which is said to be echoed by the recipient, resulting in the activation of the passive party's sexual centre and possible orgasm. G.I. Gurdjieff (1866 – 1949 C.E.) was said to have exercised this power, though again the associations with psychic vampirism and even the machinations of an incubus lend it a somewhat negative air, whether or not those involved are all willing participants.

The liberation of these sexual energies can lead to all manner of unpleasant consequences, not least if we accept the links between puberty (and frequent masturbation) with poltergeist activity, which has been a popular explanation since the investigative work of Nandor Fodor (1895 – 1964 C.E.) Whether it is believed to be a repression of sexual desires or their overuse, and orchestrated by a demonic or ghostly entity or the 'victim' themselves, the results can include manifestations of telekinetic energy, apparent materialisations, noises and physical attacks that can extend to instances of possession.

Attempts to harness such energy on a ritual basis – often with a more practical aim than that of the Tantrist – have been well documented but, as ever, notoriety and titillation fuels the myth of such pursuits well beyond any provable reality. Gardnerian Wicca is one example of this, where 'The Great Work' can indeed see a High Priest and Priestess engage in sexual intercourse either before a coven or as a private act, though with a largely symbolic rendering the most common expression (the placing of an athame – or sacred knife – into the chalice) due to issues of practicality and personality.

Sex can certainly be a fundamental rite, not least within magic and sorcery, but it can also be the main allure for those who are not exactly dedicated to the faith or cause and so seek physical gratification, ultimately destroying the ritual and potentially harming their magical partner. Particularly in the 21st century, complex social mores, along with the psychology and ideals of modern women and men and of course concerns over disease and wellbeing combine to form something of a quagmire that can override any positive outcome of sex magic, and so – in spite of the public desire for stories of nudity, frolicking and depraved orgies – the place of sex within ritual is often a small one, even where the beliefs held suggest a unique and profound power in relation to such rites.

If Shunamatism suggests one thing to us, it is that the potent youthful energies that might be associated with sex can be perceived to be the goal rather than sex itself, not least when the practitioner is an individual seeking to increase their own vitality for practical ends rather than share a heightened level of being with another party, or a deity.

The misuse of such energy has often been a concern, with precautions thus taken to ensure that (like Gilgamesh and Enkidu) hunters, warriors and magicians are focussing their attentions on a certain objective and not likely to be enticed or distracted from a common purpose – thus we read of tribal groups where warriors are asked to abstain from coitus with their partner and are later confronted with a naked female, and any resulting sign of erection is considered to be a failure of the preparatory test.

Intent and will are fundamental here, at once proving the dedication of one or all involved in an act or ritual, and suggesting that the energies built by each individual will be of a more dynamic and untrammelled nature as a result. Sex can certainly be used to increase magical potency and broaden the extent of one's consciousness, but the price of a failed sexual rite would be the subsequent failure of the magical one and so, as with the Wiccan Great Work, can be practised but may be rejected as too volatile a commodity.

Eliphas Levi clearly expounded his view on the matter in his *'Transcendental Magic'* when he stated that love is '...one of the great instruments of universal power...' borne of natural attraction, sympathy and an intoxication of the Astral Light, while sexual love was no more than an illusion: 'Woe to the Samson of the Kabbalah if he permit himself to be put asleep by Delilah.' Sex alone is often a waste of one's potency where magic is concerned, unless a form of Shunamatism is taking place and the whole aim is to capture the essence of another for one's own benefit.

Aleister Crowley would not have argued this latter point, as his own *'The Book of the Law'* explained. For Crowley, every individual had the right to satisfy his or her own desires and use every aspect of his or her being to explore and expand the consciousness, a point neatly summated in the ubiquitous 'Do what thou wilt is the whole of the Law', though he does make clear that every such act must be undertaken as a ritual or sacrament and not as a simple act of whim.

The same energies could be summoned and ritually applied by the individual alone, as is noted in the 'Conversation of the Holy Guardian Angel'. Here, the higher self is summoned, interacted with and liberated following meditation, chanting and masturbation, at the climax of which the power so built is released toward a willed effect – the very stuff of 'Magick', and a combination of mind and body that Crowley's practices frequently relied on.

One man whose work certainly interconnected with Crowley's

on at least one level was Paschal Beverly Randolph (1825 – 1875 C.E.), an occultist and trance medium who described himself as a Rosicrucian and actually founded the 'Fraternitas Roase Crucis' in 1858, which today survives as the oldest such movement in the United States.

Randolph studied and wrote on various esoteric subjects, but those most influential to Western occultism focussed on 'erotic alchemy' and sex rites, often with a clarity and forthrightness that was shocking to many of his day. He noted that a man was best placed to reach an answer to magical aims with the partnership of an 'intelligent and loving wife', with whom he shared a 'soul-sexive series of energies' with acts that were essentially prayers when two such partners exist in a condition of accord on every level of being.

The connection was vital to any success, and with that the 'superior' nature of the woman involved in that a 'harlot or low woman' would prove inefficient – supposedly embodying the physical level of connection without the mental and spiritual aspect that was vitally important. Those willing to trade their bodies, the wife of any other man, those younger than eighteen years and, interestingly, virgins were not suitable for this act, as the woman must '...be one who hath known man and who has been and still is capable of intense mental, volitional and affectionate energy, combined with perfect sexive and orgasmal ability...'

Randolph's work found a keen adherent and disseminator in Maria de Naglowska (1883 – 1936 C.E.), a Russian mystic and journalist who founded the 'Confrérie de la Flèche d'or' or the 'Brotherhood of the Golden Arrow' in Paris, France in 1932 and actively instructed in the art of sex magic, including the likes of ritual hanging within an erotic context and the broader tenets of sexual spiritualism. In her last years she collected and published much of Randolph's work on the subject, and gave his studies a wider audience that included the Western occult and magic schools, including those already practising forms of these rituals, like the 'Ordo Templar Orientis' in Germany.

The O.T.O. was established by Karl Kellner (1851 – 1905 C.E.), a Mason who has allegedly been initiated into the 'sexual current' by two Indian Tantrics and an Arab who had been much informed by the theories and work of Randolph. Sex rites were thus an intrinsic aspect of the magical syllabus of the O.T.O. from the start, though their importance increased dramatically when the group came under the leadership of Aleister Crowley in 1922.

Crowley took the core sexual rites of the group and merged these with his own 'Law of Thelema', with the intent of recreating and re-instigating the pagan ecstasies that would more assuredly part the curtains to the wisdom of the ancient Mysteries, likewise that of the Masons and Hermeticism. As a result, he linked different sexual acts with the various degrees of the O.T.O. that were perceived to confirm the developing abilities of the adherent (VII as the stage for autosexual/masturbatory works; IX for heterosexual partnering, and XI for anal intercourse, all of which Crowley had long since mastered by this point).

As noted, for Crowley sex was far from sin and its results on the mind and body were a form of ecstasy that was interconnected with the higher spiritual plains of divinity, therefore coitus was a fundamental element in any serious magical corpus, particularly where an individual was seeking wisdom or results beyond the normal ken of man and woman.

It is perhaps no surprise that one text which the normally hyper-critical Crowley vaunted as essential reading for the occult student was *'Heavenly Bridegrooms'* of Ida C. Craddock (1857 – 1902 C.E.), whose works and teachings certainly found a readership with the former's cohort. Like Randolph and de Naglowska, Craddock was a taboo-breaker in her day who most certainly paid the price for her outspoken beliefs, which extended to the tenets of free-speech and the rights of women.

Born and raised as a Quaker, Craddock was on course to be the University of Pennsylvania's first female undergraduate student before the board there rejected her right of entrance. She left Quakerism and embraced the holistic mystical leanings of the Theosophical Society, later announcing herself to be a Priestess of the Church of Yoga that continued to enjoy a long-standing erotic relationship with an angel (the intense and disruptive sexual activities with whom had apparently led to protests and complaints from her neighbours!)

Much of Craddock's notable work – and that which Crowley would applaud – revolved around this affiliation, as well as her pursuits as a sex counsellor to couples in distress which was characterised by her unique spiritual viewpoints. One recognisable teaching was here referred to as Dianism after the Roman goddess, whereby sexual intercourse with intense physical pleasure but no ejaculation was the central goal, a form of coitus reservatus that later became a popular rite for adherents of Crowley, among others.

Ida Craddock, however, suffered for her liberal views on gender, with her books on sexual rites and her own amorous adventures deemed to be offensive to the point of criminality. Not only did her mother at one point try to have her institutionalized, but she was eventually imprisoned on charges of immorality, and indeed did spend a period of time at a hospital for the insane, before an apparent suicide at the age of 45 spared her from yet another sentence when her further work was deemed to be even more scandalous than her previous efforts.

As much as Gurdjieff's abilities to activate the sex-centres of an individual without contact would find support in some quarters (and suggest an offensive and predatory manner to others), such instances were cited as examples of singular abilities that he had over mind and body, through sheer concentrated will. In fact, Gurdjieff had a similar understanding to many of the others noted in this study, in that sex may well have a useful role within human existence, but it was not in and of itself the end goal or point of revelation.

Indeed, for Gurdjieff sex was another example of the 'mechanicalness' that dominated modern life, with coitus usually performed with base drives but no application of genuine consciousness or awareness, the result being that the all-pervading sex drive serves for most as a trap rather than as any form of liberation (symbolised rather neatly by the 'Devil' card of the tarot).

In this light abstinence can be useful, but can also be damaging if one 'centre' of the self, like the sex centre, is controlled through negation but others are not; this can create an imbalance which lends an especial focus to sex and sexuality that would result in excess and perversion, rather than any meaningful growth of the individual. As with much of Gurdjieff's teachings, it is the person's awareness and alertness to reality that is important, not the engaging with or rejection of any one element of life; sex should not dominate, but it need not be absent, either – the key is to fully experience the act for it to have a meaning, and resonate for the entire self.

Where Gurdjieff does recognise the pitfalls of the sex centre is in its apparent dominance over all other such centres. The very instinct for sex is so deeply embedded in the psyche of humanity that much of what he deemed to be of the 'mechanical' modern perception was a result of its activation, and so sex here is something of a quagmire that most would not have the strength of personality or will to overcome. Instinct would again and again overtake any higher sensibility or potential for growth, crashing like a wave and obliterating the constructions that had only tentatively been built, thus sex was a threat that would require constant guard for a seeker of Truth.

For the more magically-minded, sex has continued to offer enlightenment though variations on the Tantric ideal, not least with the work of Austin Osman Spare (1886 – 1956 C.E.). His *'The Book of Pleasure (Self-love)'* defines God, morals and other such terms as 'unity by fear...bondage...' which denotes an arbitrary limitation being placed on the self and its abilities. In its place Spare espoused 'Kia' which is absolute freedom, the reality of the moment that is specific to the individual at that given time and indescribable by any overarching definition – an acuity of awareness and self that Gurdjieff may well have approved of.

Spare decried the rejection and suppressing of moods and desires, instead espousing the importance of seizing a moment and acting with the unashamed passion and attitude that is held. He termed this as being the 'kiaist', one who gives up the concepts of vice and virtue and overcomes the limitation of duality by '...riding the Shark of his desire.' His 'Zos Kia Cultus' ritualised this belief with the implantation of a sigil in the consciousness at the point of sexual orgasm, when the will and the energies are one and at a peak belying the ordinary constraints of self and existence.

The likes of Peter Carroll (b. 1953 C.E.) have extended on this ethos within the realm of Chaos magic, with Carroll's 'Thanateros' ritual seeing a practitioner meditate on the experience of birth in an environment imbued with death, and on the death of the self during a sexual (and thus generative) act. This breaking of normal constraints – and the contradictory impact of environment/act on will – extends consciousness beyond the ordinary bounds to Spare's 'neither-neither', which is a condition of true freedom that is beyond conception, existing only of itself.

The heightened, ecstatic state ultimately experienced is essentially the union of opposites that has been the spiritual focus of religious worshipper, Tantrist, alchemist and numerous magicians and sorcerers seemingly since that axe of God cleft human matter into two, if not from that initial act of creation which estranged us from our maker, some millennia ago.

III: DEATH

The most profound bond that we share with others is at the same time the most profoundly isolating experience we will ever undergo; indeed, death unites every sentient being throughout the past, the present and the future, but it is nonetheless a process wholly unique to each individual. As such, the responses and approaches to death, reflections on what it is and its meaning for those who pass as well as for those 'left behind' are countless, each offering a glimpse of a vast and complex philosophy that rather fittingly belies any one narrative.

All of the most difficult and 'eternal' questions are found within thoughts of death, such as: what exactly are we (personality, self, soul, etc.?); what is existence and what if anything lies beyond it?; is there a purpose to life and what happens if we succeed or fail? Thoughts of death confront us with the pain of regret, the pain of loss (those who leave us behind and in turn those we leave), fears of vengeance and unrest, fears of an existence beyond and fears of no existence at all – concerns and emotions that have fuelled speculation and informed religious thought for millennia, but which are no less answerable today for all of the rumination.

Ultimately, death is a vacuum in that we cannot authoritatively *know* any answer until we ourselves have made its passage, therefore its affect on us in life is open to one's own beliefs and attitudes now as ever it was. Historical context, politics, language and of course personal mores are all vital factors within each life, and so drawing comparisons – let alone conclusions – is impossible, but in spite of the difficulties of time, place, lexis and psychology, the unanswerable questions remain the same. For all our concern and attention we are ultimately ignorant – but what company we keep!

As systems of understanding go, those espoused by Arnold Van Gennep (1873 – 1957 C.E.) in his *'Rites of Passage'* (1909) do go some way to address the perceived stages that the dying and the grieving experience, namely 'separation' (a detachment that can be exemplified by ritual acts), 'liminality' (transition from one mode of being to another) and 'incorporation' (the assuming of one's new mode of being or identity following the transition).

Of course this model can be said to be better suited to those who lose a loved one through death, given that their new 'identity' or lifestyle following that death can be quantified whereas the deceased is beyond any such follow-up. However, many beliefs would attest that the liminal state of death is indeed followed by 'incorporation' into that new mode or level of existence (whether, as we shall see, a heaven, a hell or a reincarnated form), and so can be said to apply to both parties nonetheless.

The personal impact of death is perhaps more immediately apparent with Jung, who compared the energy process that is life (goals, wishes, aims and the directed will to achieve them,) to a projectile that arcs downward toward an inevitable nadir. He added that the arc was not necessarily mirrored by one's psychology and perspective, thus a conflict is apparent that can come to dominate an entire lifetime, resulting in an individual who fails to exist in a true and meaningful way because of a fear to live, only to approach old age with bitterness and regret, cripplingly fearful of death.

Jung's concern is more focused on the art of living, while Van Gennep's theory is here applied to the art of dying, but the two are again and again found to be inextricable. After all, it is far too easy to squander a life through doubt, only to begin to cling to life as it nears its denouement as though existence is the most precious thing to us – and the rite of passage that is death then becomes all the more painful for both the unwilling 'victim' and those witnessing the doomed struggle.

It seems that much that we consider when we reflect on death and mortality, be it in terms of religion, mysticism or esotericism, is centred on coming to terms with our impermanence and understanding what any meaning of life itself might be; only through finding such an understanding can we hope to be 'dying with life', which means accepting our condition and not retreating from it (and thus from living), so that we live a meaningful life while it is ours to live. This remains a fittingly personal quest for each being to wrestle with, and we can perhaps learn from those who have gone before in the hope of some inspiration, if not outright revelation...

Origins

The question of why we die has long been a fundamental one to faiths and philosophy alike, and there have been many answers and explanations disseminated across civilizations and centuries. Myths focus on the 'first death' so as to better understand what led to the 'creation' of mortality in the first instance, and every possible reason including punishment, reward, testing, a necessary transformation and the return of the innate 'spark' to its source have all been posited.

The ubiquitous James Frazer offered his own categorization of the various death myths to no small degree of success – though there are numerous variations on the core themes and certainly exceptions, his model nonetheless acknowledges the most common forms of response to the problem of death.

Frazer noted stories of 'the two messengers' as one answer, a concept prominent within African tribes where God sends a chameleon to declare to the men and women of the world that they will enjoy immortality, and in turn a lizard to declare that they will, in fact, die; while the chameleon rests, the lizard proves the more efficient messenger and so the latter edict is made fact.

Alternatively, 'the waxing and waning moon' are stories that speak of the original state of humanity as being similar to the moon (decreasing only to be made full again in due course, but never taking complete leave), only for that condition to be lost through all manner of accidents and misdemeanours.

'The serpent and the cast skin' has a messenger confusing two messages to be given and telling humanity that it is to be mortal, while announcing to the snake that it can live again by casting off its old skin, and 'the banana tree' sees humanity punished for asking for more than the stone that God regularly delivers, resulting in the new gift of the banana – and the impermanent state of the banana tree that brings forth new life only to itself die, over the solid and unchanging stone.

A search for the meaning of death – and through that, life – is also touched upon by the splendid work of Joseph Campbell (1938 – 1987 C.E.), notably in his *'The Hero with a Thousand Faces'* (1949), where something of Van Gennep's theories can be identified. Here, Campbell focuses on the 'monomyth' or 'hero's journey' common to so many narratives, not least of which are the myths of the ancient civilizations, including those of Gilgamesh, Prometheus, the Buddha and the Biblical Jonah.

Up to seventeen stages can be identified within some of these myths and their order can change, but Campbell's central argument is that the hero myths always speak of a 'departure' or separation, followed by a form of 'initiation' or transformation and finally a 'return', with the wisdom/mode of being since adopted making explicit that the individual has gained by the process/ordeal/rite of passage and to some extent transcended his/her earlier and more primitive form.

Intrinsic elements are thus those of the 'hero' who approaches and crosses a form of threshold or barrier heretofore unknown (liminality) in order to face an overwhelming adversary (in this case, death) so that its curse can be broken and the new stage or level of life can be reached and enjoyed – the deliverance, upon success, of an elixir or reward that makes more of the champion than he previously was.

As will be seen, the journey of the hero bears a neat similarity to the initiatory trials of the shaman, including the help of a spiritual guide or mentor, the crossing of the threshold, transformation within the 'womb of the earth', various trials and tortures, physical and mental dismemberment and the ultimate return to existence with a greater and deeper knowledge of all worlds – and the ability to master and control the forces and entities on either side of the 'barrier' that is mortal consciousness.

However, the process of living and dying is a frequent and profound aspect of the various hero myths, and the metamorphosed hero is a being who has faced the enemy and overcome, to a new understanding, outlook, and potentially a new mode of being. There is a sense that the concept of time and the necessary change that it enforces on all life, including death itself, is no longer a burden, and that its apparent ravages are now seen to be just that – the appearance of decay that in reality is but one further transformation, or one further threshold being crossed, in a changing of one's existence that is far from a cessation.

The hero of sorts and the ideas of James Frazer again combine in the idea of the 'Rex Nemorensis' or 'King of the Grove' that Frazer associated with all manner of sacred, sacrificial kings who were ultimately sacrificed to ensure the continuation of life through new birth in terms of human generation, fecund earth and the ongoing sustenance of sun, wind and rain. Detail of the beliefs and rites practised by those of the groves at Lake Nemi in Italy are lost to antiquity, but the legend that was passed on spoke of each incumbent priest of Diana that served there being slain in trial by combat by the individual who then became the successor.

For the King of the Grove and Frazer's broader interpretation of that position, an understanding of death led to the application of human sacrifice as part of essential annual fertility rites – as a number of gods and deities had frequently been known to do in worldwide myths and religious beliefs, it was the termination of a venerable figure and their especial life-force that would replenish and revitalise the population and the very earth itself. Death therefore served the greatest purpose in these cases, and rather fortuitously pleased the gods whose primordial sacrifice was being commemorated and re-enacted.

There are, then, a number of ways in which the idea and the reality of death is interpreted that offer either a stoic appreciation for why man and woman must die – namely due to vice, questioning a god or a cosmic error – or gives to death a sufficient worth and meaning that is seen as vital toward the continuation of all life. However, one of the most moving mythic ruminations on death takes an entirely divergent path and suggests what is perhaps the most typical and universal response to the problem of mortality, in the story of Gilgamesh.

While experiencing visions in the 'dream house' the mighty warrior is told that, due to the scale of victory that he and his great friend Enkidu have enjoyed, one of them must soon die. Gilgamesh openly weeps at this news, not least when he discovers that it is Enkidu who will be lost, and he continues to weep and wail as his proud and strong friend is eventually overcome by a dreadful illness. The pain and denial of the loss is such that Gilgamesh refuses to bury the body until the level of decay becomes overwhelming.

Following this event, which in itself is a rite of passage for Gilgamesh, he is forced to consider his own mortality, and with that his glorious life and what it might ultimately mean. Confronted by truths he would rather not accept, he initially seeks immortality, journeying through the chthonic depths and crossing the waters of death ('I am afraid of death, so I wander the wild...') and comes within reach of eternal life when he finds the 'plant of heartbeat', only to lose it to a snake that then loses its skin and finds its own re-birth.

Gilgamesh is left to mourn his own death, and acknowledges that all of his own accomplishments in life will become but a memorial that in truth will hold less and less worth as time continues to pass. The humanity of this part of the story is instantly recognisable, and all too compelling given that it is the mighty Gilgamesh that is so reduced – though it is also apparent that true wisdom lies here, both for the legendary warrior and for any who reflect on his plight, as it is in the acceptance of mortality and our own inevitable demise that we face our apotheosis and pass through the threshold of the abyss, toward a new and enlightened understanding of who and what we are.

An impressive example of our struggle in following Gilgamesh and his epiphany can be found within the changing eschatology of the Christian faith, which more than many other religious systems places death and what lies beyond it firmly at the heart of its message. Indeed, this is a somewhat ironic point given that the Old Testament gave little consideration to what if any state of being might lie behind the point of death, with Genesis 3:19 rather starkly stating: 'In the sweat of thy face shalt thou eat bread, till thou return unto the ground; for out of it wast thou taken: dust thou art, and unto dust shalt thou return.'

By the time of the New Testament's composition a much more developed theory of death and afterlife had filled the void of the earlier Scripture, though in truth any degree of detail remains lacking. Nonetheless, the books of the New Testament highlight the concepts of sin and righteousness, suffering and atonement, all with the ultimate message of death, resurrection and eternal life in the form of Christ's demise on the cross and his subsequent raising and the implicit message that those who followed his teachings and example might find similar 'life beyond life.'

John 11:25 makes clear the possibility of salvation and rebirth: 'I am the resurrection, and the life: he that believeth in me, though he were dead, yet shall he live', while St Paul claims that '...the last enemy to be defeated is death' (1 Corinthians 15:26), suggesting that appropriate worship and behaviour in life can remove the sting and import of death and ensure continuity of being.

That said, later denominations and their understanding of the Scripture did little to assuage the fear that death and dying held for most men and women, such as the Protestantism of John Calvin (1509 – 1564 C.E.) whereby the doctrine of 'double predestination' meant that those to be ultimately saved post-mortem would be those who had been fated for salvation all along, and those who would be effectively damned were similarly marked even before their birth. With no assurance that even the most Christian of individuals were to be raised come the Final Judgement and no means of escape for those who were not already blessed, the dread of death is understandable – perhaps even more so for the devout believer than the heretic, in this instance.

Just as the beliefs of one faith can change beyond recognition or in a single form find numerous interpretations, so too the panoply of 'death gods' and deities that have over the centuries been associated with mortality, passage and the afterlife is vast and impressive. As a single entity embodying and bestowing both life and death; as figures who oppose their mirror image (the creator) in some form of battle or conflict; commonly as the psychopomp or guide of the souls or deceased to their new abode, the death gods reflect the beliefs and concerns of their followers and so present us with countless characterisations of death and our responses to it.

Anubis is certainly one of the best-known examples of the death deity, and one of the most prominent psychopomps. The jackal-headed one (potentially so-formed due to the link between the jackals that would scavenge around the abodes of the dead) was the god of embalmers, who would wear masks in his image as they practised their art on a body. Associated with the deathly colours of black and purple, Anubis also served as the protector of the Necropolis and as guide to the deceased.

In the Pyramid Texts of the Old Kingdom (c. 2686 – 2181 B.C.E.) he was also the judge of the dead to the Egyptians, but was later supplanted in this role by Osiris, who was then god of the dead with a myth of resurrection all his own. At this point Anubis became the embalmer of the deceased, and would within the Roman corpus become the protector of Isis, a close connection borne from his helping her to reassemble the body of Osiris.

The fact that the role of Anubis was adapted to suit developing tastes and beliefs suggests the malleability that many deities in general have offered to adherents, but with death gods this is especially pertinent as their knowledge and power in matters of death can also suggest mastery of the life-force, wisdom of any underworld or afterlife and through that the art of magic, alchemy and mysticism.

A less nuanced figure within Egyptian belief was Ammit, the demoness and goddess who served as 'Eater of Hearts' at the judgement of the dead in New Kingdom (1550 – 712 B.C.E.) texts . A snarling, ferocious figure with the head of a crocodile, the body of a lion and the rear end of a hippopotamus, she was said to sit directly next to the scales that weighed the heart of the deceased, awaiting its failure to balance against the feather of 'maat' or truth so that it might be '...delivered to the swallower' and a new restless soul created.

Judgement was a central concern to the Egyptian mindset, and as we shall see the misdemeanours that would lead to a devoured heart and restless spirit clearly reflected the exalted position of order to that civilisation. Elsewhere, however, the rigid structure of a complex bureaucratic system would forge the figures of death – thus Chinese beliefs included a reassuringly large number of official roles that would make for a well-ordered afterlife, including the 'Emperor of Youdu' (the Underworld's capital city), the 'Kings of the Ten Underworld Palaces', the 'Four Kings of the Underworld', the 'Governors of Fengdu', the 'Four Generals of the Direct Altar' and the 'Wardens of the Nine Prisons of Fengdu'.

The philosophical bent of the Indian religions can be glimpsed in the figure of the Black Kali, the 'shade of death' that is the emaciated and voracious stalker that craves life. With protruding teeth and long sharp nails she is the archetypal hag in appearance, but as 'life feeds on life' she is nonetheless understood to be but one aspect of the goddess just as death is but one stage of existence – Kali is capable of immense beauty and terrifying ugliness, as she is filled with the life-force that at once infuses with energy and drains it away. Here she may be the waning moon of decay, but she is at the same time the waxing moon of fecund life.

Life and death most certainly meet in the presence of the Mesoamerican Mictlantecuht, lord of the Aztec underworld of Mictlan, so too his dutiful wife Mictecacihuatl. Often depicted as a skeleton with bleached white bones and bloody red spots, he commonly wears paper vestments and owl feathers, around which he bears a collar made of eyeballs.

At the festival of Tititl an impersonator of Mictlantecuht would be sacrificed at a temple which was placed at the 'navel of the world', establishing a powerful link between the living and the dead for a civilization that greatly prized sacrifice above much else and bestowed greatness on those so offered to the gods. Frequently though the death deity is, alike the Egyptian Ammit, the devourer, as that is what time and death are commonly held to be. The Balinese Batara Kala is the god of the underworld who is also the great creator, devouring individuals as the personification of time and decay just as he tries to devour the sun and the moon at times of eclipse.

Beliefs of the various peoples of the Philippines are not dissimilar to this, with the Tagbayan that devour human souls and are guarded by two-headed beasts, the serpent goddess Lakandánup who consumes a person's shadow during eclipses, leading to that individual's gradual demise, and Malakal Maut that is the angel of death, appearing as a beautiful or horrific form depending on the nature of the soul being harvested and tormenting those deemed to be sinners until the 'end of days.'

Of course death itself has been personified by many cultures and serves a complimentary role to those that assess, reward and punish the souls of the deceased. Death as an entity serves many of the same roles that the already mentioned gods and deities encompassed, most commonly that of guide to the dead, and the embodying of death as a being allows for a more direct relationship that more acutely emphasises the various responses held to the reality of cessation. As such, death is seen at points as malicious and cruel, sardonic, stoic and even benevolent.

The Persian Astwihād found in Zoroastrian works is the divider of bodies and the 'dissolver of bones', a demon that can put a man or woman to sleep with a touch, but whose direct stare means death. Somewhat more sedate is the Greek Thanatos, who is one of the twin-sons born by Nix (night); depicted in both youthful and mature forms with the ability of flight, he also leads the dead to the river Styx for their crossing – with sisters, the Keres, serving a more ferocious and vengeful role when needed for those who have died an untimely death.

Hinduism has noted, among others, King Yama, who appears as a child riding a black buffalo and lassoing the souls of the dead before driving them back to his abode, Yamaloka. A form of judgement is made once there, taking into account the individual's positive and negative actions, before a suitable place for them to reside is found in preparation for reincarnation. Yama can also be found in Chinese mythology as King Yan who wears a judge's cap and robes, through which form he also became apparent within Japanese and Korean beliefs.

Western Europe has largely characterised Death as the 'Grim Reaper' that is the scythe-wielding skeleton since the Middle Ages. The 'harvester of souls' is a common representation, but the actual name Grim Reaper dates only to English works of the 19th century C.E. and 'he' is not exclusively male even in Europe, with a female form sometimes depicted within Spanish, Italian and other culture's works, and often as the Polish Śmierć who wears a white, rather than black, cloak.

Death as a woman is most certainly the case with the Gaelic banshee that has become a legendary supernatural figure, not least for her ominous wailing or screeching that announces to a populace or household that a death is imminent. She, like Kali, might appear as a wizened old woman or as a youthful beauty, but her presence nonetheless presaged a death – and where several such figures gathered, it was said that a figure of especial importance or holiness was to be claimed.

The dullahan is another such entity, which would ride a black horse or drive a carriage led by black horses to the home of one soon to die and wait outside the property, striking the eyes of any witness with a whip made of a single spine. A more ghostly figure, the dullahan is said in mythology to carry its head under its arm, a head with a smile stretching from ear to ear.

Death appears as an angel in various Biblical passages, such as 2 Kings 19:35 'And it came to pass that night, that the angel of the Lord went out, and smote in the camp of the Assyrians an hundred fourscore and five thousand: and when they arose early in the morning, behold, they were all dead corpses.' A similar angel, bearing a sword that stretches across Jerusalem, brings King David and 'the elders of Israel' to their knees in 1 Chronicles 16:21.

The 'angel of death' is indeed the messenger of God, meting out terrible punishment to transgressors and only stopped in its destruction and murder at the assent of its creator. Such a figure also appears in the Hebrew books of Hosea and Jeremiah, while Jewish lore likewise mentions at points the 'Angel of Dark and Light' and Abaddon, archangel of the abyss or 'the destroyer' who is king of an army of locusts: 'And they had a king over them, which is the angel of the bottomless pit, whose name in the Hebrew tongue is Abaddon, but in the Greek tongue hath his name Apollyon' (Revelation 9:11).

Islam names the archangel Azrael as the angel of death or Malak al-Maut who works with others to withdraw souls from their bodies and escort them into the afterlife. We again find figures that appear benevolent and rather beautiful to those judged worthy of such, while sinners encounter wholly more grotesque entities – and in this instance the manner in which the soul is drawn from the body likewise mirrors the status and bearing of the soul in question.

A wholly more apocalyptic form of Death within scripture is that of the four horsemen depicted in Revelation, riding alongside Pestilence, War and Famine: 'And I looked, and behold a pale horse: and his name that sat on him was Death, and Hell followed with him. And power was given unto them over the fourth part of the earth, to kill with sword, and with hunger, and with death, and with the beasts of the earth' (6:8).

Death, then, is largely an agent of destruction that follows the orders of a greater power, and the verities of judgement are interlinked with his/her appearance, manner and of course the ultimate end of the soul in question. There are exceptions to this concept and, with that, less terrifying embodiments of the death process, but the majority of characterisations carry within them as much if not more fear than hope – and the shadow of death, the scream of the banshee and the scales of judgement all elicit more nightmares than reveries.

Destinations

Even more than the various characterisations afforded to the figure of death, the destinations which souls find themselves bound for exemplify the philosophies, hopes and fears of respective civilizations though, again, the similarities that underpin the kaleidoscope of hells, heavens, all in between and all beyond them are equally telling.

The Mesopotamians were a practical people, much used to arduous work and life-withering extremes of weather, including periods of drought. Post-mortem, existence was hardly more attractive – the dead were believed to stay in the ground where they were buried, and even where a spirit or ghost had a form of life extraneous from its mortal shell, the underworld was a fairly joyless and desolate place.

Known by various names including Irkalla and Ganzir (this latter meaning 'gateway'), the underworld was located either down a stairway or simply through a hole in the ground, and keepers stood on guard at each of the seven gates that led there. It was said that Ereškigal, the 'Queen of the Gate Below' and her husband Nergal lived in an abode adjacent to the main entrance or gateway, though 600 gods became associated with this particular chthonic realm as the later Babylonian culture further developed the concept.

Of all the changes made to the idea of Ganzir, however, its later guise was no more appealing: as the 'country whence none return', it was a place of dust and dirt where the deceased lived as carrion, forever flying and seeking scraps of nourishment though usually having to make the best of the filth and debris alone. The mode of one's death did have an effect on the soul's 'position' in the underworld in that, for instance, a man or woman who died in a fire was said to have been completely erased by the flames, gadim (soul) and all – thus even Ganzir was beyond them, which might be considered to be a blessing rather than a curse, given the descriptions!

Even the Greeks, who depicted both an idyllic heaven and a rancorous hell immediately recognisable to a modern mind, maintained that the afterlife may be no more than a desolate existence for some. For those whose relatives observed the correct rites and placed a coin under the tongue of the corpse, Charon would gladly escort them across the river Styx to their eventual abode, while those without the correct fare might trick their way across the waters to be torn apart by the three-headed canine guardian, Cerberus, or else stand for all eternity on the shores opposite, watching others pass over with no means of ever moving on themselves.

There is a vast amount of evidence proving the large amount of wealth, thought, labour and expectation that the ancient Egyptians bestowed on their concept of the afterlife, from elaborate funerary rites and resplendent tombs to huge numbers of grave goods and human sacrifice to ensure that the deceased would continue to be taken care of to the same standard as they had enjoyed in physical life. This is because, for the Egyptians, the afterlife was exactly that – a continuation of their existence – and so all the trappings of that life needed to accompany them to the hereafter.

For the elite there was a continued glorification in that they continued to rule in death, and having a healthy and sizeable retinue made perfect sense given this understanding. Indeed, in death a King became a god, while for many their akh spirit could enjoy a less lofty role as overseer of those they had left behind, with a farmer's akh returning to observe others of his trade, as all beings observed and maintained the same societal order that they had carefully followed while living.

Much depended on the successful observance of appropriate rites, even for the Kings, who were required to pass through the afterlife (deemed to be something of an endless rejuvenation of the being) before impressing, capturing and even consuming the gods to wield their power and prove his rightful place at their side. It was said that the sun god Re passed through the Underworld nightly on his travels, before once again rising in the land of the living, and the means of proving one's worth to bask in the warmth and light of Re's glow as he united with Osiris and became regenerated would be a fundamental and very genuine concern for those seeking acceptance and glory in the afterlife.

From the Middle Kingdom onwards a form of divinity in death was possible for most who passed over, though such a transformation relied heavily on the outcome of the judgement that was made by the likes of Osiris, Anubis and the ever-watchful Ammit, thus proving oneself as worthy and facing one's own worst enemy – oneself – continued to be the pre-eminent aspect of the afterlife, with failure an understandably terrifying outcome, as noted in the *'Book of Going Forth By Day'* or *'Book of the Dead'*, chapter 25 and elsewhere: '...save me from Baba, who feeds on the entrails of the dead, in this great day of judgement.'

Zoroastrians have also had to prepare themselves for journey and judgement as they leave the material realm. Here, the soul eventually finds and crosses the 'Bridge of Parting' where one section is similar to the blade of a sword (a common image within universal mythology); the righteous traveller would find the going relatively easy and pass across unharmed, only to be greeted by a welcoming embodiment of their good deeds in life and escorted to the 'Abode of Song', while the doer of evil reached the blade-section and had it turn under their feet, potentially slicing them in two and dropping them into the unpleasant abyss that lay below.

For the Mesoamerican cultures, whereby sacrifice and continued survival/nourishment were closely intertwined, death was firmly held to be a complimentary balance to life. Again much depended on the status of the individual and the mode of death (with those who died by religious sacrifice often regarded with the greatest of honour and respect) but most of the deceased were expected to have to make a journey that was rife with hazards such as various beasts, bats, extremes of cold, hills that suddenly clashed together and thrusting blades and arrows, before any destination was found.

One fascinating aspect of death and the underworld here is the humour that frequently pervades texts about it, perhaps unsurprising given that blood and death were literally ways of life to these cultures and so mortality was held in a very unique regard. This humour is clearly seen where the gods of the underworld are repeatedly tricked in order for objectives are to be met, such as where the Hero Twins of the *'Popul Vuh'* befuddle the gods into sacrificing themselves, and where Quetzalcoatl confuses them sufficiently to escape the underworld with the bones of a previous race of men, so that a new race can be made.

Of course, fear can be relegated to the moment of death itself and perhaps a subsequent judgement of the soul, if one believes that he or she is destined to be rewarded for a just and sinless life. If there is to be no waiting in a dusty purgatory and no descent into decidedly warmer climes, then death may be seen as a blessing or a return – not least where one has sights fixed firmly on a new existence in a form of heaven.

As might be implicit in their rather stoic understanding of the afterlife, mortal men and women had little if any access to the heavens, which were exclusively the domain of the gods – humankind was a wholly different life-form that existed on a wholly different plain, thus the only direct contact that could be hoped for would be that experienced at the temples, during worship. However, archaeological evidence of grave goods does suggest that at least some individuals believed that devout veneration of Inanna might see them rewarded in the afterlife, and few would reject an opportunity to pass to a more comfortable eternal home than Ganzir.

The Chinese image of heaven includes a notably anthropomorphic form, namely Tian who was supreme deity to the Zhou Dynasty (1046 – 256 B.C.E.) before conquest extended and broadened his prominence. In this instance, Tian *as* Heaven is aware of all actions by all men and women, and can be suitably angered, appeased or overjoyed according to their pursuits. In contrast, a more developed concept of the heavens as an afterlife was also held, whereby a fairly bureaucratic system was overseen by the Jade Emperor – with overwhelming fecundity and nourishment, along with buildings made of jade and gold, this was a paradise where stability was assured, as in life, through rank and order.

As has been noted, the Aztecs afforded a heavenly afterlife for few of their population, though it was said that those who had been sacrificed or mothers who had died in childbirth would be transported to a paradise that was perpetually warmed by the sun god. Here, souls existed as butterflies and other beautiful winged creatures, frolicking in the balmy heat with a carelessness that had been denied them in mortal life.

It must be said that although there are nuances in design and belief from one culture to another, the idea of 'paradise' is a somewhat recognisable one regardless the time or place in question – for the Egyptians, their body rested in the tomb while an aspect of spirit joined the sun god Ra on his nightly passage through the Underworld or enjoyed copious food, drink and copulation in the 'Field of Rushes'; the 'Elysian Fields' of the Greeks offered the souls of the blessed flowers and the singing of hymns to the gods, while those dwelling with Cronus in the 'Empyrean' enjoyed permanent daylight with no extremes of weather, revelry, music – and re-birth into a mortal form at will.

Islam describes a similar scene where souls rest in bliss and are served by others, the Hindu apsaras are the granters of sexual desires in the afterlife, and Vikings had the glory of Valhalla to strive for where the dead could battle as long and hard as they wished, with any injuries obtained being healed instantly to allow for ongoing skirmishes, and self-perpetuating feasts meant that even in rest the true warrior could fill himself to the brim and eat on ad nauseam without any exhaustion of supplies.

There are many such examples within worldwide faiths depicting idylls of repose and relaxation or, as with the Vikings, where one's greatest pleasures were to be lived and re-lived in perpetuity. Music, dancing, singing, basking in the glow of the sun god, being surrounded by glorious perfumes, all with an unending supply of sumptuous food and no doubt acrobatic sexual intercourse...this is 'heaven' indeed, at once a reward to those who lived in accordance with the beliefs and behaviours of their people and a suitable fulfilment of hopes and desires that were impossible in life. Wishes are here finally realised, and the hardships prove to have been worthwhile.

Even within the Tibetan Devachan, where the activities of the deceased may not rival the excesses pursued in the other mentioned idylls, it is said that the highest hopes of one's incarnation are realised. For many Devachan is reached after a long period of death and a stay in Kamaloka which is a form of purgatory, though 'initiates' with the ability are able to travel there even during their mortal life to seek wisdom and sanctity.

It should be added that one profound aspect of many of these heavens is the capacity of the deceased to act according to their own will. Perhaps not without limit and potentially alongside continued veneration of those of a divine status, the ability to choose how and when one feasts or ruts without guilt or fear, and the right to choose when and if a new mortal form is taken so that further experiences might be gained or lessons learned, is an important and pertinent characteristic of a heaven, suggesting a desire for the continuation of 'self' even where bliss is assured.

Buddhism offers a fascinating alternative to the common concept of heaven, in that several heavens are believed to exist which are still an extension of samsara or the illusionary reality that is the cycle of existence. Good karma can see a being reborn into one of the heavens, but this is not an eternal abode as the positive karma will gradually dissipate and the being will be reborn into a new mortal form in a cycle that will continue until or unless 'nirvana' or enlightenment is achieved.

Theravada Buddhism includes the heavenly realms of Yama where inhabitants can enjoy a lifetime of 144,000,000 years, Tusita where Bodhisattva's (one on the path to becoming a Buddha) live before returning to another human existence, Parinirmita-vasavartin where devas fulfil each other's hopes as to the form that they can take, and Brahmaloka were the Brahmas reside.

Mahayana beliefs include 'The Heaven of Bliss by Transformation' where we find those who lack desire themselves but will engage with desire for the sake of a partner, 'The Heaven of the Multitudes of Brahma' the resting place for those who overcome sexual desire but lack wisdom, 'The Heaven of the Ministers of Brahma' which houses those who have achieved a mind free from all forms of desire, and 'The Great Brahma Heaven' which is for those who exemplify a state of perfection.

Through this wonderfully-complex web of heavens the one constant concern is the degree of development that each individual has managed to attain during this incarnation. Release from the cycle of rebirth is the ultimate aim, and with it the bliss of enlightenment, but the process is frequently a long one involving countless challenges to mind, body and spirit; a vast array of heavens is an appropriate means for a being to dwell in a suitable environment specific to its stage in the path, before yet another mortal life is begun.

In spite of the wealth of images and ideas stirred by the Christian concept of Heaven, its Hebraic origins actually described an afterlife that was more akin to that of the Mesopotamians in that only God and angelic beings might reside there, with little or no potential for a human soul to be granted entry. There are possible exceptions, such as Elijah (with 2 Kings 2:11 stating: 'And it came to pass, as they still went on, and talked, that, behold, there appeared a chariot of fire, and horses of fire, and parted them both asunder; and Elijah up by a whirlwind into heaven') though the ultimate end of Elijah and his one potential human companion in Heaven, Enoch, is not sufficiently described to be sure even of this.

Instead, Heaven is ruled over by the God of the Israelites while most souls are destined to spend time resting in Sheol, which is described by the Old Testament as an invisible realm of the dead but also as the actual grave at which the individual was interred, as well as a realm that sinners will descend to and pray for ultimate deliverance from: 'But if the Lord make a new thing, and the earth open up her mouth, and swallow them up, with all that appertain unto them, and they go down quick into the pit (Sheol); then ye shall understand that these men have provoked the Lord.'

What is certainly apparent is that the idea of Heaven and afterlife is unclear and therefore changeable within Old Testament Scripture, an enigmatic concept which only began to receive greater thought and interpretation as Jews of the Second Temple Period (516 B.C.E. – 70 C.E.) began to follow the Persian and Greek model of a human soul as descending to a mortal existence and then striving to return to its origin upon death.

Of course, Christianity would offer much greater emphasis toward the idea of Heaven in Scripture, though there would remain a degree of nebulousness to the described realm of the 'Kingdom of God' or 'Kingdom of Heaven' where a soul might pass after death, or likewise Heaven as a state of being for the soul to attain. What was more implicit was the familiar idea that righteousness was fundamental for any such reward to be granted, otherwise a soul might, at best, be forced to reside in a form of purgatory until the End of Days – and even then fail to be lifted from its desolate state.

Islam likewise speaks of Jannah or 'Garden/Paradise', which is a heavenly destination for those who have lived an appropriately just life, though here the burden of a soul does not include 'original sin' and so the opportunity to enter this idyll is enjoyed by a larger number of souls. Judgement is once again a central aspect of the afterlife, and those who pass to Jannah enjoy harmony and bliss, expansive banquets and expensive attire, all with the company of loved ones – and the greater the good exhibited in life, the higher the level one achieves in Paradise. As is often the case, those deemed to be sinners must travel elsewhere, with loved ones, feast and harmony all but a tormenting memory until the end of time...

The *'Popol Vuh'* describes the infernal realm, known here as Xibalba or the 'Place of Fright' with obvious relish, noting the likes of 'One Death', 'Scab Stripper', 'Blood Gatherer', the Demons of Pus and of Filth, as well as areas such as 'Scorpion Rapids', 'Blood River' and 'Razor House'. A suitably vibrant concept of an underworld, the idea that a journey of sorts might be made by a being was not impossible – though the risks would be great and the challenges all but insurmountable, one could hope to emulate the Hero Twins who traverse the plains of the damned, trick the demons who rule it and return, purified, through clear waters.

Hell is of course the destination for those who are judged to have lived poorly, and again although there might be variations on the central theme of what this realm and its punishments might consist of, so too what might constitute a suitably poor or sinful life to end in damnation, the similarities far outweigh the differences and the mention of any such realm are nearly always immediately recognisable, as with the depictions of Xibalba. The term 'Hell' itself may well derive from Old English (with 'hel' or 'helle' meaning a form of underworld or abode of the dead), but the archetypal concept transcends language, time and context.

China knows it in one form as Diyu which is something of a purgatory ruled by one Yanluo Weng, its King, where souls reside while they attempt restitution and atonement for their sins in life. It is a purgatory in that atonement can certainly be made, and one of the main roles of Diyu is the gradual preparation of each soul for its next incarnation, with various levels and overseers specialising in different forms of sin – though its underground, labyrinthine construction suggests a bleak 'trap' for any souls residing there that is not dissimilar to many descriptions of Hell itself.

Zoroastrian texts offer a number of possible fates for those who have fallen short of Ahura Mazda's standards, including one whereupon souls remain in Duzakh until the end of a thousand year cycle when the god collapses creation, annihilates the force of evil and grants a re-birth for each soul back into its original state of perfection, lending itself somewhat to the Indian religions and their prevalent belief in reincarnations, a journey toward a state of unity with the divine, and cycles of existence for lives and cosmos alike.

Another, more descriptive account of where evil-doers head after death can be found in the *'Book of Ardā Wīrāz'* dating in part from the Sasanian era (224 – 651 C.E.) and completed during the 10th/11th centuries. It tells the journey of a devout Zoroastrian's passage through the world beyond our own, as experienced in a dream – and with it the torment of those, among others, who spread lies (serpents biting and feasting on their tongues) and those who failed to appropriately care for the animals upon which their own well-being depended (being trampled and crushed beneath marauding herds). The sins are those of specific concern to the Persian culture of the time, and the punishments meted out are entirely commensurate with the acts that the damned perpetrated.

The Egyptians believed that those who are damned are 'mut' and are to suffer a further death as a result of their wicked ways. As such we read of demons unwrapping the mummified remains of corpses to allow decomposition and to ensure that the ba spirit is left estranged and restless; some individuals are tied up, dismembered and eviscerated while others live in perpetual darkness and have only ordure as nourishment. Worst of all, Ra will not meet their gaze or acknowledge their presence.

There are also depictions that, again, lead us toward what would become the recognisable Hell of the Western world, with judgement of the dead taking place at a sea of fire and the flames consuming the evil heart just as Ammit did. However, one of the most remarkable aspects of the Egyptian underworld is that those destined to be sent there were 'usurpers of the divine order', those who brought chaos in life by denying or obviating their moral and spiritual obligations; again the fundamental concerns and mores of a culture are revealed and enshrined through their concept of afterlife.

Ancient Greece depicted the place of judgement and torment as Tartaros, which originally held only those who posed a threat to the Olympian gods but later came to be the home of Sisyphus, Ixion, Tantalus and the Danaides to name but a few, alongside an increasing number of mere mortals. Once more the punishment is seen to fit the perceived crime, thus we find Sisyphus eternally rolling a huge stone up a hill only for it to fall (due to his belief that he was wiser than the gods), Ixion was lashed to a flaming, winged wheel that was constantly rotating (for an unchecked passion that had led to the birth of the half-man, half-horse Centaurus), and the Danaides – the fifty daughters of Danaus - forever worked to fill a cracked and leaking tub in order to cleanse themselves after murdering their husbands.

Islam speaks of Jahannam, a term related to the Hebraic Gehinnom. As with the Islamic concept of heaven it consists of seven layers though here, as expected, it is torment that is experienced in the forms of fire and scorching waters, seas of blood, thorny hedges and no light to see by but for the flames. There are also accounts of a base to hell, Zamhareer, where it is extreme cold, snow and cutting blizzards rather than heat which beleaguer the residents.

The narrow As-Sirāt bridge has to be traversed by the dead on their way to heaven, and those who fail this task are destined to pass the gate watched over by Maalik and, ultimately, Jahannam where Iblis rules with an army of demons. There is continued debate as to whether or not this condition is an eternal one, or if a form of salvation is ultimately possible, but it is of no doubt that all those who have rejected Allah, denied the messages of his Prophets and failed to live according to their tenets will be sent there once their mortal body has given them up.

Early Jewish belief did not hold a concept of hell, though Gehinnom became a recognisable form of purgatory for those awaiting divine judgement or those who become increasingly aware of one's own shortcomings and 'sins' so that restitution can begun to be sought. All souls pass through this stage of afterlife, though it is believed that a year at the most is sufficient before a soul passes on to its next stage/level of being.

A sense of purgatory pending judgement is certainly conjured in Biblical Scripture regarding the afterlife, as in Daniel 12:2: 'And many of them that sleep in the dust of the earth shall awake, some to everlasting life, and some to shame and everlasting contempt' and Ecclesiastes, where it is stated that '...the dead know not any thing, neither have they any more a reward;

for the memory of them is forgotten' (9:5), though later beliefs and the mystical framework of Cabbalism did offer greater depth and expanse of thought when it came to punishment in the afterlife.

As with the Islam model there are seven levels, of which Sheol and Gehinnom are but two. Abaddon which is 'perdition', Be'er Shachath which is the 'pit of corruption', Tzalmavet which is the 'shadow of death', Sha'are Mavet which are the 'gates of death' and Tit ha-Yaven which is 'clinging mud' are also to be found by those so destined, with souls directed to them variously according to the nature of their wickedness.

Developed in part by many of these influences, Christianity has a typically complex and varied idea of hell and those who are likely to be sent there post-mortem. For many denominations including the Roman Catholic Church, some Greek Orthodox and the Episcopalians, Hell is the inevitable and final place of torment for those judged unworthy of Heaven come the End of Days, while the overriding Protestant credo is that those who accept Christ during their life will be absolved of their sins and find everlasting peace with their Saviour.

Perhaps more resoundingly (though not universally) accepted is that Hell is a state of being whereby God, Christ, their revelation and their love are all rejected in death as in life, estranging an individual from its creator and His son, which bears some similarity to Islamic Sufism or even the Kamaloka of the Indian faiths, where hell is accepted as a state of being rather than a literal destination for the soul. The rather haunting suggestion is that, far from ignorant, the damned are those who willingly turn from light and love toward other, more personal and perhaps more base concerns at the expense of themselves – and that, left with such a narrow and unenlightened frame of reference, hell is indeed the result.

Of course, this interpretation does not explain the vast scale of monsters, grotesques and gargoyles that peer down from churches and Cathedrals, or the scores of texts depicting in nauseating detail the geography, nature and horrors of the archetypal Hell. The likes of Hieronymus Bosch (c.1450 – 1516 C.E.) certainly bore the creativity and wit to paint panoramic scenes of torture, humiliation and degradation at the hands of gleeful demons and fanged beasts, but much relied then as now on the medieval mindset and, in particular, the works of Dante Alighieri (1265 – 1321 C.E.).

Arguably the most widely-known and exhaustive account of Hell, Dante's *'Inferno'* from his *'Divine Comedy'* (14th century C.E.) is an enduring depiction that united the various ideas extant regarding judgement, punishment and spiritual damnation and has become an active component of the collective consciousness of the Western world. From the first screams heard by Dante and his guide the poet Virgil as they pass the gate of Hell with its adorning inscription 'Abandon all hope, ye who enter here', all that has come to epitomise the state of eternal damnation is here laid out for us.

There are nine circles of Hell, and in each one are souls receiving an appropriate punishment for their sins – which extends to those left outside of Hell and across the waters of death, where those who were self-interested and non-committal restlessly chase a phantom believed to offer them some form of escape. Dante sees pagans and the unbaptized like Homer and Ovid aimless and bereft, before visiting the lustful who are tormented by endless, harsh winds that mirror the overpowering desires that they allowed to rule them.

The gluttonous exist amid 'putrefaction' and filth, while the miserly joust with great weights that they can barely move, let alone hold aloft; the wrathful fight without end over the heads of those whose animosity was internalised into sullenness and despondency; heretics, meanwhile, are held firm in burning tombs. As Dante descends still further he sees some souls turned into trees and consumed by Harpies (suicides), others covered in ordure and endlessly squabbling with one another (flatterers); he sees false prophets and sorcerers walking backwards with their heads turned clean around befitting their fraudulent attempts to know the future; he sees thieves tied and bitten by serpents and having their very identity stolen from them in perpetuity.

Dante passes through realms named after the likes of the Biblical Cain and Judas Iscariot, before reaching the centre of Hell, where the Devil – here known as Dis – stands trapped in ice from the waist down, a three-headed monstrosity held in constant torment not least for the beauty and light he once embodied, as Lucifer, before his fall from grace. Dis weeps as he chews on the bodies of those who were prominent traitors, all the while beating bat-like wings that offer further chill to his already frozen prison.

Dante's work continues to enthral and fascinate in part because it serves an encyclopaedic repository of medieval thought, faith and lore – but also because he uses the *'Inferno'* and with it his other books of the *'Divine Comedy'* to comment (with no small amount of sardonic humour) on theology, metaphysics, rhetoric, philosophy and more.

Ethics and morality are also prominent aspects of the tale, serving as a lynchpin to the Hell Dante paints with its modus operandi of punishment befitting the crime. Such an interpretation as Dante's thus owes its creator an immense debt in terms of the creativity that bore the sheer depth and expanse of detail he offers, though the fundamental understanding pertaining to the might and nature of divine punishment is something apparent within most conceptions of, and responses to, hell – indeed, those very responses to the idea of a god or gods' wrath are where Dante received his greatest inspiration!

One more fundamental aspect of the work that explains its import on the collective psyche and its universal familiarity is its central narrative. Dante tells us of a frightening and overwhelming journey that occurs to one being as he travails the depths of Hell, through Purgatory and thence on an epiphanic tour of Heaven; it is the story of one soul's deconstruction, reflection and ultimate re-birth as it passes several thresholds ('Abandon all hope...') on a mission for enlightenment and a renewed understanding of the divine, which speaks to all faiths, all walks of life, all times and all human existences.

Dante gives us terrible glimpses of torment and suffering but also shows how each and every one of us can be transformed, through that 'rite of passage' which is life as well as death, so that a certain wisdom can be gained – and the soul awarded with a return to its source, answering its cry for understanding and belonging no matter the faith, mythology or rites it frames them with.

Aspects

The soul, then, is the key. It is the 'soul' that we perceive as the vehicle of transformation both before and after mortal consciousness, and it is the soul that we understand as making the greater journey through those thresholds of birth, life and death – even where faiths and philosophies explore the idea of the soul and its timeless passage in divergent ways.

Indian faiths offer a singularly poetic understanding of being, the process of death and the afterlife, though it is more than reinforced by their scriptures which offer copious detail, reflection and wisdom on the subjects. The '*Bhagavad-gītā*' (2:20) beautifully elucidates something of the nature of the soul: 'For the soul there is neither birth nor death at any time. He has not come into being, and will not come into being. He is unborn, eternal, ever-existing and primeval. He is not slain when the body is slain.'

However, even here there is much that is not clarified and much that remains nebulous to say the least, which is perhaps the best we can aspire to when describing concepts of 'soul', 'God' and 'faith' in that they are by their nature beyond our full understanding, beyond our material frame of reference and thus beyond lexis. This may be why texts such as the *'Bhagavad-gītā'* describe concepts that might appear in this world to be extraordinary in terms that plead logic and common sense: 'As, after casting away worn out garments, a man later takes new ones. So after casting away worn out bodies, the embodied Self encounters other new ones' (2:22).

Within Buddhism it is said that rupa or pure consciousness is attained at death, and where a Bodhisattva enters a higher state of being, those not yet prepared for such an elevation enter bardo, which is a form of limbo, while they await reincarnation. The Tibetan *'Book of the Dead'* is to be read aloud to the dying as their moment of passing draws near, reaffirming that death is far from an end and is only a new stage of development and being: 'The hour has come to part with this body composed of flesh and blood…may I know the body to be impermanent and illusory.'

Hindu philosophy suggests that the spirit is the atman, the true being that lies clothed by the material form which is eternal pure consciousness, a metaphysical entity that is of its source and not of the bodies which it temporarily rests within. For the atman to break from the cycles of reincarnation it is necessary for genuine self-knowledge to be obtained, although the point of any return to life is not of itself any form of punishment – though the passage of the true self back to higher plains is the ideal to which it, and therefore we, aspire, lifetimes are the means to learn and achieve that stage of development.

Further poetry is found when we consider that the cycles of

life are not just akin to us, but to the entire cosmos. The spirit at our core pervades and is pervaded by everything else in creation, so too so much that we have no awareness of while in the mortal realm, and the 'world soul' likewise is infused with the divine and is also drawn into itself, collapsed and reformed at the end of each 'era' so that a total re-birth of all follows destruction.

This idea of a unity at the heart of all is common to many mythologies and religions, just as the 'shedding of skin' and gradual ascent to godhood/creation/other is a frequent aspect of faiths, as well as the fundamental tenets of alchemy, much mysticism and some forms of magic. Of course this raises the question of what exactly 'we' are, and where we as a being begin and end, not least given that one of the greatest fears of death in any form is the loss of our self.

One Chinese understanding of the soul suggests that it consists of two parts hun (air) which is yang, and two parts pho (earth) which is yin, though the later development of this saw the soul made up of three parts han to seven pho, which suggests the greater tie to physicality than the spiritual that our bodies present us with.

Such physicality was incorporated into the Egyptian ideas of soul along with a greater application of 'self,' in that each body was believed to have a number of associated shades or forms of energy connected to it. These included the body itself, though of course death rendered this immobile, along with the ba that is life-force or possibly the soul, depending on one's interpretation; further to these were the ka which is essentially the 'character' and the akh which is 'light', the 'effective' being that actualises the will. As such the Egyptians incorporated the material with the spiritual and encapsulated all potential levels of being from the physical to the spiritual, along with mind, energy and even the identity that imbues one's own name.

Spirit as penuma or spark alongside one's character are also found as individual forms of being in some Islamic thought, where the soul is rūh and character or ego is nafs, though the terms can each be used to refer to the other in a further example of the elusiveness of any definitive terminology or understanding, which is in-keeping with the teachings of the Quran: 'And they ask you, about the Rūh. Say, "The Rūh is of the affair of my Lord. And mankind has not been given knowledge except a little' (17:85).

Plato (c.428 – 348/347 B.C.E.) spoke of the soul of an individual as being their psyche, which was a metaphysical entity that lived on and continued to think post-mortem, just as it had existed before its physical incarnation. He broke the soul down further into three distinct parts, the logos (mind; reason, located at the head), the thymos (emotion/masculine, located at the heart) and the eros (desire/feminine, located at the stomach).

The various aspects of the soul, overseen by the logos, had to be kept in balance for any successful function to continue, but even where such balance is achieved and a worthy life lived, the soul was subject to cycles of reincarnation (here termed metempsychosis), a reasoning that was not echoed in the later works of Aristotle (384 – 322 B.C.E.) who largely appeared to deny any immortality to the soul as well as its existence as matter separate to the physical form.

Where Aristotle did meet Plato was in his appreciation of the importance of order within one's mind and body (mirroring their perception of a good and functional populace, it is no surprise that Plato frequently compared the tiered structure of the soul to the social castes within society). Aristotle suggested that plants, animals and humans all bore souls, though these were of varying levels of complexity of which the human is the most complex, being self-conscious.

Though the idea of metempsychosis or renewed lives as the soul progressed was rejected by Aristotle, the first and full 'actualization' of a being is its soul, in that its very existence bestows on it a purpose and a drive to grow, develop and become that which it is meant to be, and so by living in a state of balance the overall 'soul' of the being is being perfected as a life is lived. Later influential thinkers such as Avicenna and Thomas Aquinas developed their own concept of soul from that of Aristotle, ensuring that it was instrumental in shaping responses, with some adjustment and innovation, through the Scholastic period and into the Middle Ages.

Aquinas also upheld the Platonic belief that the soul is something separate from the physical body, so too that it can exist without it and certainly continues to exist after physical death. A suitably oblique confirmation of this can be found in 1 Corinthians 15:39: 'All flesh is not the same flesh' where, it appears, we are told that there are forms of existence beyond the mortal, and again when it is suggested that the two forms are distinct and have decidedly divergent paths to take (15:42-44): '...the resurrection of the dead. It is sown in corruption; it is raised in incorruption: it is sown in dishonour; it is raised in glory: it is sown in weakness; it is raised in power: it is sown a natural body; it is raised a spiritual body. There is a natural body, and there is a spiritual body.'

Thus the soul is delivered to the world to incarnate and live an appropriate life, with an ultimate goal of leaving its material fetters and returning whence it originated from; whether or not we allow for but one incarnation or several, the source and the destination are nonetheless one and the same, that which for the Hebrews is the life-giving breath of God, for the Gnostic the pneuma that descended from its creator, and for the Hindu the atman that is ultimately to return to the All.

The soul is something 'other' and quite apart from the coarse body that it finds itself within, even where the kernel of divinity is believed to reside in all forms of material creation. Within the Eleusinian mystery teachings, soul was Psyche and belonged in the higher world akin to the heavens, which was the only domain where it was truly alive; conversely, the human form was thus a sort of tomb within which the Psyche was trapped until it was once more released following death, an idea mirrored in the Gnostic faith.

Likewise similar to Gnostic thought was that, in spite of the fall of the soul that was implicit as well as the 'dream' or degradation that life could be held to be, it was possible if not entirely necessary for the soul to use its mortal lifetime in the pursuit of genuine revelation or remain lost from its creator and eternally confined in a lesser form. If there was a purpose to human life it was the search for insight and wisdom, which alone could deliver the final liberation of the true being, the soul (termed moksha within the Indian faiths).

The soul's journey toward enlightenment is a common theme and image within all manner of mystical schools, and however it is depicted the idea of a return to the source remains the singular goal, as described in the Gnostic *'Divine Pymander'* which is said to be the work of the legendary 'Trismegistus' or 'thrice-blessed': 'Having been stripped of all that is wrought upon him by the structure of the heavens...they mount upward to the Father; they give themselves up to the Powers, and becoming powers themselves, they enter into God.'

The *'Zohar'* of the Cabbalists represents death as chaos, which can only be irreversibly eradicated at the final end of all. Rav. Berg (1927 – 2013 C.E) described this 'tikkun' as a return to the 'pre-Fall immortality consciousness' through which the stains of existence might be removed and the true knowledge of God and existence rediscovered, though this can only be a gradual passage of the soul through a number of lifetimes of learning.

This is also reflected on a wider scale, and so is not restricted to individual beings – collectively the souls of the world can seek to gain this epiphany that unites them with each other just as it unites them with the wisdom originally held by Adam before he was made mortal and forced from Paradise. With sufficient souls thus imbued with the revelation, a tipping point would be reached and the whole of existence can be delivered into bliss.

Descent from the source to the physical realm was of course required for any journey of re-ascent to be made, and many depictions exist which explore this concept, including those within Cabbalism and the mystical Orphic teachings of the Ancient Greeks. The latter held that the process of re-birth into a new incarnation saw a soul pass through the various planetary spheres, and from them gaining specific qualities of being that related to those influences, namely contemplative reason from Saturn, the power of actualization from Jupiter, vehemence from Mars, the 'phantasy' of visualization from the Sun, desire and love from Venus, sensitivity and expression from Mercury and the operation of physical bodies from the Moon.

Alternative concepts of the soul nonetheless allow for a variety of forms that equate with the different levels of influence and energy that the spark of life is sheathed by, similar to the range of forms that were depicted by the Egyptians; thus Paracelsus allowed for a physical, elemental body within which there is an astral, sidereal soul and then, at the core, the spirit of God which is the illumined body or spirit itself. The Theosophists preferred seven such 'sheaths'; Atman, Buddhi, Manas, Ego, Astral, Etheric and Physical, which is not wholly removed from the range of attitudes and forms espoused by the Orphic model.

Theosophy was heavily influenced by Hinduism and Buddhism, not least in its response to the concept of reincarnation which as we have seen is an integral tenet of the Indian faiths. Life as we know it is here perceived as a pocket of being that is defined by one's conduct, in that thoughts and feelings from one lifetime survive death and forge something of the next incarnation – the law of Karma. Mortality, then, presents the soul with an opportunity to 'exist' in one form, learn from that existence and then pass on to another where the lessons are realised, the wishes from the previous life are actualised and any retribution that is due is sufficiently meted out.

The belief that all souls emanate from one source to which they will ultimately return is mirrored by the idea that the entire cosmos, the 'world soul' along with it, will be collapsed back into itself and made one with that source before creation occurs again. This underlines the importance of due thought and respect for all life but also offers a degree of perspective as to just how insignificant the desires, wishes and struggles of the individual can be seen to be – and Indian cosmology offers further sobering detail that certainly makes clear our importance, which is at once vital and yet trivial when applied to the broader canvas that is existence.

The 21st century is a speck in the last of the four Yugas or eras, the Kali Yuga. Each of the Yugas are successively shorter than the one before it, just as each era heralds a diminishment in the quality of existence when compared to its predecessor. However, even as the shortest such era, the Kali Yuga has endured for some 432,000 years, with the overall duration of the four Yugas being 4,320,000 years, which is known as one Mahayuga. A Mahayuga itself lasts for but one single day of Brahma, known as a kalpa – and the life of Brahma lasts for one hundred days and nights, giving us a total of 311,040,000,000,000 years!

This is noted to suggest the unique perspective on existence that is offered by the Indian understanding of reincarnation – the journey toward enlightenment will not be easy for any individual and errors may well be made, but each lifespan is but a grain of sand on several miles of beach, just as even the lifetime of the cosmos is short to Brahma. In terms of soul we are all part of something far, far greater and this is highlighted when we consider that in our pure state we are ourselves beyond duration, creation and existence and thus even several lifetimes are but dreams to the soul. Liberation lies in the profound awareness of this fact, and a life lived according to the revelation so gained.

Theories of reincarnation or the transmigration of souls unites Buddhism, Hinduism, Jainism and Sikhism with the beliefs of Plato, his teacher Socrates, the mathematician and sage Pythagoras (c.570 – c.495 B.C.E.) and offshoots of Christianity and Islam such as the Gnostics and the Druze respectively, along with the Mystery schools, Hermeticism, Theosophists, some Wiccans and even Scientology.

The idea of samsara is found in the Upanishads of the later Vedic period (c.1100 – 500 B.C.E.), and early Jainist texts from the 1st millennium B.C.E. offer great elucidation as to the role of karma and the cycles of reincarnation. Buddhist scripture, too, includes discussion of the state of Nirvana and the practices best placed to achieve this state of consciousness, along with greater detail as to the various forms of purgatorial existence, along with heavens and hells that can be entered by a soul that has not yet attained such clarity and liberation. Similar beliefs are echoed in Cabbalism and indeed Chinese Taoism, where Chuang Tzu (c.369 – c.286 B.C.E.) stated: 'Birth is not a beginning; death is not an end. There is existence without limitation...'

In spite of the efforts of early Christians to divorce any theory of reincarnation from their doctrine and the later attempt to purge any remaining believers and off-shoot movements under a banner of heresy, it did continue to flourish across the globe including Europe (thanks to the Cathars and Bogomils among others, and much earlier strands of faith that bore links to Pythagoras and his students in Germany) and North America, and would retain a place in the Western consciousness even before 'rediscovery' through religious and esoteric movements of the 19th century C.E., spiritualism and the investigative researches into it, also philosophy and psychology.

Though it shows variances across these faiths, reincarnation is nonetheless a concept with wide and deep-seated appeal, likely due to the journey of the soul so envisioned, and the sense of identity and immortality that are offered. Every form of existence beyond nirvana/moksha and the liberation from the cycles of re-birth are but plains of being for further development, and so the variegated models of afterlife including the most idyllic of heavens and most squalid of hells can here be interpreted as states of purgation while a soul prepares for a further existence.

Attachment to the physical plain, dread and fear, goals and wishes so far unfulfilled – all of these may account for the accumulation of karma that maintains one's presence in the cycle of samsara, but the very control that each individual can weight themselves down by can also be exercised, ultimately, to transform and lift them beyond what have before appeared to be impenetrable barriers. There is thus a sense of hope that however late it might come or after however many lifetimes, growth, wisdom and enlightenment are still possible for every soul.

Fears

It is striking that for many cultures past and present, the tenets of reincarnation have not always offered the reassurance and certainty that others so gain; perhaps due to the inherent metaphysical nature of such beliefs – the fact that belief is the kernel and enlightenment the result – there is frequently a stumbling block for some in that death is very much a reality for each individual, forcing transformation on the physical plain and sending reverberations through families, clans, cities, and even entire civilizations.

Even where a degree of revelation of life, death and cosmos is manifested, it may not exclude the fears that the coming of death stokes on a personal and cultural level, thus further very practical rites often follow the passing of an individual to ensure that any deceased is appropriately treated to avoid their torment in any potential afterlife, or their return to wreak vengeance among the living who failed them at the crucial time. However it is interpreted and enacted, a respect for the dead is paramount universally, which is at once a statement about the precious condition of life as well as any consequences of the hereafter.

Bodies have thus been laid to rest within or below giant monuments; they have been interred standing upright, bound, in foetal position or dismembered, often with all manner of goods to accompany them; they have been burnt in funeral pyres; they have been sent out to sea, hung from trees, and left to be devoured and scattered by scavengers or even by family, friends and neighbours. Death is indeed a rite of passage with the emphasis on *passage*, and there are countless forms of funerary rites that relate to personal as well as cultural beliefs and mores, seemingly from the very earliest times.

Though any true understanding of them is long-lost in the depths of time, burials with grave goods such as food and tools were occurring 50,000 years ago, with many buried facing West where the sun was observed to set or 'die' each day. Red ochre was applied at points to the remains – notably upon the skull – as though to give an impression of blood and therefore life, or perhaps to apply a form of immortality or continuance through what would later be termed sympathetic magic.

This evidence can be interpreted in many ways, and a great number of estimations made as to the import of such acts, but they nonetheless suggest a degree of belief for the dead either due to the loss of a loved one, their welfare beyond life, or a mixture of the two. Where we see the application of grave goods it might relate to a belief that one's belongings should follow them to the grave simply as a matter of ownership, though it might also denote concern that those items would be touched by death and so were best removed from the domain of the living. Where a corpse is bound or shaped into a foetal-position it may be the preparation of a return to the womb, or it may be an attempt to keep a troubled soul from rising, or something else entirely...

However, the scale of grave goods found across the globe, the application of ochre to remains and the sheer variety of form that funerary rites present us with does, as a whole, suggest not just the immediate awareness that death was of a unique import for the individual and those left by their passing, but also that ideas very quickly began to result from wholly natural questions about where that individual had passed to – the afterlife therefore became a real concern even where it was held to be a return to earth, or a flight to the stars, as both earth and stars were imminent and omnipresent beings that gave and took away from the living. Regardless the framework or fashion, death and the afterlife demanded consideration and the careful observance of any ritual.

Egyptian rites of burial are well-attested, including the human sacrifices that might accompany the body being laid to rest. Of course wooden effigies of servants might also be used, with the belief that magic would imbue them with life once the dead had arisen – the key was that the dead required sufficient and appropriate means to continue 'living' once the veil of death had been lifted.

Similar investment of goods and people can be found in what was the city of Ur in modern-day Iraq (where Queen Shubad was laid to rest some 4,500 years ago with the bodies of 68 servants), the Etruscan civilization of pre-Roman Italy (where tombs were likewise decked with beautiful furniture and even chariots), and Mesoamerica (where treasures including jade, chocolate and indeed attendants might be included, as well as dogs both real and ceramic that were closely linked to the dead and seen as faithful companions for the deceased).

Mummification was also employed outside of Egypt, notably by the Chilean Chinchirro people c.5000 B.C.E. where the dead, including infants, were kept in situ alongside the living for a period of time with masks placed upon their faces. A new relationship with the individual was thus developed that allowed for a sense of continuity of being, before a final departing was enacted.

The Necropolis or 'city of the dead' as it became known to the Greeks offered a specific space where the dead might be gathered with resplendent surroundings; as such great displays of art and architecture would be found there, along with a degree of beauty and opulence that few managed to enjoy even temporarily in life. A funerary cult developed from this concept, which was fundamental in that constant interaction between the living and the dead was required to ensure both the well-being of the deceased through perpetuated rites, and the well-being of the living who were at the mercy of the spectral wanderings of the dead, or their use in magic.

Less auspicious was the Mesopotamian way of death, which once again reflected the harshness of existence in life. Though the elite and wealthy enjoyed a degree of veneration and care with funerary rites (and archaeological evidence is somewhat lacking to elucidate this), most were laid to rest with little if any ritual or fanfare. This is far from surprising given that even the heroes and the gods themselves were not exclusively exempt from the murky and eldritch wasteland that was the afterlife, and so the lack of overarching rites can be seen as commensurate with the attitude to life as well as death.

More affirming is the use of jade and shells in burial sites in China, with the jade believed to preserve the body and the shells seen as a means of propagating new life given their form and link to fertility. Pearls as well as jade might be placed in to the mouth of the corpse (with pearls often serving as a model of the spark of soul held by the body), an act which has also been found in India where shells might be strewn across the path of a funeral procession to, again, offer a means for new life for the dead. Symbolism being what it is, similar grave goods like shells and pearls have been noted in Egyptian rites, so too in parts of Africa and the Americas.

Remembrance, transformation and future life can be suggested in many ways, from any kind of grave marker that denotes a cultural identity with a faith and recognises a belief in a collective resurrection, to the now-common practise of cremation which allows for a more personal and immediate means of passage, to burgeoning interests in woodland burial where the body returns directly back to the earth and replenishes the material source from which it in part emerged. Even with an intensely personal approach to death and whatever lies beyond, the need and desire to 'honour' the beliefs and wishes of the deceased can exceed the emotional and touch on the atavistic and almost subconscious understanding held by the living that due rites for the dead are 'only proper' as a means of parting ways.

Many have discovered in great shock and wonder that bodies show no evidence of desiccation, which might result from singular environments or the most carefully-upheld funerary processes, but has often been taken as a miraculous occurrence befitting the greatest of souls. So it was with the Chinese Buddhist and Zen master Huineng (638 – 713 C.E.) who was disinterred by the Mongols in 1276 and his condition found to be quite remarkable, with his skin maintaining its elasticity and his organs said to be in perfect condition.

The Capuchin monks interred beneath the church of Santa Maria della Concezione dei Cappucchini in Rome, Italy, suspended from the walls in their finery and preserved through natural mummification are another example of 'miracle' in death, while William the Conqueror (who died in 1087 C.E.) was discovered to be in such excellent condition in 1552 that his corpse was used as a model for a local artist!

Seeing the deceased in these forms stokes the same profound emotions that death in general evokes, including discomfort, sorrow, compassion, fear and of course reflections on one's own mortality, all of which continues to shape our attitudes to death and dying even in an increasingly secular age where death has been marginalised into a distant, if not absent, figure. Of these emotions it is the fear that has perhaps been interpreted and actualised in the most striking of ways, not least because in reacting to fears about death we are frequently externalising not terrors of the dead and any powers that they might possess – somewhat ironically we might not be genuinely acknowledging the reality of death at all, but responding to innate personal angst regarding our own mortality.

Sigmund Freud (1856 – 1939 C.E.) stated that beyond the 'pleasure principle' (the innate avoidance of pain in favour of the distraction of immediate satisfaction) was the 'death instinct' or 'death drive' that is the headlong descent toward an end of life, exemplified by aggressive behaviours when externalised, or suicidal tendencies when internalised. For Freud '...the goal of all life is death...' and we are frequently self-destructive as a result of both our fears of termination and our inability to actually perceive our own death – the threat of death clings to us and haunts us, but is never confronted directly and so we engage in acts and behaviours that ironically accelerate our own annihilation.

Ghosts, zombies, demons and shadows are manifestations of those fears as much as anything else, sometimes allowing us a useful means of distraction from the real horror that is our own termination, even where the fear we feel for the restless dead and other supernatural entities is a real one. Of course, for those who resolutely follow prescribed funerary rites and hold heartfelt beliefs in the soul and the afterlife, the concern for the vengeance of ancestors, the aimless and lonely and the powers tappable by the deceased in their new form can all be authentic, to the point of being overwhelming. Where the living are concerned fears about the dead are many, and they are quite literally the stuff of nightmares...

Homer's *'Odyssey'* offers a glimpse of what 'life' is like for most of the dead when a trench is filled with animal blood and the spirits are called to offer their insight and wisdom. Many, including Odysseus' own mother, approach and initially fail to recognise him but are able to gather something of their old selves by imbibing some of the blood – an empty and melancholy existence for any being, let alone the great and the good, alongside old warriors and champions, who are among the thronging 'shades.'

The *'Agamemnon'* of Aeschylus sees Clytemnestra note a perpetual sense of anger among the dead and with it a desire for some form of vengeance, whether due to what they believe to be an untimely death or simply a jealousy for those still able to eat, breath, touch and love. It is also mentioned that some may be trapped in a limbo of their own making in that their attachment and obsession with materiality (riches, power, sensation, experience) has chained them to the physical plain – though they could indeed move on if they wished it, either fear of what lies beyond or an inability to believe that there could be more than the physical renders them effectively blinds them to their new condition, and what it can offer.

Concern of repercussions where the dead have not been appropriately laid to rest or commemorated was and to an extent remains universal, and there are numerous accounts in fiction, folklore and hearsay of vengeance and haunting resulting from just this oversight. One of the most widely-disseminated is to be found in Virgil's *'The Illiad'* where Patrochus remonstrates the mighty Achilles for not giving him a proper burial, preventing him from crossing the river Styx; he promises that his spectral wandering will cease if and when his due funeral rites are completed.

The Mesopotamians believed in vampire-corpses that would stalk the living to drink their blood should the funerary rites be ignored. Offerings (Kiipū) were thus carefully chosen, including various drinks that were poured directly into the earth through clay pipes, to avoid the return of any restless spirit or gidim that was said to enter the ear of a living being and thenceforth cause illness and disease, known as 'Hand of the Ghost' and 'Seizure of the Ghost' – an ability that was afforded to the dead by many cultures including those of Mesoamerica.

Asia sees similar beliefs to this day, with the wandering dead following the living and frequently remaining near their old homes in search of some form of release. They too are believed to feed on the living if they are sufficiently starved and have been known to steal children for this purpose, while some restrict their activities to eating other members of the dead.

A common story recounted in Japan is that of the Kuchisake-onna, who was once a vain young woman and the courtesan of a jealous samurai; in a rage the samurai disfigured her and then mocked her by asking "Who will now think you beautiful?" Since that day she roams in the fog seeking man, woman and child but covering her face with a mask, asking them if they think she is beautiful – a 'yes' sees her remove the mask and ask them a second time, and those who deny her suffer greatly, with men torn apart and women disfigured and damned as a new Kuchisake-onna.

Spectral lights, known variably as 'Fox Fire', 'Friar's Lantern' and 'Will-o-the-wisp' among other colourful names are a common theme in tales and legends, suggesting that the dead are at the very least tied or drawn to their graves at certain times. This in part explains why Bohemian funerary rites were known to include mourners wearing masks after a funeral so that the attendant dead could not recognise individuals and follow them home.

In the Middle Ages ghosts were rather useful commodities for the Catholic Church in that they frequently seemed to soliloquise as to their sins in life, their anguish at belying the teachings of the Church and their warnings to the living to repent before their own time was up. With the Reformation came an attempt to quell such beliefs, and the idea of Purgatory was minimised in favour of Heaven and Hell alone and any ghost seen as something inhuman or the work of the Devil who was trying to ensnare the living…but the concept of the ghost was so tightly interwoven in faith, thoughts of death and afterlife and folklore that it maintained a place in the conscious and unconscious mind regardless.

There were exceptions to the general rule and ghosts who appeared to offer revelation, wisdom and protection, such as those who advertised the Catholic Church; Shakespeare utilised such an idea very effectively in Hamlet, and as recently as 1914 the 'Angel of Mons' in Belgium was said to appear and protect an outnumbered British regiment in what was seen as a decisive battle of World War I. Even here, where the event appears to have developed from a fictional episode (composed by Arthur Machen) the legend that built rapidly around it speaks of a need to believe in something more than ourselves and with it a message of righteousness in conflict, not least where so much loss and bloodshed would otherwise only leave a vacuum.

Of course the majority of the dead that the living encounter are far from helpful nor friendly, thus allowing for our greatest fears of death to embody and haunt us in life. As such we have the banshee or 'bansidhe' / 'fairy woman' of Gaelic lore that cries out as an omen of death, sometimes perceived as a guardian angel watching over a family line yet usually thought of with utter dread, heralding as she does the dark hand of fate and the looming shadow of the Grim Reaper.

On a grander scale still we have the widespread tales of the 'Wild Hunt' with huntsmen and demon dogs coursing through the wilderness under the full moon. Diana and Hecate may lead the throng that includes vampires, ghouls, demons and other undead who claim the lives of any who come to witness their devilish revelry and so doing add members to a band whose sole purpose on these sojourns is the infliction of madness and torment.

These stories and ideas terrified and thrilled with almost equal measure for centuries, though it is inevitable that they hold less attraction and power now following centuries of industrial development, urbanization and secularisation. However, they have not been entirely eradicated from our collective consciousness and do continue to arise from time to time, and across continents; the dispersion of land and wealth, the dispersion of peoples to distant places where vengeful ancestors are long-forgotten, the estrangement of the living from the very concept of death – all have forged a new path in terms of philosophy, belief and rites, but not yet to the extent that they have been completely subsumed.

Death remains a reality, if anything more troubling as it is pushed into the deeper shadows of a mind or a society, therefore the forms that our fears have taken over the centuries will not be easily denied. Either a new understanding of and relationship with death must be achieved and developed or the restless dead will continue to follow us with tireless and tenacious persistence, for many of them arise from within.

This is no less true than where death and magic are found, and much lore has been passed through oral tradition and grimoires that unites the two in various ways. The most prominent of these in the works of the sorcerer was necromancy (or 'nigromantia' to medieval writers, who were much taken with this divination with the dead), with its use stretching back to at least as early as the ancient Mesopotamians and maintaining an uninterrupted presence within the magical corpus ever after.

The art of necromancy recognised that either the bodies of the dead could be used, or the ghost/spirit of one deceased, though such entities were not seen as common and required careful and exhaustive rites to induce them to appear, with even greater efforts then applied to control any spirit so conjured due to their innate malevolence, jealousy and greed for life. Texts note that a 'shade' of the dead can be raised for up to one year after the passing of the individual, though the potential for a intruder of sorts – an elemental that has never known life but passes itself off as a ghost of the dead – is to be considered and prepared for.

All manner of environments can be used, but the liminal space of the crossroads is an ideal site for these rites as it is perceived to be beyond jurisdiction of town and faith, a limbo of sorts that more readily acquiesces to any efforts at thinning the veil between the living and the dead, the natural and the supernatural.

Given this, however, the dangers are immediately obvious in that he or she who summons the dead is entering the 'wilderness' and must therefore ensure that their magic circle is clearly marked, their incantations accurate and their authority sure – the placation and taming of the dead is only the second challenge, after threats have been cast from outside the circle, animal noises and growling have been heard, and the sensation of beasts prowling around the circumference of the protected area, seeking a means of ingress.

Once summoned the deceased can, it is said, be the source of much wisdom and revelation – though the common desire that brought them to bear, if the grimoires can be accepted, was a taste for riches, and the whereabouts of lost or hidden treasures, though there is a great history of necromancy as a means of fortune telling within the 'culte des mortes' of Voodoo.

An indelible illustration of the necromancer can be found in the *'Pharsalia'* and the witch Erichto, who we have already considered. She sits among the dead, with relics strewn about her that include pieces of corpses including eyes and teeth. With invocations in the names of the chthonic deities she works to summon a spirit for information, but first requires the lungs of a newly-deceased individual so as to give the spirit a means through which it can communicate.

For the serious necromancer following the grimoire, this is not so fanciful an image – success hinged on the summoning and mastery of the dead, but was founded on a closeness to the essence of death that necessarily bordered on obsession, with it clearly stated that a practitioner must surround themselves with an aura of death. Meditation on death was thus vital, and enforced by dressing in used grave-clothes and eating the likes of unleavened bread (with the absence of salt suggesting decay) and even the flesh of a dog (linking to the traditional scavenger of graves and its guardian, Hecate).

Similar extremes were necessary, and a strong constitution, when the dead were being used practically to activate or energise works of magic. Teeth, hair and nail clippings have been common ingredients in spells for millennia, with the remains of those who have suffered an untimely death believed to retain an unnatural vitality that is especially efficacious for love spells and curses alike.

The *'Petit Albert'* from 1772 and other notorious texts describe the process of creating a 'Hand of Glory': the hand of a hanged man must be cut off and the blood carefully squeezed from it, before it is wrapped and pickled for fifteen days. Following this period it is dried during the 'dog days' of July 3rd – August 11th, with the fat that runs out of the hand being used to make a candle that is ultimately placed between the fingers of the hand. Burning the candle thus transfixes and immobilises any who are in its presence, making them effectively as though they are dead.

Perhaps less grisly, one Graeco-Egyptian text instructs on how to bewitch through the use of a wax doll that must be made in the image of the intended victim and then pierced thirteen times in specific points of the figure, including those relating to the brain, the eyes, the stomach, genitals and anus. The doll was then to be placed on the grave of one who had died in youth or had suffered a violent death and conjurations recited in the names of the chthonic deities; the result was the raising of the tormented spirit, which would haunt the victim ceaselessly until they delivered themselves in body and mind to the sorcerer or witch in question.

On a metaphysical level, the 'death prayer' is certainly the most insidious and malevolent union between death and magic, with a prayer uttered and energised (by not only the ability and power of the orator, but also attendant demonic and elemental beings). With sufficient magnification of will, the prayer is directed at a victim who is believed to die as a direct result of this negative intent, whether through a forced 'accident' or an overwhelming of the mind or body.

Where such acts are concerned, (spanning the worlds of witchdoctors, magicians and others), it is not unknown for death to result if only from fear or shock, or from a cursed man or woman effectively resigning themselves to death as a result of the sword of Damocles that now hangs over them…however achieved, the summoning and direction of 'death' can be said to have been wholly successful.

The Voodoo religion certainly enjoys an especial relationship with death that includes magic, though there is much more than that at play in terms of beliefs and practise. Here the spirit is ti-bon-ange that is liberated at the point of death and remains in the proximity of the body for nine days before advancing to heaven; the soul, meanwhile, is the gros-bon-ange which constitutes the concept of a person, essentially their nature or character.

One essential act is the dessounim which is the detaching from the body of its gros-bon-ange and the dominant loa (tutelary spirit) that attached to them in life as a form of guardian. The end of this ceremony can include the attending hungan (shaman or witchdoctor) approaching the death bed or site where the body lies and straddling the corpse under any sheets or coverings; the loa is invoked, words are whispered into the ear of the corpse and the deceased is called by name. Witnesses of such scenes have spoken of the corpse moving with spasms or raising its head from the pillow (taken to be the loa leaving its host), though caution is always vital as that loa may immediately choose to enter one of those gathered to observe.

Aside from the obvious religious insult and feelings of guilt that failing to perform these rites would induce, the main concern is the vengeance that may be sought among the surviving family, by spirits trapped in limbo. Even with appropriate rites observed, a spirit of the dead may return for several days after their physical demise if only due to loneliness and estrangement, an occurrence that instils more dread than sympathy because the only relief for the deceased can be in finding appropriate company for the journey to come, which necessarily means the death of another.

It is believed that those who are themselves claimed by a ghost are likely driven to return in the dreams of others to announce the news of their murder, its manner, and to warn the dreamer of their own danger should they be sought by the restless spirit. One means of avoiding these melancholy searches for companionship in the first instance is the placing of lights on graves, particularly those of children, to offer solace and illumination before they are duly delivered.

The spirit of the dead can also become a tutelary deity and loa in his or her right though, should this be the case, ceremonies must be carefully observed that can span years before their completion. Fears of the restless dead are profound, and so where these or other rites are deemed necessary they are indeed performed exhaustively – and those with no-one to maintain the rites for them actively seek suitable candidates, to the point of adopting children, to ensure that they will not be left an aimless and wandering spirit.

There are also rituals that aim to prevent 'false life' and 'false death', the latter of which is the appearance of death through magic while the former is the vacuous and tortured existence of the zombie, a body with no soul that is owned and controlled by another who has robbed them of their mental capacity, will and character (a fear even more easily understood where slavery has been a horrific reality in the not-too distant past).

The water that bathed the corpse, nail clippings, hair and other detritus is all carefully disposed of to avoid the effects of negative magic, while any corpse feared to be under a malignant influence might be stabbed in the heart to confirm death. To appease any lingering doubt, seeds can be scattered in the grave as the body is laid to rest, to confuse the zombie should a reawakening occur and leave it counting or collecting them each night until sunrise returns them to dormancy.

To not exercise these precautions is to condemn an individual to what can be a prolonged period of degradation and unrest, as it is said that such a body that is raised following an untimely death will wander the earth as a zombie for as long as their natural life was meant to last, a belief which extends to girls and young women who die as virgins.

Death, eroticism and sex actually share close links in the Voodoo faith, to some extent exemplified by the Ghede family of loa who are the spirits of death. Their possession of a being or beings results in loud carousing, the singing of obscene songs, explicit entendres and foul language – they also happen to be innate liars and tricksters, suggesting a breaking down of morals, cultural mores and personal boundaries that once more suggests the liminality between life and death, and the graveyards, wildernesses and crossroads that are the sites where the division between these conditions is at its thinnest.

Humour is another key facet of the Ghede, who can dress as corpses and place cotton in their mouths and up their nostrils to embody the concept of death that they represent, a sense of the dramatic that is no less echoed by Baron Samedi who is one of the most prominent loa of the dead (also incarnating as Barons Kriminel, Cimetière and La Croix). Samedi is, as his various names suggest, the lord of cemeteries who can commonly be found at the crossroads, and the god of magicians – and with that, the zombie; with a tail coat and top-hat placed on a cross he may remain invisible when invoked, but will allow a twitch of the coat to signify his presence to a congregation.

Papa Legba is another prominent loa who serves as the intermediary and interpreter between other loa and the living, bearing an encyclopaedic knowledge. As the keeper of cemeteries and the remover of barriers, he is the key to passing all thresholds including those leading to the past, one's heritage and ancestors, while carnality is part of his domain also – the cross and the phallus are therefore two of the most common symbols associated with him.

The wry and sardonic humour of the Ghede is explicit with Legba, who often appears as a feeble beggar with pipe and crutch but can also take the form of a virile and horned youth, most likely garbed in the funerary colours of black and purple. He revels in revealing the all-too human desires and peccadilloes of the devout and pious, and the inevitable role he plays in every life's denouement; indeed, so assured is he of his role and his bailiwick that he rarely makes the use of any more terrifying aspect and perhaps receives even greater status as a result.

With the Ghede, Baron Samedi and Papa Legba, Voodoo offers a thorough, cultured and honest reflection of the universal responses to death and dying; there is fear, not least by the possible loss of identity that the death represents (zombie), but there is also the resultant will for life to continue (sexuality and sex drive) and great humour (the great leveller and cosmic joke that is death). In Legba there is a further form, and one that must be prepared for by those who are entered by him: the voraciousness and chaos that is death, experienced where the host has to be restrained from biting or cutting himself in an attempt to self-imbibe his body. The appetite of death cannot be sated, and will consume all in its path no matter the temporal constraints that are placed on it.

Journeys

If the soul is accepted as a separate form of being to its physical counterpart, also that it experiences some form of liberation at the point of death, then it suggests the possibility of more temporary releases for the soul, or at a least part of it, if an appropriate level of consciousness can be attained. As Eliphas Levi put it with no small degree of hubris: 'By the word of his reason man becomes conqueror of life, and can triumph over death.'

Life is perpetual change, and although it passes unseen even men and women shed their skin; all is in constant flux, and death is simply another, albeit more dramatic change, and so even in life it might just be possible to shift one's awareness and/or lift one's 'higher being' to glimpse other plains of existence – just as those who have already made that shift might return to our own plain to cause change or deliver proof of their survival.

Helena Patrovna Blavatsky (1831 – 1891 C.E.), co-founder of the Theosophical Society, was not alone in stating the possibility of not just the survival of self, but the potential for that self to be directed out by the will. She noted that if a person focussed their thought and energies at the very moment of death, it was possible to appear to a chosen other or a particularly sensitive individual in the form of a mirror image, adding that intense emotion like hate or anger could certainly result in the same effect.

If this is the case, then it may be these 'beings' that are attested to appear as ghosts or at séances, though it might be argued that a person seeking contact with a lost loved one may themselves be directing sufficient will and detail of that deceased to create a form of materialisation, though the result would be no less astounding for any witnesses.

This is also true with apparent 'sensitives' like the Fox sisters, who helped to create the Spiritualist movement in 19th century New York, numerous mediums and clairvoyants since, and those who are of an especially creative, imaginative or even imbalanced psychology – a singular perspective, unusually high energy and will power lead to thoughts and visions beyond the normal ken of humanity, whether borne of wholly internal processes or, indeed, touched by entities and wisdom quite outside of earthly reality.

There have been many instances whereby artistic endeavours have been informed by some degree of genius originating outside of the conscious mind. These include Giuseppe Tartini (1692 – 1770 C.E.) who heard 'The Devil's Trill' in his sleep, as played by the Devil himself who sat at the end of the composer's bed with a violin, and made his best efforts to recreate the exquisite piece once he awoke; also Samuel Taylor Coleridge (1772 – 1834 C.E.) who similarly dreamed his 'Kublai

Khan' – with the aid of opium – only to fail to remember it in its entirety and thus rendering it incomplete. Charles Dickens, too, was said to have dreamed of most of his characters and tales before setting to work on a new novel.

More blatantly 'spiritual' were the novels of Joan Grant (1907 – 1989 C.E.) who insisted that her books were not works of fiction but of autobiography, recounting detailed recollections she enjoyed of previous, ancient, incarnations. The Brazilian Chico Xavier (1910 – 2002 C.E.) wrote over 100 books as well as essays entirely as a medium, while similar recipients have produced musical compositions from classical artists, painted with what they say is the hand of a long-lost master, invented machinery and made scientific discoveries. Even renowned doctors and surgeons have continued their work, such as the ophthalmologist William Lang (d. 1937 C.E.), who found a suitable medium in the Phillipines some years after his death.

Revelation and portents have been received by many in their sleep, when the mind is perhaps most susceptible to any outside influence, including Richard III's warning of defeat at the Battle of Bosworth, likewise Napoleon's vision of Waterloo, and Adolf Hitler's belief that a premonitory dream saved him from death in the trenches, and convinced him that he was destined for greatness. Away from famous and infamous leaders, there have been countless examples of precognition where accidents and tragedies are concerned, notably the likes of the sinking of the Titanic and the Aberfan disaster in Wales.

Unsurprisingly there are also a wealth of examples whereby devout figures receive divine instruction or wisdom in their sleep, or while in deep meditation; we find this in the Gospel of Matthew when Joseph is reassured via dream that the immaculate child is of God and destined for greatness, likewise with the visions given to Muhammad that resulted in the setting down of the Koran, and the series of mystical experiences shared by the Benedictine abbess Hildegard of Bingen (1098

– 1179 C.E.) where she was informed and instructed by 'The Shade of the Living Light', which she experienced through all her senses.

All of these examples suggest an ability of the soul or some other supernatural facet of being to both reach out and experience plains beyond our own, and potentially reach out from those other plains, once we have passed, to touch those still living. Specific qualities of character and perception appear to be necessary, and the vital ingredients of strongly-directed will or, conversely, a total lack of direction in favour of vacuity, are for different parties the foundation of their success in this field; as such the 'ecstatic state' is key to unlocking the gates to 'supraconsciousness', but this can result from meditation, visualisation, incantation or total exhaustion (such as with the 'death posture' of A.O. Spare).

Use of the Cabbalistic Sephirothic Tree can exercise these abilities, so too the Jewish Merkabah whereby fasting precedes a prolonged period spent with one's head between the knees while reciting songs and prayers – resulting in an ascent or descent through the planetary spheres alike that ascribed to Ezekiel, who travelled the heavens in a chariot composed of divine beings: 'When the living creatures moved, the wheels moved beside them; and when the living creatures rose from the earth, the wheels rose along with them; for the spirit of the living creatures was in the wheels' (1:19-20).

A similar ability, noted in Indian works, is achieved through the successful acquisition of the eight siddhis or 'supernormal powers' as a result of meditation, one of which is known as 'flying in the sky,' as well as the stimulation of the various chakras of the body. From the Sanskrit for 'wheel', the 'chakras' are said to rotate with a speed proportionate to the energy level of the body, and through control of the chakra found at the Crown or head, a mastery of the dream state can be attained whereby a transcendence of being is enjoyed, a concept which can also be glimpsed in the prolific uraeus symbol of the Ancient Egyptians, and esoteric theories relating to the 'third eye' which has been associated with the pineal gland that sits in the centre of the brain, in the epithalamus.

One common approach to this application of the third eye and its liberation of being from body is astral projection, which became widely publicised in the 19th century C.E. as the oriental faiths found an eager audience across the Western world. 'Yram' published his *'Practical Astral Projection'* in English in 1910 which explained the various forms that the human being inhabited, so too the means of conscious will by which the inner self might travel from the corporeal form and thus to other plains and dimensions of existence.

Yram stated that each type of body we have is composed to a different degree of density, thus the physical form which is the grossest substance is well-attuned to the material realm, while our successively-finer forms have their corresponding level of existence – the key to accomplished astral travelling is accessing the appropriate level of being/degree of density for the plain that we seek to venture to.

Achieving such feats is impressive enough, but Yram also noted other risks that the astral traveller must be prepared for, noting that alongside visions he experienced of great and heavenly splendour, there were also unpleasant interactions with entities he met along the way, commonly at the more ethereal levels. Those elementals, spirits and demons that arise ubiquitously in similar theories and their texts are no less apparent here and however and whatever they are believed to be they represent potential danger to the naive wanderer.

Detail of analogous adventures came in 1929's *'The Projection of the Astral Body'* by Hereward Carrington, who chronicled the journeys and teachings of the self-instructed astral projector Sylvan Muldoon. We are told that Muldoon's first experience was intensely shocking and discomforting, coming as it did unexpectedly and without aim or warning, and involving as it did a period of catalepsy and a suspension of his etheric body in the air over his reposing, physical form.

Muldoon stated that the unseen, astral form was no less affected by material life, in that any change of environment, shock or impact on a body had a corresponding effect on the astral being, which is easily made 'out of sync' as a result. The awareness of one's astral form, so too a closer link to it, might be said to aid a vast number of physical and mental ailments with this in mind, in that the full being would be able to equilibrate and exist in a manner of harmony with itself.

The text makes clear that the 'internal' means of projection and then movement is provided by a type of 'elastic' cable that extends between the brow of the physical body and the back of the astral form's head, which has been associated with Biblical Scripture by way of confirmation: 'Or ever the silver cord be loosed, or the golden bowl be broken…then shall the dust return to the earth as it was: and the spirit shall return unto God who gave it' (Ecclesiastes 12:6-7).

These studies were not the first of their kind and they were certainly not the last, with countless tomes following them exploring the possibilities, means and results of the great astral experiment. Raymond Moody (b. 1944 C.E.) is a recent notable writer on the subject, who is not alone in expounding the verge of sleep as the ideal 'stepping off point' from which astral projection can be achieved, not least due to the number of testimonies from people (like Sylvan Muldoon) who found themselves free of the physical body during a deep sleep, as well as those who had 'Out of Body Experiences' and 'Near Death Experiences' while comatose or under anaesthesia, to which we will return.

An immense lore has been constructed that describes and explores *where* the astral form travels to, which understandably links the esoteric with religion, mysticism, symbology and psychology among other schools of thought. It is said that the astral plain is contiguous with space, a realm permeated by the astral light or Akasha (from Sanskrit, meaning 'luminous'). It is the fifth element that binds the other four together, and is the realm of the unconscious of humanity, where the universal memory and knowledge are stored (the Akashic records that medium Edgar Cayce and others have attested to visiting) and the symbols and archetypes of Carl Jung maintain a presence and existence all their own.

Indeed, Jung suggested that the collective unconscious is where thought, ideas and images either become associated with existing archetypes or themselves 'become' archetypes, following which they make an indelible mark on the astral plain – the subconscious depths of humanity – that ensure their continuance and accessibility thereafter. Israel Regardie in 'The Philosopher's Stone' (1938) suggested that the likes of renowned sages, too, leave their lasting imprint on the 'Anima Mundi' or world soul, which is akin to the astral plain and its store of collective memory.

It is said that at death, as the veils slip away and the blinkers of the physical self are dropped, the energies and entities of the astral level become visible. What is left behind are but the 'shells' of a denser existence, such as the physical remains and any lingering shade or ghost, while the etheric self finds its own appropriate level until any further state of development is chosen.

The astral body that is able to traverse this plain is also known as the sidereal body, the Ens Astrale and Linga Sarira. It is believed to be the 'desire body' that is imbued with the emotional self, thus its colour, shape and size are changeable and reflect the state of the being at any given time (with those of a lesser level of spiritual advancement appearing as grey and of loose or chaotic form compared to the resplendent colours and forms of those who have attained a greater degree of insight) –

seen as the aura that is recreated, it is said, in Kirlian photography and by sensitive individuals.

Theosophists Annie Besant (1847 – 1933 C.E.) and C.W. Leadbeater (1854 – 1934 C.E.) produced studies on the nature of the aura as a 'thought-form' and published images said to recreate the forms created and projected into the atmosphere during services of worship and prayer, and Besant, in 1897's *'The Ancient Wisdom'*, clearly encapsulated the nature of the plain where this constantly-shifting, kaleidoscopic being might exert its influence: 'Life is more active there than on the physical plain, and form is more elastic.'

Eliphas Levi stated that the soul, like the material body, breathes in and out including the 'breathing in' of ideas from 'inner sensations'. He believed that the astral body, at the point of corporeal death, '...evaporates like pure incense...' to higher plains of existence, which conjures an image not unlike the illustrations in *'Thought Forms'* (1901) already mentioned.

The risks of venturing into this realm either before or after one's passing are manifold, but most dramatically encapsulated by the other beings that might be encountered along the way – nature spirits (elementals), the astral beings of animals, fellow human essences awaiting reincarnation, even psychics who themselves are exploring the astral vistas and may well be lost, as well as 'diseased' souls who continue to haemorrhage their negativity and create unwholesome and harmful currents; the inner being is reflected in this astral light, and so while there is no pretence or hiding from one's doubts, fears or malignancies, those qualities can nonetheless bring harm to others.

Chroniclers speak of entities attacking them on the astral plain, or trying to tempt them from the path to claim another lost and wandering soul, while the physical body can be overwhelmed with headaches, fainting, hysteria, obsession and complete mental breakdown, not least in those who desire to again and again return to a state of being and understanding that has only been glimpsed and who tip the balance of consciousness firmly into the subconscious. Whether in the mind or perhaps on another level of existence altogether, the risks of opening up oneself to a 'higher plain' are, for many, as great as if not greater than the rewards.

However, the idea of this intermediate astral level between the corporeal and the spiritual can be found among most forms of faith, including Islam (where it is, among other titles, the Barzakh), Cabbalistic Judaism (where it is the 'World of Yetzirah') as well as the various forms of shamanism and magic (with it being stated that meditations and visualisations made over time can construct an 'astral temple' that is the focus of magical works which are ultimately directed to affect the material world). The rewards are manifold, and they are tempting even for those without an overriding taste for personal development.

Gurdjieff was typically dismissive of any individual who chose not to identify with, experience and develop their 'body Kesdjan' or 'vessel of the soul', noting that the true being remains unformed and but a shadow of what it can and should be where this work is not undertaken. Indeed, the idea of spiritual development is fundamental to the astral plain and what it represents – after all, emotion and desire underpin the efforts of those who seek its wisdom, and are the foremost aspects that are said to be visible to and experienced by others once in that realm.

The concept of the astral plain is an affirmation of soul and, through that, of life beyond physical death, as well as a sense of order lying at the heart of all existence, a means to repent, learn, grow and thence transcend, a cosmic meaning that might be grasped – not to mention the survival and expansion of archetypes, collective images and beliefs and of all wisdom – along with that important freedom of the inner self to continue its own journey. It is compelling on many levels, not least where it informs and is informed by a diverse spectrum of mystical frameworks, because it addresses most of the greatest concerns and questions that men and women spend their waking lives seeking answers for.

This is why the astral realm is such an inherent aspect of the life and work of a shaman, who regularly pierces the veil to seek advice, help and guidance from that higher plateau, where unearthly spirits, ancestors, animal guides and universal wisdom all lie, waiting to be tapped. It should be noted that the very process of becoming a shaman requires a form of death, which can include being daubed in ashes to resemble a corpse as well as symbolic burial, with the understanding that to make this passage and return is to exist from that point on as a being with a foot in each world, never being wholly human again.

Shamans suffer extremes of physical, mental and, they would attest, spiritual ordination, with tortures and dismemberment undergone when in a trance state, whether attained through meditation alone or with the addition of hallucinogenic narcotics. Long-deceased forebears, fellow shamans and animal spirits can all appear to 'deconstruct' the initiate, thus allowing a passage through death and back to life, in a new form – with, perhaps, an ancestral guide now serving them as a result of the ordeal or, where it is an animal that has marked a connection with the new shaman, that animal appearing henceforth as a spiritual conduit.

Much of the work of the shaman involves communication with those who have died and the various spirits that populate the astral plain, as is the case where a person's sickness requires a journey to find that individual's lost soul, or a descent into infernal regions to learn the wisdom of demons so that a suitable cure be composed, or a specific means of exorcism obtained. There is a similar need when the soul of a deceased requires guided transport to their next level of existence, an offering needs to be made to a god or battle must be done with the spirits of the dead.

Even more so than with others' infrequent rambles through the astral plain, whether we share the beliefs of the shaman or not, the risks that they expose themselves to in achieving their rank and then exercising their skills is profound, as is any way of life where the lines of reality are so frequently and dramatically blurred.

As we have seen, those who 'ramble' may not do so with regularity – once may be all that is experienced, and may be quite sufficient! – but the number of those who have shared experiences akin to those of the medium, the mystic and the shaman does suggest a state of mind or consciousness that can, with the right means and circumstances, be granted to any individual.

At points termed 'travelling clairvoyance', this temporary liberation of the astral being from the body (Out Of Body Experience or OOBE) is of course a common theme in Near Death Experiences (or NDE), all of which can result from meditation or visualisation but can also be given a helping hand with the addition of anaesthetics and hallucinogens; William James (1842 – 1910 C.E.), the American philosopher and psychologist, reported first-hand experience of this through the use of nitrous oxide, after which he wrote that beyond normal waking consciousness '...there lie potential forms of consciousness entirely different.'

OOBE's are effectively instances whereby an individual sees the world, including themselves, as a spectator. At points classed as 'autoscopy' which is the seeing of oneself from a distance, the common experience is of floating or levitating above one's reposing physical form on a journey that is beyond the constraints of normal space and time. Of course, these episodes profoundly whet the appetite of any individual, whether in terms of the ultimate consequences raised regarding the abilities of the mind, as well as the potential ramifications for any form of self beyond the physical.

The term 'Out Of Body Experience' was coined by G.N.M. Tyrrell in his 1943 work *'Apparitions'* and quickly gained popularity as a means of charting the scientific investigation – and resulting empirical data – of the subject, rather than continuing to discuss 'astral projection' with its blatant and complex connotation of faith and mysticism – the focus was firmly being placed on the objective analysis of data, over and above the bias and wish-fulfilment of an overarching spiritual schema.

As the 20th century progressed the studies on OOBE's grew in number and scope across the globe, perhaps as a result of the widespread application of anaesthetics during surgery, larger numbers receiving more complex medical treatment and indeed the slackened grip of religion on the psychological framework of those who experienced such events on the operating table.

With more controlled investigation came insight in to the various circumstances that would most frequently induce an OOBE, of which the most common still appears to be a specific point of sleep, notably when an individual is on the verge of lucid dreaming. As described by Sylvan Muldoon, sleep paralysis often accompanies this event, and the likelihood of an occurrence is increased if the 'dreamer' is in a state of stress, high emotion or exhaustion, whether physical or mental.

Indeed, 'bilocation' can occur with either a peak of mental/physical arousal or the total lack of any such stimulation, thus we find that meditation and a certain vacuity of mind is a further means of attaining OOBE, and sensory overload including the results of hallucinogens is another – both of which have been widely-documented within esoteric circles, shamanism and magical practise for hundreds, if not thousands, of years.

NDE's are a final means of induction, though here we find

variations on the above in that a severe shock or injury might lead to the event, as well as the aforementioned use of anaesthetics during the aftermath. As such the experience may be related to an individual being on the brink of death, but the core aspects of sensory overload, followed by potential sensory deprivation, do suggest something of the brain's struggle to process a chain of events in its normal manner.

Raymond Moody carried out extensive studies of NDE's and summarised the well-known aspects common to most, including the ubiquitous 'hovering' over a scene and/or oneself, witnessing events that they cannot explain having witnessed, an overwhelming sense of peace, calm and love, a viewing or 'reviewing' of one's life, along with the presence of deceased loved ones, 'beings of light' and the appearance of a tunnel that seems to beckon. The overriding emotions that appear to be attached to these experiences are a positive form of detachment, a feeling of belonging and a degree of revelation that stays with the person for some considerable time thereafter.

Psychology has a different understanding for the causes of OOBE's, so too what the episodes themselves consist of, though again we find parallels to ideas already sited; here, OOBE's are dissociative experiences that take the form of an altered state of consciousness. As such dreams and imagination are understood to factor in the same category, as well as psychosis and hysteria, all with a focus on the projections of the subconscious where the brain is struggling to maintain its normal narrative and consciousness – and with it, reality – are infused with images, symbols and creations of the inner mind.

Tyrell himself stated that the events were hallucinations constructed by the subconscious, while Nandor Fodor concluded that OOBE's related to any threat of death and the subsequent defence raised by the inner recesses of the mind; Carl Sagan (1934 – 1996 C.E.), meanwhile, postulated such 'astral' events as a type of re-birth fantasy, which clearly interprets the image of the 'umbilical cord' that has often been seen to maintain the link between human and ethereal forms.

More recent studies have shown that the brain can be stimulated in such a way as to induce an OOBE, though we again find that the motivators are especially high or low levels of stimulation and shocks to the running of the brain, thus we are left with an appreciable consensus as to what might lead a person to experience an OOBE, but no single explanation of what lies behind the images and adventures experienced. Examples of OOBE's or astral projections do frequently return us to a realm of faith, religion and mysticism, though how much of this is a result of psychological bias and how much is divine action is impossible to identify.

The great Apollonius of Tyana was said to appear in two places at once through will, while Bede mentions in his *'Ecclesiastical History of the English People'* a monk called Fursey who recounted a number of heavenly and hellish visions while apparently asleep and even suffered a burn on his arm as a result of one of his more nefarious visitations. The Portuguese friar St. Anthony of Padua (1195 – 1231 C.E.) was, it seems, even more adept – having knelt in contemplation during the speaking of a sermon one day when he remembered that he was also due to read a lesson at another site some miles away, he duly appeared at that site to the congregated monks, observed his duties, and returned to the sermon.

Witches most certainly attested to attending two places at the same time, such as Isobel Gowdie who was seen to be listening intently to a sermon in her local church while she revelled with her coven in the wilds some miles away. Those who joined the Witches' Sabbat often believed that they had left their bodies behind, which explains some of the more fanciful means of transportation recorded as well as the sometimes vast distances mentioned. More recently, Carlos Castaneda (1925 – 1998 C.E.) recorded his shamanic experiences of projection through the use of datura or the 'Devil's Weed', as well as his later efforts to induce astral travel without the use of intoxicants.

The concept of the 'mythopoeia' is fundamental here, in that myths or stories that can be seen to stand as proof of projections, past life experiences and indeed visions of any heaven or hell can also be understood to result from existing archetypes that have been read, seen, heard or even drawn from the minds of others, and stored subconsciously in the mind – thence arising at an appropriate time as an original and unique event, something potentially alluded to by Milton in the seminal *'Paradise Lost'*: 'The mind is its own place, and in itself can make a Heaven of Hell, a Hell of Heaven.'

One's own frame of reference may therefore shape what is seen, as well as how it is later perceived, a point which can negate bias to the fields of faith and science in equal measure. However, a salient point in considering the NDE in particular does return us to the focus of this chapter, namely the concern for and understanding of death: Kenneth Ring's 1980 study suggested a common throughline for these experiences, beginning with 'Peace' and then a separation from the body, before the entering of darkness, a vision of a form of light, and finally an entering into that light.

NDE's may well be a 'little death', a fleeting and unfinished experience that is the same as the experience of dying but for the completion of the journey, but the sense of 'passage' from one state, through another and into a new level of understanding, returns us firmly to the work of Joseph Campbell and others, and the frequent result of the passage – a change of outlook in life, a shifting of beliefs that shape a new attitude or behaviours – is certainly akin to many of the ideas that we have discussed related to death and dying, not least as a form of rebirth for the 'hero' that has faced his or her apotheosis (the relationship between mortality and self) and returned to embody and spread the word of revelation.

Conclusions?

Duly informed but only bearing elucidation, not total clarity, we return from the quest to the point of our original departure. As we might well have stated at the offset, death has a form and meaning wholly related to the frame of reference of each individual even where a broader belief system or framework informs that understanding; as was most certainly stated, death is an experience shared by all but remains the passage of each individual alone, as it must forever be.

Fear compels many of our questions and imaginings on the subject, but as has been illustrated there is also the application of dark and ribald humour not just to alleviate those fears, but because of the very situation whereby death so dominates one's life and stimulates beings to all manner of behaviours, actions, obsessions and rituals as a means of finding expression and meaning.

The Ghede family of loa carouse with abandon and Papa Legba gnaws on his own arm to show us that death is a joke, a mockery of the importance that we place on our existence, while Dionysus is glimpsed in the form of the tree and fruit of the fig which represent female and male generation, just as he is associated with death, and Ovid (43 B.C.E. – 16/17 C.E.) writes '...let me go in the act of coming to Venus, in more senses than one let my last dying be done.' Life is death and vice versa, thus pantomime and excess sit happily alongside those most primitive drives like sex even as we feel the chill of the condemned.

Obviously there is much more to the uniting of sex and death than that. Effigies in the form of the phallus are placed in graves to simulate a return to the great womb, generating new life and re-birth thereafter, and the copulation of Shiva and Shakti or the union of bliss that is the Yab-Yum reminds us that birth leads to decay and death, from which new life is stimulated – copulation is a dynamic release of directed energy that at once encompasses existence and non-existence, thus Ovid and others see the likes of the flaccid member as a symbol of death, and the dissipation of life once the energy is spent.

The dying gods Osiris, Adonis, Attis and the son of God, Jesus Christ are mythical embodiments of this understanding, with the dismembered Osiris proffering life from his demise (most profitably from his phallus, which fecundates the Nile) and the cross upon which Christ is crucified showing signs of re-birth with leaves sprouting even as he suffers his physical end. We see it, also, in the tarot such as with the lemniscate form (8) of the hat adorning the Magician where we touch on matters of infinity alike the cycles of the Indian faiths; death is an end, but not *the* end, and where we are able to see our place within the macrocosm it is infinity that we begin to grasp, a thing of countless ends and beginnings.

Away from myth and mysticism, however, it has to be acknowledged that death is nonetheless a reality that requires consideration if only for its inevitability. Plato's *'Republic'* states that the various perils of life, likewise loss and death, are scoffed at by the young, only to become a matter for more serious thought as the years progress and the arc of life begins its descent, which Jung interpreted as the psyche preparing the individual for death where focus on ideals, dreams and future give way to remembrances and retrospect.

This is not a sign of defeat but of stoic acceptance at worst, with a potential for genuine growth where the individual is able to accept and appreciate the nature of their own existence amid all others in the cosmos. More optimistically it is what Soren Kierkegaard (1813 – 1855 C.E.) suggested as a crucial aspect of personal development – the rejection of what has become atypical 'death-denial' and the realisation and acceptance of one's mortality in order for a full and passionate life to be lived.

All of this is potentially more challenging to achieve in a world that emphasises youth and vigour over experience and wisdom, so too where death is removed from sight and mind – and in turn the popular consciousness. The singular perspective of humanity which can acknowledge and ruminate on its own demise is thus lost, at least until that demise becomes a reality and the opportunity for any understanding is all but passed. Secularism has delivered spiritual freedom but has barred the door to decay and death as an unwanted visitor, and the respect and thought afforded to once grand funerary processions and rites are minimised into near-obscurity, as those rites fall from favour and disappear.

Obsession over one's mortality is unhealthy and ultimately stifles any true expression or experience of life, but this is equally true where death is an uncomfortable thought kept at bay no matter the consequences. Both states of being are capable of becoming Milton's idea of hell, with the man or woman and their soul, whatever that might be, trapped in a prison of their own making. Death is a natural consequence of life and so is part of life, and a finer understanding needs to be attained if a person is to genuinely live well and with personal meaning.

Myth and mysticism, then, continues to hold an especial place for the conscious mind and the subconscious depths of self. The collective knowledge of humanity, the Akashic records if you will, are at least in some evidence here, the eternal questions along with the expressions of any and all possible answers, waiting to be tapped and invigorated with new energy and new life, as we see in contemplating the response of Gilgamesh to thoughts of mortality that spoke of the human condition thousands of years ago, speaks profoundly today, and will continue to speak for it for thousands of years to come.

Where we are able to consider these explorations in stories, in the meditations of the sages, the astral voyages of the shamans and the attempts to control life through death in magic, we begin to gain an insight into the universality of the condition of life and its end – revelation can be gained here, as the separateness of being is itself seen to be a common link, of which death and dying are especially striking examples.

By considering scripture, the life of Buddha, the adventures of the Aztec Hero Twins and the work of Gurdjieff and Muldoon we step outside of time and space and grant them a form of immortality or re-birth that we are ourselves capable of through our works, our progeny, and perhaps through our own additions to the vast Akashic record, where matter and spirit find equal merit and exert equal influence on those who follow.

What is certain is that thoughts on death and our attempts to better understand it continue to suggest depths of being that are as yet unknown, or at least alien to our concept of reality. All of humanity's hopes and fears lie within this sphere, so too the anxieties that drive us, the inspirations we bear and that desire to know, to truly know, who and what we are. Our approach to death very much informs our approach to existence, therefore it maintains the closest relationship with us regardless how irrelevant or distant it is held to be at any given time, and true wisdom in this offers one of the greatest gifts imaginable – that of a life well-lived.

MACROCOSM

IV: CORRESPONDENCES

The human condition is as predictable as it is profound. One example serving both of these traits rather neatly is the perception of universal 'common' experiences, unifying lives across the globe and through the centuries, that has shaped and in turn been shaped by the innate need of the human mind to understand its situation and indeed control it, or at least find a degree of stability through a semblance of control.

There are of course immense variations in form and nuance due to the environment and mentality specific to the individual, but from the first humanity has strived to comprehend its own existence and the world it is born into and has found that 'common experience' is one powerful means of establishing an intensely needed sense of order, even where the patterns and correspondences that are demarcated are stretched to the limits of credulity or make the familiar assumption that 'man' is at the centre of all such order and meaning. The results may be somewhat blinkered, but they reward the yearning mind with an invaluable frame of reference all the same.

As such we might find demons associated with fire due to the parching heat that meant hell to one tribe or culture, while another found death and damnation in the form of water and terrible flooding; the results of each existence would be clothed in different vestments, but the overall pattern of order versus chaos and good and bad fortune would nonetheless be entirely apparent and wholly relatable to both.

Of course, there has to be a common basis of understanding

for any such order or normality to be achieved – without a consensus between people there can be no law, no morality, no faith (or lack thereof) and certainly no cohesion or growth. This extends to practically every facet of human endeavour therefore it is not surprising that the arena of spirituality, faith and magic are constructed firmly on commonalities of perception and experience that have actually been used to add weight and meaning to later manifestations, when ancient wisdom is sought and ancient power tapped.

To sum up rather crudely what could be a vast discourse in its own right, patterns emerge in the earliest of beliefs that connect with later myth and then religion and establish what can be perceived as an uncanny network of correspondences that unite all of what we are, think and do. Thus we find global myths of creation, the sun, the hero, death, the soul, and post mortem worlds of reward and punishment that speak of much the same hopes, fears, jealousies and biases in spite of colourful variations.

Likewise we see the same patterns adapted for the various forms of religious faith, from the animism that sees fire, water and stone as divine beings, to the polytheism that affords individual fire and water gods that one might offer obeisance to, and mythologized accounts of the fundamental concerns whereupon the setting and rising of the sun becomes the death and re-birth of Osiris, a story which in certain forms lends itself to monotheism and beliefs of salvation.

The innate need to *know* sees connections between past and present experience and styles the answers in a suitable form for the time, frequently framing them in decidedly poetic and beautiful ways. Herein we find order, stability and a vital sense of continuance that links each new mode of being with those that went before it, allowing a degree of freedom to interpret and apply that which has been discussed and cogitated over for millennia. Whether we conclude that these similarities are meaningful to a broader picture or not, it certainly becomes clear that the human mind abhors a vacuum, and so any sense of ignorance or unknowing stirs the greatest seeds of dissent and disturbance.

This can be glimpsed in the struggle to understand the place of evil in the Western world from the birth of Christianity. Where the Old Testament God was a being of immense power that delivered both love and vengeance, the New Testament God offered His son to suffer on behalf of humanity and instilled hope in eschatological salvation and was an altogether less threatening figure (it might be said that the dynamic and holistic 'yin and yang' was jettisoned in favour of a more blatantly dualistic sense of good and evil akin to that espoused within Zoroastrianism).

The result was a need to find the corresponding figures to God and Christ as exponents of pain and suffering, namely the Devil/Satan and the Antichrist, a development that was perhaps more stark and polarising but was also an easier concept to fathom for the everyman seeking a sense of right and wrong, and a more potent weapon for a Church desiring greater dominance as the true faith.

The concept of 'Oneness' where a God is both positive and negative figure is a difficult belief for a literally-focussed mind to countenance, thus dualism took hold as a means of dividing form, matter and 'evil' from the domain of the spirit, the 'good' and God – the development is a significant one, but the place of correspondence remains to ensure that all concerns and perceptions are acknowledged.

Correspondences (or the 'signatures' that might be perceived to reveal them) are particularly striking when they arise from what might be simply an unusual or unlikely event. For the human mind to conclude that chance or accident led to the fire that destroyed a home, the flood that drowned the year's crops or the sighting of an anomaly such as a meteor or eclipse has always been a challenge, more so where the effects of an event are personally affecting – the instinct of humanity is to seek a cause for the misfortune so that the vital sense of order is preserved, fears of ignorance and chaos banished, and efforts made to avoid such a calamity or event from being repeated.

The results can range from the procurement of amulets and lucky charms to deflect malicious witches and blood sacrifices to appease gods, to obsessive prostrations in places of worship as those who have been wronged seek forgiveness for perceived sins; indeed, all manner of prophylactic rituals and magics have been entirely based on such attempts to avoid further misfortune, just as revelations in faith have occurred to right what have come to be seen as errors of the past in both religion and deed.

However, it is the desperate efforts to find a reason for ill-luck, blight and disaster that are most important to this study, so too the fundamental need within the human psyche to be in control and able to exert an influence over matters regardless how random and cosmic they might initially appear to be...cultural stability, survival and sanity are at stake, it often seems, where the possibility of chaos (and with it the inability of any being to gain any true knowledge from experience) rears its terrifying head.

And so patterns are found to establish a form of agreed wisdom and insight, frequently perceived by those deemed to be more gifted in this area than others. These patterns draw together the experiences of individual tribes, cultures and civilizations, and the accumulated patterns of all these can be united in still further, overarching patterns that can be seen to constitute eternal truths that belie space and time and reveal on a grander scale answers to the ultimate mysteries of existence.

They can, of course, also be rejected as nonsense and the stuff of dreamers, but the intrigue of mystery – the belief that answers to the riddles of life, death and all else are around us and awaiting discovery – is another instinctive aspect of humanity, and so the patterns are sought, perceived and explored in ever more intriguing systems of thought, sometimes easily derided but never lacking in vision or meaning.

Jung certainly appreciated what he termed 'synchronicities', those coincidences of seemingly random events that appear to have the same or a similar meaning. He noted that these synchronicities could result in a profound transformative experience for the inner being, as the very fact of a person's recognising an 'uncanny' importance in an outer event suggests a need or desire of that person to find a meaning, or seek an answer to some riddle that has no other outlet or conscious presence for that person. Even if we reject any form of universal import for these correspondences, they most certainly reflect an intense and insightful aspect for the individual that perceives them.

Exploring this area (and with it the 'archetypes' that Jung held to be the timeless and subconscious meanings attached to myth, alchemy, symbolism and more and retained by the 'collective unconscious') he made close study of the 'I Ching' and ultimately studied the cards of the tarot and their imagery, both of which suggested frameworks of meaning that informed and impacted on the mind even where acute knowledge or use of the practises was lacking.

For Jung, the tarot in particular was a result of a shared esoteric knowledge that might be framed differently at times, added to or 'developed' for specific needs, but was ultimately a timeless and placeless expression of a deeper, wholly more atavistic level of consciousness which, it might be said, adds credence to any belief in correspondences of experience and belief, and indeed the signatures that are signs of those correspondences.

As Above, So Below

One of the most compelling symbolic archetypes in this area is the 'chain of being' that took various forms in ancient doctrine but always espoused the order of creation and with it the paths that existed between creator and created, and vice versa. This idea informed orthodox faith as much as it did mysticism and magic, as it illustrated – often quite exhaustively – the composition of all life, at all levels, and the means that exist to rise and fall from one state of existence to another.

Medieval thought held that the cosmos is no void, but an expanse housing angels and all manner of celestial entities at the centre of which is humankind; moreover, the cosmos is itself a living entity that links the creative agent to all forms of life within it. Given this and the fact that all life, from angels to planetary spirits, to elemental beings and then to the mundane beings of earth consist of varying densities of the same cosmic matter, emanating from one source, it is understandable why the concept of correspondences, the possibility of drawing lines between perceived causes and effects to reveal hidden truths, gained such a hold on the imagination of both practical minds and dreamers alike.

Emmanuel Swedenborg (1688 – 1772 C.E.) may be deemed to be a rather brilliant dreamer, but for him the role of correspondences was a vital and revelatory one that spoke for itself. Influenced as he was by Neo-Platonism and Cabbalism, he held that every sub-lunar object was the result of a spiritual cause, therefore '...every natural thing is the replica of a spiritual thing, and this, in turn, is the replica of a divine thing.' The spiritual progenitor created the 'idea' of life which resulted in the 'image' and life itself, and so patterns can be identified in all aspects of existence as it shares one source, and ultimately one substance. Correspondences would thus be rife.

The cosmos has commonly been represented as concentric circles where the outermost is that of Pure Spirit, the next holds the eternal stars, the next again demarcates the limits of time (which for the medieval mind was Saturn, hence the images of Saturn, as time, devouring his own children), before all forms of mortal existence are depicted with the grossest of forms, humanity, at the innermost centre. Elsewhere a simple circle with a dot at its centre represents the soul encompassed by the limits of the cosmos, while a circle holding a cross depicts incarnation within the limits of time and space, the soul immersed in and surrounded by matter and therefore influenced by all that lies outside of it.

Human life is at the base of the chain of being, but bearing the divine spark it seeks to climb the chain and unite with its creator, thus it was not only possible but necessary for appropriate correspondences to be identified and interpreted in order to transcend the material limitations and gradually achieve a form of epiphany that might unlock the soul and at the very least raise it to the next level of being. The order of creation, patterns of experience and the occult significance of the 'synchronicity' – for Swedenborg and others of his ilk these are the means of revelation, and through it the path to God that God Himself laid down for us to follow.

The chain of being and the idea of correspondences are wholly in evidence when we consider the concept of Microcosm and Macrocosm that held great sway until the 17th century C.E. and even now appeals to the spiritual and occult mindset. Derived from Greek terms, the Microcosm is the 'small work' or 'small arrangement' of the created, material realm while the Macrocosm is the 'great work' or 'arrangement' of the celestial, heavenly realm.

In uniting these two worlds, scholars and thinkers suggested a cosmic order which underpinned all that existed within creation – a harmonious structure that was evidenced in pattern and synchronicity – while also acknowledging that the created world bore copious reflected images of the creating essence exactly because it derived entirely from that source. Not only does the human mind thus recognise *order* which assuages the panic against chaos, but it also defines patterns in form and event that suggests something of divine *meaning*. To observe the material is to glimpse the eternal.

It is not surprising that Pythagoras is believed to have been the first philosopher to apply the term 'cosmos' in describing the created universe, as that term also denotes order – a defined and intentional system – over randomness, given the importance of balance and harmony to his understanding of existence. As we shall see, the observation of the 'design' within materiality allowed for knowledge of form, number, music and architecture to flourish alongside a spiritual ken whereby the world around us can be seen to equate to one exquisite kaleidoscope of correspondences between the realm of the creative force and our world, its creation.

Plato did not employ the language of Pythagoras in his understanding of the universe, but he did rather succinctly describe the belief that underpinned the concept of Macro- and Microcosm in his 4th century B.C.E. *'Timaeus'*: 'Therefore, we may consequently state that: this world is indeed a living being endowed with a soul and intelligence...a single visible living entity containing all other living entities, which by their nature are all related.'

Greater elucidation on this thought was offered by Plotinus in the *'Enneads'*, where all matter is united due to its emanation from the one creative spark, and thus from the one creative source. Here, 'the One' created both the soul or intellect of humanity as well as the 'anima mundi' or 'world soul' of the earth, therefore we are more still than a chain of being; we are, rather, one with the cosmos in all of its forms and gradations, and while the creator remains something 'other', all else beyond the creator is linked inextricably because nothing exists that did not emerge *from* it.

Neo-Platonism was a key ingredient of manifold philosophies that followed through the patristic and medieval periods, notably those of Origen (c.184 – 254 C.E.) who stated 'Understand that you are another world in miniature and that in you are the sun, the moon and also the stars', Thomas Aquinas (who placed humanity between spirit and animal worlds and so suggested that it was a central link in the chain of being) and Paracelsus (who developed much of his medical and scientific works upon the belief that within each man and woman was something of an 'inner heaven', and that for all illness of mind and body there is a corresponding remedy existent in nature).

In support of this belief was the English doctor Robertus de Fluctibus or Robert Fludd (1574 – 1637 C.E.) whose works prominently featured the Macrocosm/Microcosm and gave stunning examples of imagery that are ubiquitous even today. For Fludd, the original chaos had been transformed by divine Light into the water of life (Spirit), a trinity of substances that neatly mirrored the Scriptural trinity as well as the Paracelsian trinity of Salt (thought), Sulphur (will) and Mercury (emotion).

A more cohesive cosmology was described by Fludd, who held that the sun was essentially the house of divine light, while the human heart was the house of divine emanation within the body – with the sun the lynchpin of the cosmos and the heart as the lynchpin of man, God was omnipresent, timeless and fully infused within the planetary spheres, the Earth, and all life carried upon it.

'Oneness' is inherent to the idea here described, and there have been various forms which that oneness have taken by those depicting the unity of creation, including the idea of the cosmos as a tree (such as the Jewish Sephirothic Tree) which is often inverted so as to offer its branches to the earth and its roots to the life-giving creator, and the linked idea of the

Macrocosmic Man (often named 'Adam Kadmon'), the brain of whom also bears roots that link the conscious mind with its spiritual progenitor. In this instance, the 'fruit' of the 'tree' are the creations and acts of the man or woman whose limbs are the branches forging them.

The Indian concept of the 'Universal Man' clearly defines the gradations of form that humanity enjoys in conjunction with the Macrocosmic order: the Superior aspect is the higher state capable, while the principles of sun and moon are linked to the right and left eye, respectively; the fire principle is the mouth and the directions of space are the ears, while atmosphere is associated with the lungs; finally, the space between the earth and the heavens is connected to the stomach, and the earth itself is the lower body.

Adam Kadmon features heavily in the idea of 'cosmogenesis' where we see humanity as a model of the universe. Though the Monad or creator remains impenetrable and unknowable, those signatures or traces that we have mentioned can be glimpsed and experienced as reflections of the creator – this reflection is Adam Kadmon, said to have been described in scripture: 'The first man Adam was made a living soul; the last Adam was made a quickening spirit...the first man is of the earth, earthy; the second man is the Lord from heaven...and as we have borne the image of the earthy, we shall also bear the image of the heavenly' (1 Corinthians 15:45-50).

In magic this same principle is succinctly defined by Eliphas Levi in his *'Transcendental Magic'* when he describes the 'Symbol of Solomon', two interconnected triangles where one is directed heavenward and the other is pointed earthward: 'The Double triangle of Solomon, represented by the two Ancients of the Kabalah: the Macroprosopos and the Microprosopos, the God of Light and the God of Reflections; of mercy and vengeance; the white Jehovah and the black Jehovah.' The human mind therefore appreciates a sense of unity that it ultimately belongs to, alongside a means of understanding order in the cosmos – and the potential of controlling/affecting the cosmos through that understanding.

Numerous understandings of the chain of being exist, though one of the most recognisable certainly belongs to Robert Fludd: the 'regio intellectus' are the stars of the heavens that are the extent of creation, which equate to 'Selfhood' and objective wisdom in humanity; within this sphere lies the 'orbis solis sen cordis' or orb of the sun, which equates to the human heart and the seat of emotion; finally, there is the 'regio elementaris' or elements, which equate to the condition of mortality and the eventual return of all matter to the grossest substances of the earth.

This system is close to that which names the outermost sphere as the 'Empyrean' (fixed stars), the next as the 'Aethereum' (planetary spheres) and the lowest as the 'Elementarum' (earth), while other understandings maintain a greater focus on the immediate environment – as such we find the solar element associated with the creative impulse and thus the brain and/or heart of humankind and God, the lunar or earthly elements associated with desire (frequently sexual, and potentially demonic), and humanity itself as the third element, embodying consciousness and emotion.

Fludd certainly exercised an understanding of a 'three-fold' being in a similar vein, with one of his most recognisable and laudable illustrations depicting a woman at the centre who wears a chain on one wrist that is connected securely to the heavens, and a chain held in the opposite hand that reaches down to a studious monkey; the message offered is one of hope for humanity, in that while it consists of soul, body and desire, only the link between the soul and its creator is eternal and sure – the link to base desire and impermanent knowledge can be severed at any time, should we so choose to let go of the shackles.

Ultimately, there are countless expressions of this model, though the consistent point is that man and woman stand at the centre of creation, housing the spiritual within the corporeal and sharing its aspects with all of perceivable creation. Such an idea smacks of anthropocentrism and may well depend on this view, though it should be remembered that the attempt to define a chain of being and correspondences between the Macro- and Microcosm is a decidedly human concern, and so placing man at the centre of all does not necessarily suggest dominance.

Of more immediate concern was the need to identify the various substances inherent within humanity as a creation in order to better understand it – if similar substances could be observed within the wider creation then all the better, for it united human beings with the cosmos in an inextricable manner and suggested that we might learn from all that stands around us, however grand or small. Similarly, where earthly substances could be defined within the human being, it became possible to see forms of character, general aspects of health and even fate and fortune written within the body – humanity might be chained to the heavens through its soul, but its form owed much to the gross materials of the elements.

As such, Fire was linked to the choleric temperament and those with an active and impulsive nature; Earth suggested melancholy and a wholly more slow and cautious attitude; Air resulted in a sanguine mode that was volatile and mercurial; Water was phlegmatic, sensitive yet unstable. Made from the substances of the created world, we are all here interpreted as compositions of the four elements in differing degrees that essentially make us what we are in being, meaning both metabolism and psyche. By association, Fire has been associated with the astrological signs of Aries, Leo and Sagittarius, Earth with Taurus, Virgo and Capricorn, Air with Gemini, Libra and Aquarius and Water with Cancer, Scorpio and Pisces.

Further East, within the Indian philosophy, the correspondences of the elements were afforded the form of the 'Tattva' which are at points an aspect of a god as well as elements and constituents of reality. The term tattva is Sanskrit for 'principle' or 'truth' which adequately defines their import on existence – though the number of tattvas is changeable, depending on the school of thought consulted.

Jainism considers knowledge of the tattvas to be essential to any form of development of the self toward liberation, and describes them in terms instantly recognisable as a metaphysical chain of being, akin to the Cabbalistic Tree of Life:

1: Jiva – souls and living forms

2: Ajiva – non-living forms

3: Asrava – incursion of karma

4: Bandha – bondage of karma

5: Samvara – cessation of karma

6: Nirjara – shedding of karma

7: Moksha – liberation

In this system a gradual ascent is perceived from the corporeal, through the limiting and constricting cycles which surround the self, through to an ultimate liberation that can only be achieved through following that chain of being back to its source.

Within Hindu tantrism, the tattvas are as follows:

Element	Tattva	Colour	Shape
Earth	Prithivi	Yellow	Square
Air	Vayu	Blue	Circle
Water	Apas	Silver	Crescent

| Fire | Tejas | Red | Triangle |
| Spirit | Akasha | Black | Egg |

Here the tattvas constitute the various elements that compose reality, while also being associated with a colour and form. Further still, each tattva represents a mode of energy that is globally active each day as a 'tattvic tide'; each element exerts its influence for a set period of the day before a transition takes place into the next, until a full cycle of all elements has occurred and a new day dawns.

Beyond the philosophical and religious applications of this concept, magical systems such as that of the Golden Dawn made use of this 'wave' cycle in harnessing appropriate energies/elements when they were most accessible, and the association of colour with form, aspect of reality and character have long-been an intrinsic aspect of magical rites, whether in the form of meditation and expansion, conjuration or invocation.

Attention must certainly be afforded to the Cabbalistic tradition which greatly influenced the Golden Dawn as well as copious mystics, alchemists and magicians into the Islamic world and the West. The *'Zohar'* a text which has been described as the 'garment' worn by humanity through which the inner mysteries can be revealed, and the Merkabah tradition which is the meditative passing through the spheres in the style of Ezekiel, both centre on the various emanations of God that must be traversed in order to reach from the material, back up to pure spirit and the ultimately unknowable creator.

The Tetragrammaton 'YHVH' is here applied to a clear chain of being which consists of the worlds of Atziluth (Y) the higher plain of consciousness, Father and Fire; Briah (H) the creative image, Mother and Water; Yetzirah (V) the astral embodiment; Son and Air; Assiah (H) crystallized form; Daughter and Earth. The progression through active element to primordial water, and thence generative energy to the nurturing womb of the earth is clear in this system, just as are the gradations of being that see a descent to corporeality, along with a demarcation of the path from that gross state back to higher modes of existence.

This is also the case with the 'Sephirothic Tree' or 'Tree of Life' of the *'Sepher Yetzirah'*, which has arguably had the most far-reaching influence over modern-day Western occultism than any similar schema, and as a result has had the most exhaustively-analysed bodies of correspondences. The tree itself presents the ten emanations or stations of God that are knowable to humanity, linked by paths that themselves represent modes of being before each new 'gateway' is reached.

'Ein Soph' is the creator that lies beyond the reaches of the tree while 'Kether' or 'crown' is the tree's apex, and the chain reaches down to the corporeal realm of 'Malkuth'; all is framed by the left-hand, passive (female) Pillar of Severity, the right-hand, active (male) Pillar of Mercy and a central pillar of balance, with the sephira located on each pillar denoting something of the pillar's character as well as that of the proceeding and resulting sephiroth.

Among other associations applied to the Tree is that whereby the top three sephira (the Supernals) are the head of man and also the point of incarnation, which is penetration and birth; the middle three sephira are the body and arms of man and the points of growth and nourishment; the lower three sephira are the genitals and legs of man and the point of completion and form.

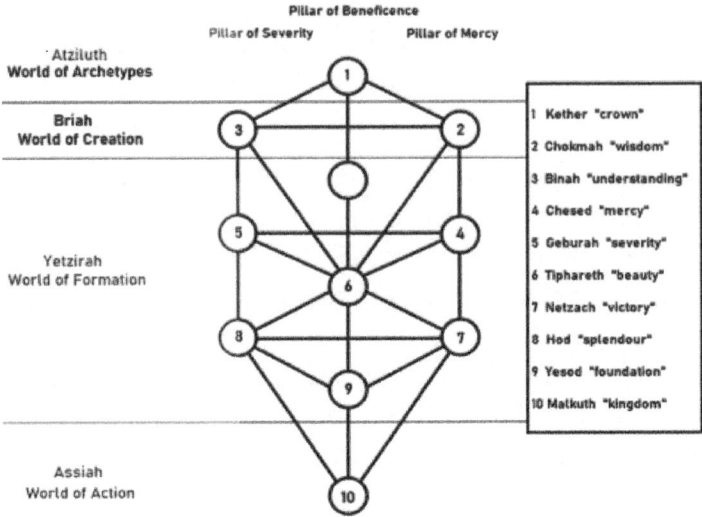

Later Cabbalism associated Microprosopus (the Great Face) with Kether, that heralding the nine further emanations. The left-hand pillar was here the Great Mother 'Aima', also the Holy Ghost and the right-hand pillar was the Great father, 'Abba' which is the universal wisdom and the Son and Word of God. The six sephiroth from 4-9 are the Microprosopus or Lesser Face', and the tenth sephira of Malkuth is the Bride of Microprosopus, Eve as a creation from the rib of Adam and the combination of the four elements that is humanity.

Beyond this, the twenty-two paths of the tree have received a great deal of attention, resulting in an array of correspondences (an example of which can be found in the next two tables). Eliphas Levi linked the paths to the cards of the tarot, and though there is no evidence to suggest this as a long-standing (and intentional) design, the numbers certainly match and the result proved sufficiently impacting on psychological and occult beliefs for this connection to withstand critique and be accepted by many as revelatory, if not divinely-wrought.

The Twenty-Two Paths & The Tarot

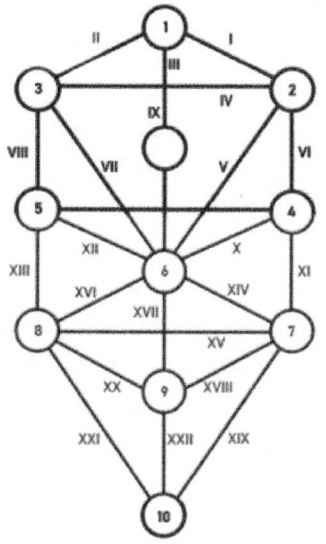

I	The Fool	XII	Justice
II	The Juggler/Magician	XIII	The Hanged Man
III	The High Priestess	XIV	Death
IV	The Empress	XV	Temperance
V	The Emperor	XVI	The Devil
VI	The Hierophant/Pope	XVII	The Tower
VII	The Lovers	XVIII	The Star
VIII	The Chariot	XIX	The Moon
IX	Strength	XX	The Sun
X	The Hermit	XXI	Judgement
XI	The Wheel of Fortune	XXII	The World

Indeed, Levi saw numbers, letters and the chain of being as self-evident and fundamental, just as it was to Robert Fludd, though in this instance the Cabbalistic philosophy was integral to this wisdom as he noted in his *'History of Magic'*: 'The Zohar is a kind of light, the Sepher Yetzirah, a ladder of truths. Here are explained the thirty-two (the ten sephiroth and the twenty-two paths) absolute signs of the word, the letters and the numbers. Each letter reproduces a number, an idea and a form, so that mathematics is as rigorously applicable to ideas and forms as to numbers, the proportions being exact and the correspondences perfect.'

All of what we are, our constitution, attitudes, drives and potentially even our ultimate end in life begins to be definable as a result of the concept of a chain of being, the correspondences between heavens and earth and the signatures that are signs of those correspondences; from a basic and rather beautiful concept we head into a veritable labyrinth of ideas that cross much of faith, mysticism and magic because of that human need to *know*. How much reassurance this ultimately offers is questionable, but the drives that forged these systems remain apparent today and show no signs of dissipating, regardless our faith or creed.

Forms

The majority of occult systems across the globe recognise that numbers hold especial significance. Indeed, numbers correspond to letters and thus words, as well as ideas and symbols, while also exercising influence in sound – they are frequently held to have their own unique character and collectively form an esoteric web that underlies all of created reality.

At what is perhaps the most basic level, numbers are the key to the universe and the commonalities that are shared throughout it. Where one is the single point that is the spark of being/the first expression of creation, two is duality (divergence into opposite states), three is the triangle that demarcates the trinity and four is the tetrahedron that exemplifies the entirety of space:

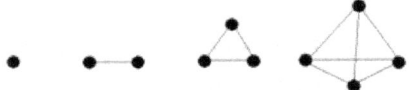

One expression of this belief was extended by the Ancient Egyptians, for whom the 3 of the trinity was the creative power of Osiris, the 4 was Isis as the base or womb of all life, and Horus was 5 – the hypotenuse or progeny. Thus we can chart the origin of existence through to form, but all subsequent products contain that same original 'spark' or point within, an understanding that lends to numbers the concept of 'perfection' and 'completion' and so can easily be equated symbolically with wholly more spiritual pursuits and beliefs.

Number and mathematics was central to the faith and wisdom of Pythagoras, who was born on the island of Samos in Asia Minor. Having travelled extensively, he benefited from studies in the East which gave him a singular understanding that was somewhat revolutionary to his forebears and cohort – the result was a popular movement consisting of men and women who practised vegetarianism and profound introspection, even if they were rather dour of manner (excessive laughter, for instance, being forbidden).

Pythagoras taught that there was word and speech which was the act of expression, the hieroglyph that constituted mystical concealment, and symbolism which was the realm of 'signification', the hidden truth made tantalisingly (yet deceptively) close. It was number, though, that underpinned all of reality and served as the purest and clearest link to the creative force, in mathematics, in geometry and indeed music: 'Everything is disposed according to the numbers.'

God, for Pythagoreans, was the Monad or Supreme Mind which was the cause and creator of All. With the Monad as the eternal wellspring, the worlds of the Superior (the Immortals) and the Inferior (Materiality) existed 'below' and completing the three points of the triangle, the trinity, that contained all in existence and, through that, the answers to all 'problems' that the mind of man might seek an answer for.

In terms of the innate characters of individual numbers, within this system **1** was the Monad, the Mind, but could also serve as the chaos and abyss of pre-creation. 1 came to be associated with Proteus who had the ability to change his own form, and Jupiter in his role as head of the gods.

2 is the duad, potentially evil and certainly suspect because it represented differentiation and division. 2 is darkness, instability and misfortune – but offers hope in the form of the union that is marriage. Associated deities included Isis, Venus and Juno.

It should be mentioned that 1 and 2 were not perceived as numbers, as we would see them, within the Pythagorean system. Rather, they are the supernal spheres that exist before the material realm, hence the interpretation of 1 as the primordial chaos. The first true 'number' is therefore the 3 that is the product of the first two, the pinnacle of the triangle that rises above the creative waters and instils form amidst the formless.

3 is the triad, seen in forms such as the tripod of Apollo. It is the first unification of opposites and as such embodies the qualities of peace, virtue, temperance and justice. 3 were the Furies and the Fates, and the associated god was Saturn as the lord of time – time being created at the point that form is established within the vacuity of space. In the form of the triangle, 3 is the womb of gestation and the direction of matter to spirit.

4 is the tetrad, the root of all things. Establishing the first geometric solid, it is the form of the human soul (which here consists of mind, science, opinion and sense). 4 is associated with Hercules, Mercury and Vulcan.

5 is the pentad which is Nature, and with it all superior and inferior entities. It is reconciliation and providence, and is linked to the likes of the Egyptian Bast, as well as Pallas and Nemesis.

6 is the hexad, which is the perfection of the constituent parts, and the creation of the world. It is the maker of souls and the conjunction of marriage (as two linked triangles).Orpheus is associated with the 6.

7 is the heptad, which is religion and life. Herein lies fortune, judgement and all things that lead to an end. As a sacred number to many cultures, 7 is associated with Osiris, Mars and Chirst.

8 is the ogdoad, the first cube and as such a sacred number. 8 of course divides equally to four, and thence to two and finally to the Monad, which means that the figure 8 is the return to the source, as well as love and prudence. Neptune and Themis are among those linked to it.

9 is the ennead, which is a mark of failure in that it is one short of the 10 that is completion. It is a boundary, as it contains all that has gone before it and stands on the border before ten. It can also signify the life of man and woman due to the nine months of gestation, and at points has been linked to the principle of evil as the inverted 6. Jupiter, Prometheus and Proserpine are those connected to it.

10 is the decad, which for the Pythagoreans was the tetractys (one on two, on three, on four) that was held to be 'eternal nature's fountain spring':

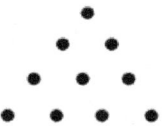

10 is perfection of number and the totality of earth and heaven, as well as the balance and comprehension of opposites.

As might be expected, the ideas that came to be associated with each number are manifold and somewhat changeable, though the commonly-held aspects are no less compelling when applied to either philosophical or spiritual endeavours, and have not strayed far from the Pythagorean system of the 1st century B.C.E.:

0 The form of zero suggests both the World and God/Creator, but the void or space at its centre defines the external vastness around it, rather than its intrinsic limitation. The space in the 0 can, however, be perceived as eternity, likewise the womb or the 'doorway of life'. It is nothing and everything. Zero can be non-being, and so is closely linked with the concept of unity and completion.

1 One is commonly the masculine, active principle. It is a constant force of potency which is also the ego of humanity; thus it is the divine Monad as well as the material creator/architect and the driving force of the personality. One is aloneness and aloofness, that which stands apart in isolation, the origin and measure of all. It is the delivery of the spiritual essence to humanity, and is therefore the unifying principle.

2 Two is the feminine, passive principle. It is also the union of spirit with matter, which suggests a link with the fire of creation. Two is duality and opposition, as well as choice in life, love, marriage and conjunction. It is the echo, the shadow and the bisexual. Pythagoreans, as already noted, at times deemed two to be 'unclean', in part due to its deviance from the unity of one.

3 Three is the result of the union of one and two. It is therefore the cosmic breath issuing forth, as well as the genitals of procreation. The form of the three (3) consists of half-loops, therefore it suggests a mercurial and potentially androgynous element. Three, as the progeny, is the fruits of the earth. Three's relevance within earthly schemas have often been cited – past, present, future; length, breadth, thickness; faith, hope, charity. Three was also posited as a perfect number due to its association with the trinity – with three-fold repetitions of names a common undertaking in conjurations, love spells and charms.

4 Four is the material form, that which is the base and supports all else (as with the tetrahedron and the place of Isis within Egyptian belief). As such it is tangible experience and worldly wisdom, as well as the sphere of action. Regularly noted, among other correspondences, are the four directions and elements, the four weeks of the month, the four phases of moon and the four seasons. The four evangelists/gospels are another potent association linking Biblical Scripture to the world that it spoke to.

5 Five is the quintessence, the mystical fifth element that holds the other four together – sometimes equated with the life-giving spirit of God. It is a notable number as the result of adding the feminine and receptive two to the masculine and active three. Five is the number of Venus and can be seen to be similarly changeable in its aspect – the very form of the numeral 5 shows this, with the beginning and end of its lines pointing in opposing directions. The five senses of man and woman are notable, and the five can be symbolically represented by the head and limbs of the human form within the circle of creation, the square of matter and the pentagram that unites all elements with the human intellect and will.

6 With its open top and closed base, six is a number of conflict and opposition (with the top suggested to represent aloofness, in contrast to the base that speaks of closure and a separate, fixed isolation). However, the interlocked triangles previously described by Eliphas Levi offer something decidedly more balanced and nuanced, thus in certain forms the six is equilibrium. Six are the days of creation before humanity in Genesis.

7 Seven is the 'complete man', which is the unification of the lower three and upper three through the art of the seventh. Seven is ubiquitous, whether in the days of the week, the planets of the solar system, the length of the moon's phases, the colours of the spectrum or the notes of scale. Pythagoras held seven to be the addition of the one as Monad to the six of impulse, likewise the product of the four elements and passion, desire and reason. Seven cannot be produced by multiplying other numbers, nor is it capable of producing the other numbers between 1 and 10 and so has an uncanny character that, like 1, stands alone and aloof. Seven can therefore be a holy number denoting a higher state of being, but it does not necessarily suggest peace that can only be achieved through the balancing of forces.

8 Eight is justice and balance, suggestive of eternity if not that which exists and occurs outside of the limitations of time. It is regarded as versatile and secretive, and though diffusive in its nature can also be isolated when focused upon itself. The eight is linked to the eighth, life-giving orifice of woman and also with the second birth which is life after death. Eight can take the form of the octagon which is the intermediate form of the square as it becomes a circle, which is a sign of regeneration. '8' is also the form achieved by the intertwined serpents of the caduceus.

9 Nine is the 3+3+3, which is the triad or trinity multiplied by itself, which is perfection. As such it is the complete image of the 'three worlds'. The form of the 9 suggests an open connection with the earth and matter but a fixed and complete connection to the higher realm (much like Robert Fludd's chained lady of the macrocosm). Given this form, the nine is seen to gather spirit and deliver it through to matter, which by association links it to the 'T' which is incarnation, as well as a form of cross. Nine are the muses and the moving planetary spheres, and both a multiplication of the nine and the total of the individual numbers 3,6 and 0 results in 360, which completes a full circle when applied to degrees. Nine is the end and the beginning.

10 Ten is the addition of the mystical seven to the generative three and is often deemed to be the perfect number of completion. However, the form of the 10 also suggests the individual (1) aloof from the world of creation (0). At points the space between the 1 and 0 have been identified as a force in and of itself and in these cases 10 is interpreted as a reflection of trinity. With the number ten we reach a sense of completion if only due to the repetition of figures that follow it – ten is therefore the process of separation through to unity, and then a return to separation, though in other forms (such as the Pythagorean tetractys) ten is the totality of all which holds all else within it. Notably, there were ten days of initiation in the Ancient Mystery schools.

11 Eleven is God/Creator (1) and the creation (10). It is said to be the highest level of being; the condition of revelation. Conversely, eleven can also be a number of transition and of excess, in that it is beyond the completion of the ten and potentially frivolous or dangerous. Connected to this latter understanding is eleven as the number of the martyr.

22 Twenty-two should be noted as it is the number of letters within the Hebrew alphabet and so is understood to signify the manifold aspects of creation, which are themselves emanations and manifestations of God.

Here the characters and natures of the numbers themselves are explored, while in the study of numerology it is the association of letters and words with number that are considered, and with that a form of divination based on observed correspondences. It must be added that in contrast to the apparently ancient lineage of numerological practices, the term itself was a 20th century C.E. appellation and so the many forms that the art took and the roles that it played are at best summarised in the established system, and certainly not exhausted.

The authority lent to numerology was a product of the Pythagorean attitude that numbers were Truth, and that which underlay all of existence. Augustine of Hippo for one shared this belief and held numbers and mathematics in the highest regard as intentional markers passed to humanity by God as a means of fully understanding creation, and potentially securing revelation, and though numerology would eventually be disregarded at best (otherwise denigrated) as the stuff of superstition or magic, sufficient following saw its tradition disseminated through the centuries in both wholly disposable and decidedly more mystical and meaningful forms.

Given this, there are several systems of numerology in evidence, including those of the Babylonians, the Hebrews, the Arabs (the Abjad system), the Chinese, the Japanese and the Indian – which is to be expected given the need for a form specific to the alphabet concerned. There are therefore variations in form and content, but the general approaches (and the most common traits) remain recognisable across systems where letters are associated with number values so that names, words and phrases take on especial significance and power through the total value which they produce. We shall consider the Pythagorean system in due course, within a study of letters and their correspondences.

However, one of the earliest applications of number as a means of unlocking the divine mysteries was that afforded to vibrations in pitch. It was noted that, when sounded together, the first and fourth strings of an instrument produced the octave – in doubling the weight, the string was halved – and the subsequent investigation of notes in relation to number resulted in a wondrous conclusion: 'musical intervals may be represented in terms of simple ratios of whole numbers.'

Such study was believed to reveal the 'harmony of the spheres', the melodies of the celestial bodies and indeed all of creation that could be unlocked and experienced given the correct application of number, and if number was the proof offered by the creator of a divine pattern, then music of this kind was actually the music of God, and the act of revealing the celestial harmonies was a pure and unrivalled epiphany.

Students and followers of Pythagoras continued to explore this area, with one Nichomachus of Gerasa (c.60 – 120 C.E.) publishing a *'Manual of Harmonics'* alongside texts on arithmetic and standard mathematics. His conclusion was that there existed a discernible 'systematic method' in the arrangement of the universe, in accordance with number '...by him that created all things', and the result offered a decidedly mystical opportunity for humanity to perceive the often unheard song of creation, described perfectly by Pythagorean aphorisms such as 'The wind blowing, adore the sound.'

In this light, all of life can be understood to be singing a song in praise of God which is frequently disregarded or unheard by humanity due to the grossness of matter that encompasses and distracts us as corporeal beings. The truth, however, was held by the Pythagoreans that through the application of number, the universe had been revealed to be a giant, cosmic monochord (illustrated as such by Robert Fludd) with a single string reaching from earth to heaven; to experience this cosmic harmony was to experience God, and the use of musical compositions especially created to treat mental and physical imbalances was not uncommon as a result.

Johannes Kepler (1571 – 1630 C.E.) utilised studies in science and mysticism to conclude that all true order was that designed and maintained by God alone, that mathematics revealed musical harmony and that the movements of planets were modulated to harmonic proportions, and so sang their own tune as they proceeded on their cosmic paths. Plato, too, certainly agreed with this understanding to an extent, with his *'Philebus'* noting that measure and proportion equalled elegance and beauty. As ever, order from chaos represented intent, design, and a degree of excellence that only a divinity could manifest.

Number and balance were also central to the discovery of the 'Golden Ratio' or 'Golden Mean/Section' or 'Divine Proportion' that sees perhaps its earliest mention in the *'Elements'* of Euclid (mid 4th – mid 3rd century B.C.E.) where it is described as the 'extreme and mean ratio'. Numerically the Golden Ratio is 1.618, and it is the ratio of a line cut into two parts of different length, where the ratio of the whole length to that of the longer segment is equal to the ratio of the longer segment to the shorter segment.

Frequently appearing in geometry, when applied to art and architecture it was believed to offer the most aesthetically pleasing results and so became a common feature in these spheres, potentially including the works of Leonardo da Vinci (whose 'Vitruvian Man' composed around 1490 C.E. is a related work), Salvador Dali (1904 – 1989 C.E.) and the Swiss-French architect Le Corbusier (1887 – 1965 C.E.). Classical music composers such as Debussy and Satie also incorporated the Golden Ratio into their works.

The fact that mathematics unlocked patterns and correspondences in the very make-up of creation was itself remarkable and compelling to many; however, the fact that the products of the application of these patterns were more appealing to human perception was overwhelming to the artists, whatever his or her particular field of creativity. On another level again, where the proportions of the human form could be equated with the same correspondences and thus the same divine pattern, it appeared that number truly did reveal the hidden reality behind all of existence, just as Pythagoras and his followers had espoused.

Attempting to tap and potentially harness the kind of power that the hidden reality was imbued with was the bailiwick of magic, and numbers were perhaps most common in that area in the form of magic squares, which continue to enjoy a place in recreational mathematics. These squares are essentially numbers (usually positive whole numbers or integers) placed together in a square form in such a way that each row, column and main diagonal lines all add up to the same figure.

Magic squares were seen in China (the third order or 3x3 square named the 'Nine Halls' among some of the earliest mathematicians c. 190 B.C.E.), India (with the fourth order or 4x4 square dated to 587 C.E. at least), pre-Islamic Persia and then disseminated through Islamic works and translations across the Middle East, Africa and, later, Western Europe. Texts by the likes of Jabir ibn Hayyan (who may have existed as an individual circa the 8th century C.E. or served a role as a legend) and al-Ghazali (1058 – 1111 C.E.) offer examples of magic squares as charms with specific uses, and notably within the art of alchemy which both figures are often most associated with.

Europe's introduction to the magic square was in the *'Book on the Influences of the Planets'* by Ibn Zarqali (1029 – 1087 C.E.) where they were named 'Planetary Squares' and linked in their various forms to the respective planets then known, before being included in the popular grimoire the *'Picatrix'*, Agrippa's *'Three Books of Occult Philosophy'* and also in the studies of Paracelsus. Albrecht Durer's 1514 engraving *'Melencolia I'* offered a 4x4 square in all its glory, directly above the predominant figure.

Each of the planets thus had their own magic square, such as that of Saturn:

4	9	2
3	5	7
8	1	6

Saturn's magical numbers are 3 (the amount of digits in each row and column), 9 (the amount of digits that are used in total), 15 (the total of each row, column and main diagonal) and 45 (the total of all nine digits added together). From this were defined the 'names of intelligence' for the planet like 'Agiel', all of which equalled totals of 3, 9 and 15 when translated to number, and the name of the planet's spirit, 'Zazel', with a numerical equivalent of 45.

'Seals' or sigils that are essentially the signature of an entity or character were also formed from this use of numbers, identified as a mark which theoretically crosses the path of all numbers within the relevant magic square, such as that of Saturn:

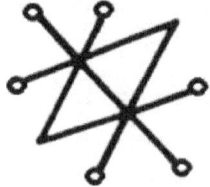

Used as part of a talisman or amulet, sigils like this could be used for protection, to ensure good luck or to summon the intrinsic character of the planet in question, and those seals attributed to the 'intelligence' or 'spirit' of a planet (drawn using the relevant numbers) could be used by one seeking wisdom of one sort or another to invoke that entity or quality.

We will return to the subject of correspondences within ritual anon, though what is fundamental here is that numbers were held to be a unique chain of being that reflected the patterns of God in His creation of the cosmos, and were thus seen as revelatory keys in the unlocking of nature, personality, fortune and indeed the higher wisdom inherent to the higher emanations of God in the firmament and even the heavens. All knowledge could be found through their use, and at their heart they offered balance, music for the spirit and powers and abilities previously known only to the Creator – making them a universal and timeless language with incomparable relevance to the human condition.

Words

If numbers are the building blocks of existence, then words are the concrete which forges them together. Letters and words have frequently been held to be the very stuff of creation, with no 'existence' as we understand it until the designs of God or the gods were spoken. One example of this can be found in the

Memphis creation myth of the Egyptians, where it is said that Ptah conceived the world in thought, before uttering the all-important words in order to give form to that design – an act of creation that is echoed somewhat in the Biblical Word of God that establishes the world in the Book of Genesis.

Words, written and spoken, are therefore of immense meaning to all living beings, and unrivalled in their potential power both to create and to destroy; thus we see Elijah writing the secret name of God on the forehead of a clay man to give him life in the Hebraic legend of the Golem, countless incantations in and out of grimoires that name deities, angels, spirits and demons with the aim of harnessing their wisdom and abilities, and Solomonic instruments such as a large brass vessel inscribed with seals in order to trap and bind spirits – words are a potent force that afford men and women the might of a deity.

It is worth noting that illiteracy further compounded this belief, with the mystery of words beyond the ken of many people until relatively recent times and even then retaining a sense of awe among those who had sufficient learning to appreciate exotic and occult texts. This was certainly a boon to 'cunning folk', wise women and men and other forms of 'witch doctor' who could allow a simple bookshelf to purport to their clients an intellect far superior to their own, and indeed one willing to tamper with the very fabric of existence!

One mystical work that lent itself to this belief is the Hebraic *'Sepher Yetzirah'* which Eliphas Levi described in his 1860 C.E. work *'The History of Magic'* as transforming '...the known to the unknown by the help of analogy.' Unity is the key here, and with it the ubiquitous chain of being, with the understanding that all creation emanates from God, and is bonded together by the 22 letters of the Hebrew alphabet (a belief beautifully depicted by the 'Sephirothic Tree' or Tree of Life, which has ten stations or sephira that each represent a name of God).

It is said that there are actually 72 separate names of God and one 72 syllable name, the Shemhamphorasch, which is said to have immense power when the name is known and – crucially – pronounced correctly. It is this name that some believe to have parted the Red Sea for Moses as he led the Jewish slaves from their captivity in Egypt, as the Biblical account of this in Exodus 14:19-21 consists of verses of 72 letters when in the Hebrew language.

The search for the names of God has understandably been a long-held and ardent pursuit of certain theologians and mystics, as well as magicians and sorcerers, though the work of the German scholar Johann Reuchlin (1455 – 1522 C.E.) attempted to link the Shemhamphorasch with the four letter name frequently applied to God, 'YHVH' or 'Tetragrammaton' that gives us the names 'Yahweh' and 'Jehovah'.

Reuchlin suggested that the Yod, He, Vau and He of the name were a derivative of the longer name and noted a numerical translation by way of evidence: With Yod as 10, YH as 15, YHV as 21 and YHVH as 26, the total was the 72 of the Shemhamphorasch and so it could be said that all that was necessary to be known could be found within the shorter name – to arrange them appropriately was to reveal that elusive and impressive name that would bestow upon the learned the power of the deity.

The Tetragrammaton therefore contained all, just as the Hebrew alphabet was held to be the Word of God given form, and as such was the fabric of all creation. The application of number values to the letters along with the esoteric pursuit of playing with words and phrases to reveal hidden truths behind texts (and hidden wisdom behind reality) is one of the foremost concerns of the Jewish mystical works that would become a predominant concern of seekers of revelation across various forms of mysticism, magic and alchemy.

As can be seen from just a basic model of correspondences, the letters were applied to all aspects of existence and so were an omnipresent and accessible 'chain of being' between God and humanity.

One popular derivative of this correspondence of letter with form is the aforementioned art of numerology, which largely focuses on the cumulative values of names to reveal inherent characteristics, abilities and fortune. There is more than one framework that can be used for this, among which that of the Hebrew alphabet and a modern Western equivalent are the most prominent:

Hebrew

1	2	3	4	5	6	7	8
A	B	C	D	E	U	O	F
I	K	G	M	H	V	Z	P
Q	R	L	T	N	W		
J		S			X		
Y							

Modern

1	2	3	4	5	6	7	8	9
A	B	C	D	E	F	G	H	I
J	K	L	M	N	O	P	Q	R
S	T	U	V	W	X	Y	Z	

A name can be translated to numbers, added together to make a total figure and that figure reduced to a 'root' number (i.e. a total of 26 would be reduced, by 2+6, to 8) to reveal various aspects about that individual, with the root of the full name giving insight of the overarching character, the root of the vowels in a name suggesting the inner being or 'heart', the root of the consonants exploring the outward personality and the date of birth offering further insight to character, and predicting the fortune of the person in question.

Individual numbers again offer specific traits:

1: those who are assertive, ambitious and possibly aggressive. They are independent, sometimes to the point of excess where they come to dominate lesser wills.

2: those who are quiet and may serve as peace-makers. Diplomacy and sensitivity are positive abilities, though this can lead to intense shyness and introspection. 2's can also be rather cruel and deceptive.

3: those who are imaginative and energetic, well-suited to the arts. Fortune favours them. The ease of their successes can lead to a lack of awareness for the efforts of others. 3's can be too whimsical and light-hearted, and they are often keen to please and gain popularity.

4: those who are less creative, but are reliable and solid figures – though this can extend to dullness and predictability. They are workers who may resent those who need not apply the same effort to achieve, and may be predisposed to melancholy.

5: those who are bright and rather impatient. Wanderlust is a mark of 5's, as is the endless desire for new experiences. Active in the pursuit of sex and love, they can be more passive when it comes to commitment, just as responsibility and the 'planting of roots' can be undesirable to them.

6: are those who offer domestic harmony. They are caring and happy in close-knit circles, but can be idealistic and in certain matters somewhat self-satisfied and parochial.

7: are the philosophers and mystics. Often of an insightful and impressive intellect, they can be lost in their own thoughts and imaginings, and be aloof as a result. Pessimism is another unfortunate trait.

8: are those who feel the intensity of success and failure on the material level, with nothing gained without considerable focus and effort. Highs and lows are equally affecting, and 8's can be intense and grim as a result of their experiences and philosophies.

9: those of a spiritual instinct, who engage themselves passionately. Investors in others, they can nonetheless be egocentric and belligerent if they are not paid due attention.

10 would be reduced to **1**, but consideration is offered for those few who might find that they are the rare and lofty **11** (the visionary, who is quite possibly the classical martyr figure) and **22** (the master, a standout character who embodies all of the best qualities of all of the other numbers).

This said, the latter two numbers are most often removed from the numerological system due to the particularly rare characters that they relate to – and the potential to warp a personality and bring out the very worst of their nature where such a plaudit should be incorrectly applied!

The various modes of applying numerology within the Cabbalistic system deserve a sizeable study all their own, but in brief they are 'Gematria', 'Notatikon' and 'Temurah.' Gematria again considers and analyses the calculated value of words, with those of the same value sometimes being interchanged to offer further insight to a given passage or text, or the value of a word being used to identify other words that can expand a given meaning. Essentially, the central belief here is that words of similar numerical value relate to one another and so can be brought to bear on a phrase to unlock what are perceived to be hidden meanings and esoteric wisdom.

Gematria was in evidence in Assyria of the 8th century B.C.E. and so certainly has an ancient lineage, though its application within the Bible is much more contested, even with the 666 of the Beast in Revelation being equated numerologically with both 'Nero Caesar' and the 144,000 that are 'the saved' (with 144,000 being reducible to 9, just as the 6+6+6 = 18, which reduces as 1+8 to 9).

Notarikon focus on words as abbreviations, with each letter of a given word being taken as the initial of a new word, or the first and last letters of a series of words being re-arranged, so as to make a new and relative word, term or name. This system has long been a popular one on the composition of talismans, such as those inscribed with 'AGLA' which has no single proved meaning but has commonly been regarded as an acronym of 'Atah Gibor Le-olam Adonai' or 'You, O Lord, are mighty forever.'

Temurah is that where letters are substituted for alternatives that are taken from a specific order, such as the first letter of a word being replaced with the last letter of the Hebrew alphabet, the second with the penultimate letter, and so on. A similar application instead sees the first letter of a word changed to the twelfth letter of the Hebrew alphabet, the second with the thirteenth, and so on, while a third form replaces each letter with that which precedes it in the alphabet.

What can be concluded from all of this is that letters and words certainly are power, and immense time and insight has been applied to their creation, just as great efforts have been made to reveal truths that sacred words, sayings and texts conceal from the majority of their audience. As we have already seen with the Shemhamphorash and Tetragrammaton, names have most frequently been seen as imbued with something of the power and character of those that they denote, and the desire to uncover hidden messages and reveal potent energies from name and word has produced numerous associative lore and compelling legends along the way.

A long-held belief is that whereby a name is used to gain mastery over an individual, attack them or otherwise control their fate – a person shares a genuine bond with their name, therefore the name can expose any man or woman to great risk where there is a malefic intent. Thus we see the Egyptian practise of both a greater name ('true', relating to the Ka) and a lesser name ('false', relating to the public image) being bestowed upon a child at birth to ensure protection from any unwanted powers; we also see in Plutarch how early Romans withheld the name of any local guardian deity so as to avoid any attack that might be made upon it, or Rome itself). Further to this, we have the story of Rumplestiltskin!

Conversely, names have been used to instil a sense of power and, indeed, an aura better suited to one's concept of self, a well-known example being Aleister Crowley's 'Perdurabo' or 'I will endure to the end.' It may be considered self-promotion at best, but this use of names and titles to create an effect makes use of ancient beliefs and can still impact the self and others psychologically and just possibly spiritually.

Finally it should be noted that a number of diverse systems including Celtic Ogham, the runes of the Scandinavian Vikings and both the Arabic and Greek alphabets offer esoteric associations for each letter or figure. The English alphabet has also where possible been linked to the Hebrew letters and, where this is not possible, occult interpretations using various languages, philosophies and symbols have been associated to ensure a continuation of beliefs that can be applied outside of the Cabbalistic framework. The following is a brief but insightful consideration of this latter alphabet, where God, the words of creation and modern antecedents are united by the perceived hidden power of the letter:

A: Having the value of 1. The Hebraic form of Aleph, derived from head of the ox, which is Taurus. Alpha, residing at the side of Christ. The 12th century C.E. Italian theologian Joachim di Fiore associated the letter A with the trinity, and recognised it as a holy letter.

B: 'Beth', which is the door of the house. The twin enclosures suggest duality. In both of these interpretations, the underlying principle is transition toward a state of being.

C: The lunar crescent; linked to the number 8.

D: Value of 4. The sound value of 'Daleth'. In its modern form, a doorway, potentially a division. Hieroglyphically it is 'hand'. D is incarnation/expression.

E: 'He'. Value of 5, which is Virgo and Venus, as well as the pentagram. Cabbalistically it is the womb, while in its modern form E it is 'window.'

F: Associated with the Greek 6, due to the largely lost usage of the 'diagamma' which at points had the form of the upper- and lower-case F.

G: The Hebrew 'Gimel' which, with the C, is said to have derived from shape produced by the neck of the camel. The modern G is derived from C, (Gamma, the third letter of the Greek alphabet). The Grail, in its aspect of both the source and the destination of life.

H: 'Heth', which in form is vestigial of 'fence'. Helena Blavatsky linked H with the womb, and the 5 of Venus.

I: 1 + 10, which is consciousness and the external world. The phallic symbolism is unavoidable.

J: Jod/Yod within the Hebrew schema.

K: Kaph – bowl; spirit-container. Its sound value is the severed 'C'.

L: Numerical equivalent of 30. In Egyptian hieroglyphs L is the lioness, a solar letter. A sound value of changing form, mirroring the letter itself which presents as a volume without form – hence light and liquid.

M: For Phoenicians, M was a depiction of waves of matter. In Hebrew, 'Mem' is water. In Sanskrit it is 'ma' – Manas – which is the mind or higher ego. This can extend to the being of maker or master, who creates as a result of skill and wisdom. Value of 40, which reduces to 4.

N: The female principle, with further associations with the womb. In Egyptian hieroglyphs N is the line of water. In Hebrew it is 'Nun', the fish, which is Christ. The value is 700, which resolves to 7, the sacred number of Christ.

O: Associated with 11. The enclosed circle. Seen with a horizontal line through it, it is death. Seen with a dot at its centre, it is sun/life/God.

P: 80, which then resolves to 8. The Hebrew 'Pe', which is the 'mouth'. P is the 'point', in that it is the orientation of existence, to which the Word gave form.

Q: 'Koph'. 100 or 90, which then resolves to 9.

R: 'Resch' Value of 200.

S: 'Samech' Blavatsky stated that this was a sacred name of God. Saturn. Value of 60.

T: 'Tan'. Value of 400. The S as serpent around the T of the cross, which is the caduceus. S (60) + T (400) = 4+6+0 = 10 = 1. As such, this is the reintegration of the self into the cosmos. T is also the direction of an intent; the realisation of a goal.

U: In Cabbalism 3x7 = 21 = 3, which is the trinity. The 21 days of the alchemical transmutation period which sees base matter refined to silver – and perhaps also its spiritual equivalent.

V: 'Vau'. Vibration and energy from a fixed point outward, in the form of a continuum.

W: The double 'v' is the celestial waters. The Anima Mundi.

X: The unknown quantity, but also perfection. The cross, which is the sacrifice of the Logos.

Y: 'Yod' , with the arms denoting choice, such as that between good and evil.

Z: 'Zayin', which is the sceptre. Its form, like the S, suggests movement but here it is the state of existence in perpetuity, on the threshold of non-being.

Signatures

With a belief that everything in existence shares one source, also that a constant flux of energies affects all beings and that perceived patterns defines this activity, the understanding that copious 'signs' would be apparent to offer insight to the cycles of life is hardly a far-fetched one. 'Signatures' of countless varieties have been acknowledged and exhaustively studied, it seems, since the earliest known civilizations, and frequently with common results in terms of character and symbolism.

One of the oldest known forms of divination is geomancy, a system based on changes in the state of 'Oneness' resulting from the interplay of the principles yin and yang and best known for many through the '*Yi Jing*' or '*I Ching*'('*Book of Changes*'), a work composed c.3000 B.C.E. that Richard Wilhelm (1873 – 1930 C.E.) considered to be the root of both Taoism and Confucianism.

The philosophy at the heart of the work is to an extent recognisable as that central to Pythagoreanism and Cabbalism: 'The One produced the Three, the Three produced the Seven, the Seven produced the Ten; these Ten are all things.' However, here the system is applied to divination and simple 'yes' and 'no' questions where a yes is represented as an unbroken line (yang, the phallic symbol of active energy) and no is the broken line (yin, the receptive symbol of gestation and change), the combinations of which saw the creation of the eight 'trigrams':

☰ ☷ ☲ ☵

The trigrams represent every possible occurrence in existence, though fundamentally the yin/yang principle of flux – the potential and act of change – is understood to be a constant that affects the cosmic interplay. Transition permeates all, and so what is represented by the trigrams is never an end in and of itself, but a trend or movement towards a potential end, hence *'Book of Changes.'*

The eight trigrams, with a third line added to each, were used to form the 64 hexagrams (six-line patterns), with each line denoting a stage of transition (essentially a microcosm) within the broader change said to be occurring.

Initially sticks were used to 'cast lots' and find the relevant trigram, though a widely-applied 'modern' alternative sees the throwing of three coins, where each throw results in one of the six lines. Decidedly mystical in their framing, the trigrams of the I Ching fell from favour in their native China in the 20th century C.E. but nonetheless retained import as the civilization's most ancient text, with a popularity in the West to a large extent attributable to the work of Richard Wilhelm and Carl Jung, who saw in the trigrams a source of immense wisdom befitting the theories of synchronicity and the 'archetypes'.

Before this development, though, the idea of correspondences and signatures, with the latter held to be the mark of higher beings on the mundane world, were inherent within much of the global mindset and rife within certain religions and most certainly later alchemical and magical pursuits. Plato himself suggested the worth of recognising and divining the message in given signs, with his *'Symposium'* noting that the divinatory arts are 'communion between god and man.'

Astrology is, of course, one of the more famous (or infamous) systems of divining the signatures, dating back to at least the 2nd millennium B.C.E. when the study of celestial bodies and their movements informed agricultural pursuits as much as it revealed divine wisdom and offered portents of both fortune and disaster to come. The ancient Chinese and Hindu peoples certainly indulged in astrology, though a throughline of practise – if not worship – clearly saw Mesopotamian and Babylonian usage disseminated through Greece, the Roman Empire, through the Islamic world and thence to the further reaches of Western Europe.

Indeed the religious tower that was the ziggurat was akin to the celestial spheres for the ancient Mesopotamian. Itself a model of the world, the ziggurat consisted of seven 'stages' from the black Saturn at its base to the gold Sun at its apex, a microcosm that was a fitting domain for any god to reside in (as was the belief). The blessing of a god or gods was fundamental to balance as much as it was to any fortune for a city, and to lose the patronage of that god or see a change from one deity to another would be believed to herald dramatic changes for the populace, therefore stability was dependent on an active mix of faith and worship, and these pursuits were frequently dependent on the observation of the heavens.

Alongside the carefully surveilled omina and patterns of the sky, correspondences were defined that linked each known planet to a god, a character and a metal among other elements (an approach that would only gain in popularity and complexity as the art of astrology was passed to ever more cultures):

Jupiter: Marduk (the creator); ruler of the sky; former of diminishing chaos; tin.

Moon: Sin; changeability; waxing and waning influences; silver.

Sun: Samas; changeability; warmth and growth, but potential excess; gold.

Mercury: Nebo; knowledgeable scribe, though potentially herald of ill-fortune; mercury.

Saturn: Adar; the hunter; misfortune, the vagaries of conflict; lead.

Mars: Nergal; evil; war and death; iron.

Venus: Ishtar; love and motherhood; copper.

The Mesopotamian system gave the images of the bull, the twins, the lion, balance, scorpion and fishes to modern astrology, though was in itself a much more exhaustive and involved area of study in its main focus of sky and celestial omina (with the *'Enuma Anu Enlil'*, a collection of 68 or 70 tablets recording such signatures that was completed c.1000 B.C.E. offering up to 7,000 pertinent observations).

A special caste of priests existed to decipher these divine omina, and they alone stood as the rightful conduits for the messages writ in the heavens. Such was the prestige of the Babylonians who developed such a corpus of reflection and understanding that one descendent, 'Berosus' established a college in Cos for astrologers and ultimately had a statue erected in his honour! The Romans, too, regarded astrology as a laudable area of study and termed its study as 'mathesis' or 'the learning'.

Even Plotinus, who was highly wary of the magic arts and believed that man was able to choose his own destiny, saw astrology to be something capable of incomparable profundity due to the fact that the stars are more divine than human, for him unchanging and beyond the influence of passion and will. This baton of sorts would subsequently be passed to Christian Scripture in the form of Genesis 1:14 ('And God said, Let there be lights in the firmament of the heaven to divide the day from the night; and let them be for signs, and for seasons, and for days, and for years) and the wheel of fortune apparently being borne by the four fixed signs of the zodiac – man, lion, ox and eagle – in Ezekiel 1:15.

The developed forms of astrology are Judicial, which is that of individual and nations, and natural, which relates to the weather and the natural world. The affect on the human being was such that in some quarters it was held that certain patterns of the heavens were imprinted on the brain, the place of the intellect which reflected the macrocosm and the various archetypal forces, and their images that existed there.

The twelve zodiacal signs consist of six diurnal/masculine and six nocturnal/feminine signs that are applied successively diurnal, nocturnal, diurnal, nocturnal, etc. The first 6six signs are those termed Northern/Commanding, and the latter six are those classed Southern/Obeying, and of course numerous correspondences have long-been linked to them, including each of the four elements and, not least, their link to individual characteristics and bearings when relating to individuals:

Aries: Mars. Dry, fiery, possibly violent. Links to the head and face. Typical ailments include headache, epilepsy and apoplexy. Countries influenced include England, France, Germany, Poland and Switzerland. The associated colours are red and white.

Taurus: Venus. Cold, earthy, potentially melancholy. Slow to ire but then hard to quell. Links to the neck, throat and voice. Sites influenced include places of cattle; also Russia, Sweden, Persia, Ireland.

Gemini: Aerial. Hot, moist. Active, vital, with business acumen and good judgement. Links to the hands, arms and shoulders. Sites include places of high ground (internally stairs, externally hills); also Armenia, Egypt, Sardinia.

Cancer: Moon. Cold, moist, fecund. Some weakness and sickliness. Links to the chest, lungs, ribs, breasts. Sites include seas and rivers, wells etc. also Holland and Scotland.

Leo: Sun. Hot, dry, fiery. Generous and cautious but capable of cruelty and brutality. Links to the heart, stomach and sides. Maladies such as fevers and plague. Sites include woods, deserts; also Italy, Turkey.

Virgo: Mercury. Earthy, cold, dry. Benevolent; good wit. Links to the viscera. Sites include libraries, places of study, also the cornfield; Assyria, Mesopotamia, Greece.

Libra: Venus. Hot and moist. Upright and just. Links to the kidneys, navel, loins and the buttocks. Sites include mountains and felled forests.

Scorpio: Mars. Cold and watery. Stagnant waters and ruins. Links to the sexual organs. Places include Norway and Fez.

Sagittarius: Jupiter. Fiery, hot, dry. Intrepid and generous. Links to the hips, thighs and muscles. Sites include Arabia and Spain. Colours are green and red.

Capricorn: Saturn. Earthy, cold and dry. Cheer and talent, though potentially hysteria and melancholy. Links to the knees and hips. Sites include workshops; India and Mexico. Colours are black and brown.

Aquarius: Saturn. Airy, hot, moist. Fair and honest. Links to the lower legs and ankles. Sites include mines and quarries; roofs of houses. Denmark. Colours are grey and sky blue.

Pisces: Jupiter. Cold and moist. Fruitful, but not to the extent of the moon in Cancer. Lacklustre, but well-meant. Links to the feet. Similar sites to Cancer, but not rivers. Normandy. White.

Given that the stars imprinted their form on the human brain, it is understandable that the sign of the zodiac that a person was born under the influence of would make a similar, though more apparent, mark on an individual, though astrological lore has it that one's overall appearance is directly related:

Aries: Slender, with a long neck, broad forehead and curly black or sandy hair.

Taurus: Stocky, with broad shoulders. Wavy brown hair.

Gemini: Tall and well-proportioned. A long nose, wide mouth and brown hair.

Cancer: Somewhat shorter, with a round face. Brown hair with a light tinge. Smaller hands and feet.

Leo: Tall and robust. An 'ornate' complexion. Grey eyes and wavy hair.

Virgo: Lean, with a square jaw and prominent cheekbones. Brown hair.

Libra: An oval face, with healthy complexion and good teeth and nails. Brown hair of a rich colour and texture.

Scorpio: Stocky and swarthy. Bright, possibly piercing eyes. Wavy or curly hair.

Sagittarius: Tall and well-developed. Long features and expressive eyes. Brown hair.

Capricorn: Prominent features. A relatively small stature. Dark hair.

Aquarius: A good complexion. Blue eyes and light brown hair.

Pisces: Small of stature, but robust. Pale blue eyes and black hair.

There are a number of types of horoscope, with perhaps the natal form (drawn according to the arrangement of the constellations and heavenly bodies at the time of a given birth) the best known. As an insight to order and correspondence, though, the form of the horary horoscope should also be mentioned – just as the horizon and meridian are divided into twelve to identify the various 'houses' that form a horoscope, the twelve hours of each day and each night are here divided with an especial hour for each of the fundamental subjects being probed, namely the person themselves, riches, brethren, parents, children, sickness, marriage, death, religion, magistry, friends and enemies.

Alike the stars and their constellations, the planets are fundamental to astrological systems, and the character of an individual born under their influence is said to be imbued with something of their nature also:

Moon: One who broods, the introspective. Favourable to the Sun, unfavourable to Mars.

Mercury: One immersed in creativity and the arts. Favourable to Jupiter, unfavourable to Saturn.

Venus: One inclined to love. Favourable to Mars, unfavourable to Saturn.

Sun: One associated with riches. Favourable to Mars, unfavourable to Saturn.

Mars: One associated with war and conflict. Favourable to Venus, unfavourable to the Moon and Mercury.

Jupiter: One who is innately honourable. Unfavourable to Mars.

Saturn: One linked to accident and tragedy, potentially death.

Echoing Plato, the German Dominican Albertus Magnus believed that the planets shape all that can be divined, while the Normandy-born astronomer and Cabbalist Guillaume Postel (1510 – 1581 C.E.) wrote that the Hebrew letters themselves can be seen among the heavens, serving as omnipresent signatures of that divine, creative wisdom that number, form and word were accepted to be.

Such was the credit afforded to astrology that it was not anathematized by the Catholic Church like so many other forms of magic and divination. Far from it, as common depictions of the heavens and the zodiac placed Christ at the centre and so were applied frequently within Christian art and architecture, such as on baptismal fonts. With the planets and stars those fixed and immutable bodies that linked humanity and the heavens, Christ here became the symbolic chain of being that stretched betwixt the two spheres.

Empires, governments and royalty had sought the wisdom of astrology and its talented augurs to shape matters of diplomacy and conflict aside wholly personal affairs, and the likes of William Shakespeare included the subject in plays due to its familiarity, if not outright popularity, with much of his collective audience, as in 1602's *'Troilus and Cressida'*: 'The heavens themselves, the planets and this centre, Observe degree, priority and place, Insisture, course, proportion, season, form, Office, and custom, all in line of order.'

Use of stars and the planets to unravel symbolic knowledge

and prognosticate over affairs of the individual, country and civilization was in its earliest days the stuff of the scholar and interconnected somewhat with pursuits like alchemy, medicine and of course astronomy, though the once lofty and ubiquitous presence of astrology nonetheless declined rapidly as scientific knowledge and hard-edged empiricism became de rigueur; what had at points shaped the destiny of nations became at best a frivolity, if it was acknowledged at all.

The case for the mantic arts was not aided by the sheer scale of forms it had long taken, whether reading facial features (physiognomy), the lines of the forehead (metoposcopy), moles or scars (naeviology), hands (chiromancy), or even, as attested by the astrologer Michael Scot (1170 – 1232 C.E.) one's sneezes! Dreams, the casting of lots (sortilege), the spinning of a sieve (coscinomancy), the cake that cannot be swallowed by a guilty party (aleuromancy) and the sprouting of onions (cromniomancy) are still further attempts to unravel hidden truths and fortunes that may have been more palatable than the disembowelling of sheep or the observation of smoke as a person was burned to death, but they exposed the act of divination to mockery as the masses became more articulate, informed and less prone to superstition.

It goes without saying that divination did not simply disappear as a relic of the past, and even today there are earnest and vocal supporters of its cause, but the ever-more focused efforts of science to deconstruct and understand illnesses and cures, body, mind, the network of life within the elements, space and beyond – not to mention the greater understanding of the movement of planets and lives of stars – all relegated this form of 'signature' to the position of a pastime, or an exercise in escapism.

There is no doubt that observations and discoveries were made, so too associations of symbols and correspondences, that remain of meaning and importance to the 21st century mindset, but the acceptance and belief in one single pattern of life emanating from a creative source and imparting the cosmos with something of its nature, then again inscribing esoteric truths in the fabric of existence, is no longer even seen to be a luxury, but an outright delusion.

That said, the mystical approach which perceives very real proof for an individual of a 'cosmic web' uniting all, a chain of being uniting the corporeal to the spiritual or a simple sense of 'oneness' still exists. So too does a search for further laws of nature, which – whether through holy design or simply the necessary limitations of the human mind – recognises patterns across its experience. And even where the intellect frequently denies any plausibility to the pattern glimpsed, there are still many who see the complexities of the ancient correspondences and feel awe, or who look to the stars or minutiae of nature and cannot help but feel that there is an order apparent that simply cannot be overlooked, even if it cannot be fully revealed.

Applications

The language of alchemy is most certainly symbolism but even a cursory study of its texts and teachings, however obliquely expressed, exposes the overarching belief that correspondences are a ubiquitous and vital aspect of existence. The Greek *'Poimandres'* or *'Divine Pimander'* states: 'Before the visible universe was formed its mold was cast. This mold was called the Archetype, and this Archetype was in the Supreme Mind long before the process of creation began.'

The concept of the Monad producing thought and then form is thus introduced, linking this text with earlier Cabbalistic works and the teachings of Pythagoras: 'The darkness below, receiving the hammer of the Word, was fashioned into an orderly universe. The elements separated into strata and each brought forth living creatures. The Supreme Being – the Mind – male and female, brought forth the Word.'

As creations from the one source, all in existence thus shares origin and substance, even if the degree of the latter can vary greatly – and, by extension, the keys to unlocking one form for another through a transformation are all around us, if only a given substance can be sufficiently refined and re-modelled. This is the core belief at the heart of alchemy, whether the substance being sought is gold or Pure Spirit.

The '*Tabula Smaragdina*' or '*Emerald Tablet*' of the 2nd – 3rd century B.C.E. is perhaps the single-best known and most succinct statement on the Hermetic art, and declares with disarming clarity the role that 'correspondence' plays in any work of alchemy: 'Tis true without lying, certain and most true. That which is below is like that which is above & that which is above is like that which is below to do the miracle of the one thing....The Sun is its father, the moon its mother, the wind hath carried it in its belly, the earth its nurse. The father of all perfection in ye whole world is here...So was ye world created.'

The irony implied by many alchemical treatises is that the transmutation of one substance to another is actually a simple act, if only the blinkers and wilful ignorance of humanity can be removed, which is a central teaching in the New Testament of the Bible and other faiths, notably in Matthew 13:15: 'For this people's heart is waxed gross, and their ears are dull of hearing, and their eyes they have closed; lest at any time they should see with their eyes, and hear with their ears, and should understand with their heart...' The means for change (and salvation) are there to perceive, if only men and women are able to sever the binds of base passions and drives...and the ingredients for change surround us in every form we see around us (and those, too, that we do not).

Cosmic forces permeate and affect humanity and spirit lies at the core of the higher self – alchemy strives to reduce the corporeal and invigorate it to such an extent that a total transformation is realised, but this magnum opus relies on a sound understanding of the unity at the heart of all, be it number, form, the elements, the cosmos and any symbolism that they are broached with. Knowing the true self is part of this, and the acceptance that any meaningful search must start within, as it was explained by the Polish alchemist Michael Sendivogius (1566 – 1636 C.E.): '...the soul in man, the lesser world or microcosm...is the king.'

A similar concept underpinned the theory and practise of magic, which had developed an ever-increasing system of correspondences not dissimilar to the central ideas of Robert Fludd that was informed by Cabbalism and widely disseminated through works like Cornelius Agrippa's *'Three Books of Occult Philosophy'* where the author summed up the chain of being concept and all other esoteric practises more succinctly than any other, citing Plato: '...all is in all.'

Agrippa, like many others of his time, firmly held that man was created as a miniature of God, with the world made to human proportions. Every facet of humankind was imbued with the various emanatory substances of God, and the efforts of man to become as God through the grasping of these 'higher natures' was the uniting of macrocosm with microcosm, and the very basis of magic.

One clear example of this is his description of a man or woman moving with harmonious gestures as achieving a magical ends, such as curing illness, by recreating something of the cosmic dance; everything is connected and bears an intense relationship with all else. Agrippa's occult philosophy states that the universe expands with the same instincts and aims as man, and that by tapping the forces of the universe man is able to discover extensions of his abilities and expansions of his being (which may be used as an understanding for magical acts such as evocation and invocation).

Ideas of patterns and correspondences have always been integral to the workings of magic. Even where spontaneity is prioritised (as in certain modern forms), the 'association of ideas' that effectively catalogued all manner of connections between matter and spirit, symbol with form and one being or substance to another has long been held to be a powerful tool for practitioners, if only due to the psychological assurance that such collected 'wisdom' affords them; desire forms a goal, will incises the change, but the foundation that this all rests on is the arcane knowledge passed down through the centuries, and correspondences are a large part of that knowledge.

The Sephirothic Tree found many supporters in this arena, with the Golden Dawn in particular applying much of the extant Cabbalistic wisdom to develop their own corpus such as their understanding of the chain of being as a means of spiritual progression:

1: Spark of creation. Unity

2: Father, and giver of the spark. The male principle.

3: Mother, and womb – where the spark gestates. The female principle.

4: Collective unconscious, and the limits of manifestation.

5: Purification / Purging. The direction of will to eliminate the needless elements of self.

6: Sun as sacrifice and re-birth, toward a higher level of existence.

7: Instinct (drive) in the form of passion. Love.

8: Intellect over animal instinct. Perception of form.

9: The receiver, bestowing grosser form. The astral waters and sex energy.

10: The everyday existence. Earth to subconscious, and vice versa.

Where more practical magic is concerned, numbers, forms and shapes with all of their correspondences are readily and frequently applied, not least due to the ancient lineage of ideas associated with them. As we have seen the three of the triangle serves as an image of both unity and trinity, and of course in magic its orientation shows the nature of the work being practised / the positive or negative forces being tapped; it is further held that the three-sides of the triangle represent the 'idea', the 'declaration of intent' and the subsequent form that those two takes.

The two triangles that make up the Seal of Solomon which Levi described as 'the science of all things' are considered to represent the microcosm. The triangle pointing up represents infinite height at its peak and signifies East and West with its inclining lines, while the triangle pointing earthward extends from the realm of tapped energy to the 'abyss', thus the two of them together create a microcosm of all space and time.

Four here represents the totality of existence as it applies to the elements, the fixed signs of the zodiac embodied by man, eagle, lion and bull and the alchemical substances salt, sulphur, mercury and azoth. This is a fixed centre, such as man and woman, where the composite substances that reality is subject to coalesce and find balance. Four of course can have many other meanings depending on the work or philosophy at hand, including the concept of babe, youth, middle-age and old-age as well as the four states of spirit, matter, motion and rest.

Another potent symbol of the microcosm is the five-pointed figure that is the pentagram. With the human form (head and four limbs) reaching to its points, this shape is an especially dynamic one when used for conjuration. Said to be the form of star that led the Magi to the birth of Christ, the five links the four elements with the fifth element of quintessence, suggesting the place of will and/or spirit in the ritual being enacted.

Goethe for one was well-versed in the symbolic power of the pentagram and wrote, in his version of the Faust legend: 'Was it a God who traced this sign which stills the vertigo of my soul…and, in a mystical rapture, unveils the forces of Nature around me? Am I myself a God? All is so clear to me. I behold in these simple lines the revelation of active nature to my soul.' The pentagram thus concentrates the four substances and, through the quintessence, directs will to achieve real change, which is the heart of all magic.

One of the forms of the pentagram has an 'A' as each of the five points, which is an arcane arrangement of the five A's in the word 'Abracadabra.' As a word of magic, this is perhaps the most frequently applied if only due to its adoption within popular culture, but it is sufficiently powerful simply as a result of this widespread usage and the identity it has managed to build within the collective psychology.

The Hebrew phrase 'I will create as I speak' has been cited as the origin for 'Abracadabra', though similar has been suggested with regard Aramaic terms and the Greek/Latin 'Abraxas' which was utilised prolifically by certain Gnostic sects. The truth, however, is that no firm evidence exists to explain the origins of the word, and its earliest use is similarly shrouded in mystery.

One Sammonicus, who was physician to Roman emperors, was potentially the first to record the word in the 2nd century C.E., just as his illustration of it in triangle form for use as a prophylactic amulet is the earliest such reproduction:

```
A B R A C A D A B R A
A B R A C A D A B R
A B R A C A D A B
A B R A C A D A
A B R A C A D
A B R A C A
A B R A C
A B R A
A B R
A B
A
```

This word of power was commonly used to rid a patient of illness, but was apparently also popular more generally to ward off misfortune and maleficia. As a protective amulet it was often inscribed or attached to the outside of properties for exactly that purpose, to the extent that Daniel Defoe felt compelled to comment disparagingly on the efforts of Londoners to avoid the plague in 1665 C.E.

Protection was again the desire where the 'SATOR Square' was instituted. Its earliest incarnation read 'ROTAS' along the top of the square, but most later applications headlined the SATOR; why this would be the case is not fully understood, not least because the exact meanings of the words that compose the square has long been lost to posterity.

The square is a two-dimensional palindrome that can be read the same from the top, from the bottom, from the left, from the right or rotated 180 degrees. There are a number of ideas about the origins and meaning of the words, but none that are by any means conclusive, though a general consensus states that they are the derivates of a proper name that either held significance at the time of the original composition, or one that was created specifically for the square:

```
S A T O R
A R E P O
T E N E T
O P E R A
R O T A S
```

Churches in Europe bear examples of the SATOR square, with some appearing to rearrange the letters to make 'PATER NOS-

TER' and present the talisman in the form of a cross, though its common use was in easing illness, defending cattle against witchcraft and reinvigorating weary travellers. The true meaning may have been long-lost, but its rather profuse application even within churches and cathedra suggests a keen belief in the power of the word, particularly that which bore occult meaning (or at least no commonly-known meaning) or that which could be linked to ancient faith.

Words of power were readily applied among many cultures including the Egyptians who inscribed 'hekan' on tomb walls as well as on scrolls to serve as an ongoing manifestation of power and protection, both for living and dead; the *'Book of the Dead'* as it is commonly known to the West contains twelve chapters discussing words of power, such as those said to transform a person into a crocodile, a hawk and other beast-forms.

The all-powerful Shemhamphorasch, the 72 names of God, was used to create 72 magic circles in *'The Keys of Solomon'* and, from those, 36 talismans that each bore two of the divine names, while the aforementioned seal of Solomon used a circular inscription of sigils to entrap spirits in a specially-constructed bowl, often referred to as a 'Devil Trap.' However, letters and words were commonly used not just because they were believed to contain divine power, but because they made manifest the intent of the sorcerer or witch, just as the Word made manifest the original design of God.

The vital importance and large-scale practical application of correspondences within magic are beyond question, best exemplified by the 'law of sympathy' where like produces like (as with the use of a wax doll to inflict harm on a chosen victim) or like cures like (where a substance believed to be the antipathy of another is used to control or eradicate unwanted effects). Sympathy can rely on simple observation (such as when Paracelsus stated 'Behold the Satyrion root, is it not formed like the male privy parts?' and waxed lyrical as to its properties toward stimulating virility) but can also be applied to immerse a worker of magic into a desired state where specific energies and attributes might be more readily activated.

In this manner we find the association of Saturn with lead and the colour black, both of which suggest density, heaviness and melancholy, if not death. Alternatively, Mercury is linked to quicksilver which suggests energy and pace, and Mars is linked to the iron that is used to forge weaponry, as well as the colour red which denotes anger and blood. Elsewhere iron, being 'from the heavens' is said to ward of demons due to its heavenly source as opposed to their chthonic one, and salt, as a preservative, is believed to ward off demons and other unnatural creatures because theirs is a being that prays on decay.

Correspondences are manifold and they are genuinely meaningful because they impact on all the senses and allow for a shifting of mental states that is unique and of paramount importance for any success to be achieved. Their application can take the form of sound through mantras, music and rhythm as well as the Word which gives form to intent as well, with Agrippa noting of rhythm that it '...alters the celestial influences and changes affections, intentions, gestures, notions, actions and dispositions.'

Smells are an especially potent use of magical correspondence, warding off spirits as well as attracting them, and being used in suffumigation to arouse aspects of mind and personality within the practitioner to the point of intoxication. The following is a brief idea of substances linked to the planetary spheres:

Saturn: Mandrake, opium, sulphur, henbane and asafoetida.

Jupiter: Cedar, ambergris, saffron and aloes wood.

Mars: Blood and hellebore root.

Sun: Cinnamon, frankincense, myrrh and cloves.

Venus: Coral, musk, rose and myrtle.

Mercury: Cinquefoil, narcissus, white sandalwood and wormwood.

Moon: Camphor, menstrual blood, jasmine, mandrake and ginseng.

Vision is something that has already been touched upon, and is a sense that relies heavily on accepted knowledge, such as a belief in the circle serving as a model of the cosmos which demands order within its centre and can be surrounded by God- and angel names to ensure spiritual protection. In a similar vein, the triangle is a definition of finite form and the hexagram is the balance of opposites (fire and water) that can invoke and banish planetary forces.

Colour can play a very significant part in magic, and colour correspondences feature regularly in grimoires and occult philosophies due to the powerful effect that tones of light and shade have on human psychology (such as a concentration on 'red' to link to Mars and with it an impulse of anger or vengeance, if not outright violence). Again and again the importance of mental associations are apparent as they instil a subconscious, 'gut' feeling within an individual that imagination alone is unable to achieve.

The very tools of magic are themselves a visual and psychological aid toward manifestation of a specific intent, thus the wand, dagger, cup and pentacle serve as vehicles of the four elements, the letters of the Tetragrammaton and the suits of the tarot while also being used physically as a conduit within ritual – a target for both psychic energy and the external forces being tapped.

As has been suggested by much of the above, the planets of our solar system are rather exhaustively catalogued within magical rites and remain popular bodies to focus the mind upon, along with any number of the associations linked with them, in order to heighten the energy of the practitioner. With that in mind each of the days of the week have a corresponding planet (Saturday – Saturn; Sunday – the Sun; Monday – the Moon; Tuesday – Mars; Wednesday – Mercury; Thursday – Jupiter; Friday – Venus), and the hours of each day from midnight to midnight have allotted planets whereupon that particular sphere enjoys a more active influence.

We have already seen that number squares have long-existed for each celestial sphere and, from those, their occult signatures have been revealed, but the correct procedure must be followed to invoke the character and energies of each planet, so too the appropriate ingredients for any given ritual – as such we see that the brains of a cat are necessary to appease and grant the energies of Saturn, while the blood of a black cat or of a man can engage the favour of Mars, and the brain of a fox or weasel is a suitable astral offering for Mercury.

Once summoned, the planetary spirits take a variety of forms in-keeping with the traditional image of angels and demons in the Solomonic works and other grimoires: among other guises Saturn may appear as a bearded king riding a dragon, an owl, a sickle or a black garment, the Sun may arrive as a king with a sceptre, riding a lion, a bird, a cock or as a yellow garment, and the Moon enjoys appearances including a king as an archer riding a doe, a female hunter, a cow, a goose, a many-footed creature or a silver garment.

Finally, it is of course vital for the sorcerer to know the appropriate archangels and angels whose bailiwick they are entering, as is sensible within any form of invocation:

Saturday: Cassiel – assisted by Machatan and Uriel – the South Wind.

Sunday: Michael – assisted by Dardiel and Huratapal – the North Wind.

Monday: Gabriel – assisted by Michael and Samael – the West

Wind.

Tuesday: Samael – assisted by Satael and Amabiel – the East Wind.

Wednesday: Raphael – assisted by Miel and Seraphiel – the South-West Wind.

Thursday: Sachiel – assisted by Castiel and Asasiel – the South Wind.

Friday: Anael – assisted by Rachiel and Sachiel – the West Wind.

What can be concluded is that, regardless how complex and varied the correspondences at points became, they did share specific and usually very clear links to the archetypal image that the planet had within occult lore and, partly through that, popular consensus. For workers of magic these correspondences were and are not frivolous, but a means of immersing themselves totally in the essence of any desired body or being, whether that be a planet, a demon or an emanation of God, and even if success results from associations that in reality only exist in the mind of men and women, the success is all that matters.

In magic, correspondences are a means to an end, where the practitioner places him- or herself at the centre of a created universe, harnesses the latent energies within and without themselves and creates a desired link with another or a desired change in the environment – and if the knowledge and application of correspondences aids in the ultimate outcome, then correspondences do indeed exist and serve their purpose, even if their validity is destined to remain occult.

Other writers expounded the use of such associations, but the likes of Aleister Crowley's '777' remains one of the foremost compendiums of correspondences which includes those of Greek, Arabic and Coptic letters and Greek, Roman, Hindu and Scandinavian gods, forms of Buddhist meditations and magical powers and weapons. Crowley himself acknowledges that this vast and interlinking system can be easily denigrated as daydream and fancy, but clearly states that the true import of the correspondences of esoteric lore and magic lies beyond reality, and transcends the human intellect; again, this is an area built on faith as well as knowledge, and the results must speak for themselves.

This remains the key to any appreciation of correspondences today when, in spite of the diminishment of the image of macrocosm / microcosm, the fall of alchemy and magic to a point where they are held to be legerdemain at best, and increased areas of knowledge that have branded belief as myth or outright nonsense, the old associations and with them the ancient symbols retain something of their power over the human imagination, and at times over the human mind itself.

Even if this is the stark truth and much that has been discussed in this chapter now exists as archetype more than an active belief, the distant fears and drives that originally created them and the millennia of study that reconsidered them within ever new frameworks has made them timeless and placeless and so no less transformative. They continue to impinge on our thoughts, hopes and dreams if only from the root of our subconscious – which is perhaps where they have dwelled throughout history, and indeed where they arose from in the first instance.

V: SYMBOLS

The 'cosmic connections' explored through recognised correspondences and signatures have frequently resulted from symbols, on occasion they have been used to create symbols and they ubiquitously rely on them to communicate to a given audience. Indeed, correspondences are inherent within the study of symbols, but at the same time they may only enjoy a superficial and transitory relationship with one another.

This is due to the fact that correspondences represent the often exhaustive responses of man, woman or movement to a stimulus, while symbols (though they certainly can serve the same role) are wholly more succinct, less distinct in terms of any direct meaning and thus universal in their application. Where correspondences join the dots of an idea or experience and wax lyrical thereon, the symbol is an immediate and revelatory thing that instils the initial inspiration.

By extension, where correspondences are the 'microcosm' where investigation and analysis forges knowledge, symbols are that which speaks to the 'macrocosm' that is the higher mind, informing the subconscious and triggering involuntary responses more in line with the creative, imaginative and perhaps spiritual capacities of humanity.

It would be unfair to generalise that the former always enforces a rigid framework through which the world and the cosmos is explored, but correspondences undoubtedly define on an often intellectual level, where symbols impact visually on a personal and emotional level – their affect and meaning expanding with reflection, but in wholly independent directions given a specific time, individual and context.

Semiotics is the applied study of the symbol, which is effectively any sign that communicates a meaning to an audience that is not restricted to, if speaking at all of, the meaning of the sign in itself. Through Greek culture and no lesser personages than Plato and Aristotle, and then later with Augustine of Hippo and John Locke, the idea that symbols are active, immediate and malleable disseminators of profound meaning on the human consciousness has long been believed. The relatively recent efforts of Freud and Jung in psychoanalysis was another perspective on what was therefore an ancient theme, where symbols suggest another level of understanding beyond the everyday, to the extent that symbols themselves could be regarded as something other.

Wheel Of Fortune

As with much that symbols speak of themselves, theories and responses about their importance – and as to exactly what symbols *are* – have recurrently appeared, in cycles, from the earliest eras of human history. What unites these theories regardless their provenance is a recognition of the impact that imagery has on the mind and general consciousness of man and woman, with otherwise ethereal and metaphysical properties and meanings being encapsulated in a more concrete, and relatable, form.

Symbols neatly summarise vast quantities of information, including the cornerstones of world faiths, and impart a sensation of knowing on the observer that may be somewhat changeable and nebulous but is nonetheless penetrative, sometimes to the point of being transformative. Within the realm of the occult, symbols have been applied by exoteric religious frameworks, in arcane alchemical tracts and as sigils and seals in grimoires and works of ceremonial magic to name but a few salient forms, but the power and potency that that they carry remains omnipresent, and a fundamental reason for their use.

The complexity of symbols can be readily identified by considering their use within the ancient Egyptian culture, where they have been said to have been the primary form of thought. 'Medu-Neter' or 'Words of Nature' that effectively make up the hieroglyphic language of Egypt had various aspects reflecting different functions and levels of being; containing at once a 'spiritual' or archetypal element, a potential of the thing being symbolised and a link to the unrealized potential of that thing, each figure of the language also had a name association which alone afforded great power to the object or entity depicted.

Symbols could therefore represent an object, creature or individual, but were also capable of being a manifestation of a god, thus more than one plain of existence could be denoted in one instance, just as more than one meaning could be applied at any one time. We have considered similar in mentioning the 'true' and 'false' names given to all to ensure that one's inner being and innate power would remain hidden and free from misuse at the hands of others (a person therefore known and yet fundamentally aloof on a spiritual level), suggesting the power and malleability of the symbol in declaring and disseminating wisdom without necessarily revealing its whole, or perhaps its true import.

With more than one meaning applicable to each symbol – and the relevance of symbolism within the movements, gestures and sounds of ritual – it is clear that immense flexibility of mind was applied in establishing and developing the hieroglyphic language and its counterparts within Egyptian culture; a similar flexibility is thus much needed in any attempt to unravel meanings when that language is encountered.

One example of this can be found within the use of colour symbolism, which was an integral part of the Egyptian 'lexis'. Black potentially represented the fertile soil of the country as well as the Underworld, neither of which is a psychological stretch for the modern mind, less so if the connection both share with Osiris is acknowledged; a similar logic of thought applies to the application of turquoise, which might suggest the sun, the dawn, funerary rights and the process of re-birth.

Green was understandably linked to vegetation, and through that was associated with the skin of Osiris, which in turn carried connotations of rebirth and regeneration, while red bore recognisable links to fire and blood and therefore also to life and death. Somewhat more esoteric connections were established for silver, however, which was said to represent the bones of the gods, and for gold which alongside use for depictions of the sun was utilised as the flesh of the gods. The precious lapis lazuli was a composite symbol with its blue signifying the ground and its gold flecks suggesting the stars.

Elsewhere, there can be more immediately discernible roots for developed symbols such as with certain planetary signs as used in ancient papyri (where Saturn and Jupiter equate to monogram images of the letters from their Greek names, and Mercury is in an elaborated form of caduceus). The more widely-recognised zodiacal symbols in use today largely date from the Renaissance, but these were forms developed from classical sources and so there was a degree of continuity which maintained certain logical links between the symbol and that which it symbolised.

Often, though, the use of symbols is of the Egyptian variety where there is distinct multi-valency in application, such as within the traditional Chinese system where few represent natural objects and most are composites where a graphic image is united with an associated link to the phonetic, essentially suggesting how the name or title of the represented figure should be pronounced. Even where there is a practical reason for the various meanings inherent to a symbol, the result is an image of exceptional and singular dynamism that represents something of a 'polysymbolic' existence or reality – there is more than one meaning, and so more than one truth supposedly being revealed.

At the purest level symbols are *experienced*, following which their meaning and impact can be internalised before any real sense of interpretation is achieved, and even then that interpretation can consist of a sub- or supra-conscious understanding rather than any overt external statement. As such dreams and visions are often the domain of the symbol, where the esoteric realms of mind and consciousness exert their especial influence and the means of communication and understanding are wholly more malleable than that of our waking consciousness.

The experienced symbol is supposedly ruminated on in ways that we do not comprehend let alone understand, and so the prominence of dream analysis is unsurprising where the reading of symbolism is concerned. This is even more readily the case where the work of Freud and Jung concludes that symbols in dreams are the result of efforts of the mind to restore a form of psychological balance and 'psychic equilibrium' from the chaos of waking life, including the relentless intake of information, emotion and any resulting complexes and neuroses – symbols both create and result from subconscious interpretation, as their 'language' is singularly-suited to the acquiescent rather than the rigid, and so to the suggestive realm of dream rather than the comparably clinical light of the everyday.

The combination of atavistic response, subconscious rumination and no small degree of imagination means that even the most routine of events can ultimately have a profound effect on the human mind, its behaviours and certainly its philosophy and faith, on an individual and collective scale (the latter of which Jung most certainly believed). The fact that a symbol can be raised to a new level from all of this and used as a tool with which to stir further responses, imaginings and belief is all the more moving, attesting to a rare power that symbols can innately bear.

A more apparently 'concrete' symbol can thus come to represent what is otherwise an abstract concept or reality, concentrating the mind of the initiate who truly understands what is being denoted while also stirring the senses and deeper recesses of the total novice. More than this, a symbol used in the appropriate manner can suggest a wealth of ideas and ideals that may not necessarily exist at all in any organised and workable capacity, a point that is arguably proved through the rose and cross of the Rosicrucian movement where the symbolised union of opposites served as a clarion call for a form of spiritual revolution that certainly made an impact (and still does, to this day) without any actual movement of that name requiring existence.

A symbol, serving as an emotional commodity as much as an intellectual one (again suggesting the importance of our relationship with them in dreams where we are at our most suggestible and responsive) impacts on the mind, stimulating feelings and responses that little can rival. Where the initiate might perceive a language or 'algebra' by which thought is guided through the otherwise incomprehensible, the ignorant nonetheless feel a power through mere suggestion, that herein there is collective wisdom, or at the very least an individual's revelation.

It should also be noted that, alike the grand symbology of

the Sephirothic Tree, symbols are not a static and/or historic form of understanding, but an ever-expanding and growing mode of thought that cannot be delimited or clearly defined. Symbols are constantly evolving, both within themselves and in relation to one another, and maintain immense historical meaning while remaining immediate and active, to be held, explored and manipulated within the consciousness of the individual who experiences them; in this light, the idea of the emanations of a creator, or the world (and ourselves) as thought-forms of a god are wholly appropriate, as that in some respects are what symbols are to us.

Rene Guinon (1886 – 1951 C.E.) was an influential thinker on the subject of symbols and their use, whose interest in Hinduism, Taoism, Sufism and Islam (the latter of which led to an eventual citizenship of Egypt) certainly informed his appreciation of the expansive symbol over that which he deemed to be of more far more limited meaning.

For Guinon, the occult groups of his time were misguided in their 'syncretistic' use of symbols whereby a traditional form was employed with a specific meaning or import in mind, and thus without any regard for a greater and more holistic 'truth' that stood behind it. In this understanding, movements like the Theosophists maintained close affinities with fundamental symbols but only recognised a fraction of their total meaning, resulting in a loss of depth that in turn disseminated but a refracted and much-diminished teaching.

Symbols, rather, required a form of 'synthesis' alike that which Guinon recognised in the use of the cross, which might be presented in various guises with specific meanings for a number of peoples, but never loses its true 'unity of meaning', that underlying principle which the form of the cross represents. This is a cornerstone of Guinon's understanding of the symbol, in that a pure example of the type is at once a source of knowledge and spiritual epiphany – with the source meaning and wisdom retained and not diminished through any misguided changes or modern innovations.

Symbolism is here a 'metaphysical language' beyond measure, delivering a total understanding of all to the total being of man and woman, in comparison to the limited and limiting written form which defines and regulates to the point of sterility and emptiness. Plaudits are given to the East where this mode of thinking has remained accessible and imminent, while the West is regarded as lost, to an extent, in its own created limitations and the symbolic has become an alien and misunderstood form (including, for Guinon, the psychological interpretations of Carl Jung).

Both the glory and the danger of symbols is in their acquiescent nature – at once revelatory and ambiguous they thrive where they are experienced again and again, within countless new contexts and frames of reference, but this in itself allows for what might be seen as misuse (unless this is accepted as an innate quality of the symbol that is natural to its dynamic and shifting form). In the same vein lists of correspondences can be linked to one or more symbols that appear to concretise any meaning but which might instead limit any worth.

There is a degree of this thinking in the work of the theologian Paul Tillich (1886 – 1965 C.E.), who held that where symbols maintained an active meaning for people they were effectively 'living', but that they could die where that meaning waned or was forgotten. He made the striking point in recognising the danger of a symbol coming to be idolised over and above the 'thing' that it is meant to represent, echoing some of Guinon's concern for wayward interpretations of symbols that lose their heart, or core, due to misguided or misleading interpretations. However, Tillich as much as Guinon recognised the potential power of the symbol as that by which the deeper recesses of being and the more remote levels of reality might be glimpsed and experienced.

The Hindu philosopher Ananda K Coomaraswamy (1877 – 1947 C.E.) succinctly stated that the symbolic is 'the act of thinking in images' and, similar to Rene Guinon, focused much thought on modes of thinking and communication that existed before writing became preponderant. For Coomaraswamy the more traditional symbols harked back to a point in time where the usual means of transmission of knowledge relied on imagery rather than words, therefore symbols offered insight into genuinely ancient responses and reflections on existence.

Like many of his cohort in this sphere of study, he held that with increasing reliance on words in place of images, vital depths and extents of meaning had long been lost that remained inherent within the schema of symbolism but had been warped beyond recognition through the derogation of the idea of the image. In this manner the more purposive and intrinsic metaphysical mode of thought had given way to the blinkered and limited language of philosophy, which resulted in the broader impoverishment of the human condition (not dissimilar to Rene Guinon's embracing the Eastern worldviews over their Western counterparts).

Coomaraswamy suggested that symbols were intended to relay ideas and concepts rather than instil an emotion, and so much of myth, religion, folklore and indeed art made use of core symbology to achieve a specific end and disseminate beliefs. He noted that a great many examples of these common themes/symbols exist within everything from world faiths to fairy tales, including the idea of primordial waters, great floods, symbolism of the sun and of the wheel, symbolism of snakes, so too that of birds as psychopomps, the figure of the hermaphrodite as a unity of opposites and meanings linked to the sacred tree and its like (in both standard and inverted forms).

The core of the idea here is that certain concrete beliefs/actions were immortalised in symbol so as to propagate and spread the knowledge held, and that – in spite of various different reconstitutions through religious divergences and the apparent excesses of folklore – those same concrete origins were long maintained, until symbols became seen as abstract and, in some instances, nothing more than their own image or figure. To return to a means of thinking where the symbol communicates its truth is to return to an earlier and, some might argue purer, state of being that would re-establish a long-lost balance to the individual being, as well as to its relation to others and the collective consciousness of humanity.

In a more general sense this returns us to the domain of the psychoanalyst, however we might judge their conclusions, as the consensus holds that to be separated from the language of symbols, their meaning and the responses that they stir within us is to separate the conscious from the subconscious entirely, if not the waking mind from the soul. This is the stuff of neurosis, aberration and, at its extreme, total mental-breakdown as a core aspect of the self has been effectively banished and thus lacks a vital component of what it in truth is; alongside the knowledge of 'wisdom' we lose the means to communicate it or to even recognise it as wisdom if glimpsed, resulting in symbols being experienced as fantasy at best, or as downright nightmare at worst.

Paul states in Colossians 1:16 'For by him were all things created, that are in heaven, and that are on earth, visible and invisible...' and the idea of constants emanating from central cosmic or divine points and offering insight to ourselves and the wider world is a compelling one that offers some solace to that creative, imaginative and spiritual aspect of our make-up that wastes away to naught if left to logic, rationality and everyday experience. If symbols represent another level of reality which we are, by simply existing, a part of, then they are part of what we are, and to lose them totally would be a devastating point in our evolution.

Mircea Eliade frequently argued the importance of the idea of the 'centre' to man, woman and culture (be that the temple at the centre of a town or city, the city or country where one lives as the centre of civilization or faith, or the simple act of placing oneself at the centre of everything else in existence as the sole means of gaining any frame of reference).

Eliade noted that symbols were a means of integrating one 'fragment' of being (humankind) into the All that can be perceived and believed to exist – the relationship is innate as everything, including humankind, constitutes one Whole, and so as a means to knowing the 'total self' and finding a degree of understanding as to where we or 'I' fit into the cosmos, symbols are of paramount importance.

This brings us to the concept of fundamental 'ideas' and 'archetypes', to which this entire study owes a debt of gratitude. Though at points tangential to the subject of symbols, it is vital that we consider it as it underlines the at points ancient attempt to identify pure truth from the mere perception of truth, which is a fundamental concern within the study of symbols and will continue to raise its head as we consider the forms, faiths and applications that have been built for centuries around many central and ubiquitous forms.

Plato's doctrine of 'Ideas' states that there can be various forms of a thing which share a common nature, and while the individual forms are temporal and many, the root nature or Idea which they share is timeless and universal. Simply put, we instantly recognise a dog or a tree as a dog or a tree in spite of the countless varieties that we encounter – and it is the shared Idea of 'dogness' or 'treeness' which we recognise as uniting them that is ultimately real.

It is a common theme in Plato's work that knowledge is innate, and so while we can learn through experience, we must apply rigid analysis and introspection to fully discover and understand any absolute truth from that experience; the living world *exemplifies*, but we must essentially dig down within ourselves in order to realise *truth* and *knowledge*. Plotinus followed this train of thought and championed the idea over mere matter, and likewise the soul over the body, as the means of knowing harmony and a good life; to be enamoured by the corporeal to the extent that it is taken as true reality is to embrace disharmony and evil.

The symbol thus takes on something of a prestigious role when it is combined with the concept of the archetype, which was expounded by the likes of Cicero, Pliny and Augustine of Hippo among many others. Cicero (106 – 43 B.C.E.) aired a thought akin to that of Plato and Plotinus when he stated: '...the creator of the world did not fashion these things directly from himself, but...from archetypes outside himself' and it was the 'archetype' that came to strongly represent the Truth so vital to Platonic, Neo-Platonic and, much later, Jungian systems of thought.

For Jung, the archetype is the aforementioned innate knowledge which can be rediscovered within us through the correct processes of self-analysis, a counterpoint to instinct in that it is a timeless repository of wisdom holding intensely personal meaning, while existing as a product of the collective unconscious of humanity. Archetypes, like symbols, are beyond time and context – they result from and direct human action and understanding, even where they are not consciously recognised, as they represent the sum of all knowledge.

Archetypes, however, hold specific meanings for each man and woman, just as they enjoy specific and unique relationships with each being given the environment and broader context that they exist within. The prominence of particular archetypes within one's consciousness can suggest the level of individuation, with disharmony and a troubled relationship with the self (and thus the world around the self) resulting from a lack thereof.

Jung later expanded his theory of archetypes to the point that they are seen to exist within the human psyche but also as a 'psychoid' entity that has an existence beyond the levels of the ordinary human consciousness. Here, the archetype is a singularly metaphysical thing which lies beyond our ken but forms innate tendencies of action and repeated patterns of thought and behaviour; it links 'true reality' with the everyday world of matter, and serves as a means of passage to the unifying truth that underlies all in existence. Little greater prominence could be afforded to the concept of the archetype, nor those recurring images within myth, faith and magic that appear to again and again arise to represent otherwise intangible knowledge that is perceived as being spiritual or divine in nature.

Hermit

Individual examples of these forms may have less lofty pedigrees than those of Jung's archetypes, but they are instantly recognisable and sufficiently commonplace within both exoteric and esoteric frames of reference to suggest an impressive lineage and, through that and its applications, a rather profound influence on the human mind. A consideration of a select few symbols is sufficient to demarcate the depth and breadth of meaning that is covered, as well as the frequent connections between forms that tell us almost as much about the central and recurrent questions – and responses – inherent to humankind.

Graphics have often been used to offer a somewhat clearer and more explicit meaning than many symbols, and are all the more suitable to the task of dissemination and stimulation given their relative economy of form:

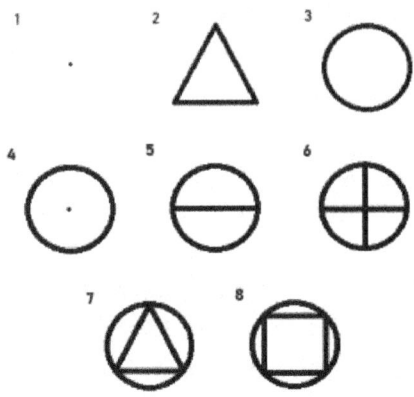

1 Unity. The point of origin.

2 Form. The state of evolution.

3 Infinity; totality.

4 First cause. Emanation (link to the point of origin).

5 Movement. Separation of waters from heavens.

6 Elements (on the microcosmic scale); spirit (on the macrocosmic scale).

7 The spirit within the All.

8 The material within the All.

One ancient and common symbol is that of the tree, which in one ubiquitous facet is the 'world tree' that is a model of all creation. It of course appears within Jewish and Christian scripture as the 'Tree of Life' in the Book of Genesis, where the tree also serves as a cornerstone of the Fall from Paradise, as the 'Tree of Knowledge' from which Eve takes the forbidden fruit, and is also apparent as the Nordic world tree of Yggdrasil where it is a huge ash tree that is the centre of creation and a highly venerated body which houses various supernatural beings.

World trees, however, enjoy a much wider prominence and can be found in forms within the folklore and mythology of North Asia, the ancient Tengrism of the Mongols, the Siberian Samoyeds and the Maya, Aztecs, Mixtecs and Olmecs (among others) of Mesoamerica. Common in many depictions of the world tree is its place at the centre of existence, and its role as a form of pillar or axis mundi where the four directions meet, and the 'ladder' extends between the realms from Underworld, through creation and up to the heavens.

There are of course exceptions and more singular applications of trees within mythology and ritual, such as the pine being associated with Attis and the oak being linked to Jupiter and holding especial significance for the Celts, but the frequent application of the tree focuses on it serving as a model of the cosmos, and as either a symbol of existence or the stages of growth/development and immortality.

The Sephirothic Tree certainly utilises the tree-image as a symbol of microcosm to macrocosm, so too the cosmic ladder of ascent and descent (with the roots often depicted as being in heaven, the trunk passing through the realms of divine emanation and the limbs and fruits of the tree being that which finds existence on the corporeal level). This idea of the inverted tree was not unique to Cabbalism, and H.P. Blavatsky suggested that the pyramids had been constructed with this image in mind.

Elsewhere the Upanishads name the branches of the great tree as those of the four elements and aether (the composition of matter and the quintessence that binds all together), while Yggdrasil is depicted with nine branches that, similar to the Sephirothic Tree, represent the various spheres of existence that are encompassed within a tenth.

The form of the tree lends itself somewhat readily to the concept of matter and spirit / birth, life and re-birth among other progressive trends, just as the ladder and sacred mountain. The tree perhaps offers more grist for the symbolic mill, however, and we find the roots frequently associated with the primal and chthonic dragon or snake, the trunk with the lion or stag of elevation and aggression, and the limbs with the bird which, again, frequently serves as the psychopomp that bears the soul to the next, and higher, realm.

With the tree as a cross we are offered a symbol of redemption that suggests a potential for everlasting life, while as an image of life and death there is, once more, the possibility of immortality, though here with a degree of risk in that the true path can be difficult to comprehend, and the wrong paths are numerous – it is no accident that Romanesque decoration often employed vines of 'entanglement' – when we recognise that the idea of the forest suggests chaos, the wild and unknown that can devour the unwary or ignorant who search for lost glory, as well as the Mother- or feminine principle and the subconscious (the shaded land where the canopy fails to allow the sun to penetrate).

In spite of the potential hazards, though, the tree of knowledge offers stimulation and wisdom of self toward personal growth, so too a higher level of insight and revelation, thus the risks may well be said to be outweighed by the possible benefits. The key is to only enter the arena of growth, knowledge and transition armed with sufficient wiles and awareness to offer the chance of success; the ignorant will become ensnared in base passions, daydreams and material distraction and will lose any meaningful sense of self along the way.

The tree can also be the spine (both micro- and macrocosmically speaking) around which winds the snake that we previously found at its roots. The unwound serpent-and-tree motif is representative of mind and the temptation toward knowledge, while the serpent can here also suggest the spiral which equates to the principle of cosmic energy and creation, and through those rotation and outward expansion. The unravelling of this serpent from the tree is the activation of Kundalini which further links to the third eye that is capable of sight beyond the material (and which Jung linked to the Egyptian Uraeus).

Indeed, serpents enjoy even greater usage as symbols than trees, from the divine energy of Kundalini to the popular image of the Ouroboros where the snake/dragon/bird or hybrid of these creatures serves as a figure of time, existence and immortality. With one notably early use of this symbol dating to the *'Codex Marcianus'* of the $10^{th}/11^{th}$ centuries C.E., it can appear as a two-tone, black and white symbol representing unity within duality, but always serves as a powerful image of self-fecundity and the passage from the source, through a cycle of existence and thence back to that original source.

Where we reject unity from duality, the snake is the figure of treachery and seduction, as in Chinese thought where the serpent can appear as a female or male influence. The snake promises wisdom but may deliver only lies and deception, among those who badly wish to believe its deceit because it appeals to the basest instincts of the human being, a tradition perhaps best-known within Biblical scripture such as Isaiah 27:1 ('that crooked serpent') and Revelation 12:9 ('And the great dragon was cast out, that old serpent called the Devil').

The influence and character of the snake largely revolves around the issue of its duality / unity, and one's attitude towards 'worldly knowledge', sexual energies and the revelation of self. Where its wisdom was regarded balefully within the Bible, the Greek Python – the chthonic god that bestowed prophecy to its Priestesses through rising fumes from its lair – was the means of ascension for the individual to a higher level of being. Revelation from and to the realm of the 'unconscious' was the reward for those in communion with Python (clearly symbolised through the composite imagery of the snake, the 'below', the void and the female principle), which might be dangerous to the uninitiated but was genuinely epiphanic to those gifted with true vision.

Quetzalcoatl was the feathered snake that represented the raising of one's consciousness and regeneration and elsewhere, too, the snake is resurrection (in that it sheds its skin and is 'renewed'), and frequently appears as a symbol of spirit over matter and metempsychosis. As with the application of the serpent to the unifying quality of the Ouroboros, the association of the snake with immortality, revelation and with pure energy (similar to electricity), all suggests an ambivalent nature that is deep-rooted and natural, beyond the petty characteristics of good and evil. It is a force waiting to be tapped, and the result of any interaction with it reflects the character of the communicant and not that of the serpent.

The dragon is, of course, the 'great serpent' that as a mythological image represents a more grandiose nature and qualities, though the application of the Greek 'drakon' to both dragons and serpents in general suggests that they are somewhat fluid as symbolic constructs and interchangeable, depending on the context.

Where the dragon is most widely-recognised is as a fantastic beast and monster, or the formidable adversary which we encounter frequently in the New Testament of the Bible such as with Daniel 7:7 ('...I saw in the night visions, and behold a fourth beast, dreadful and terrible, and strong exceedingly; and it had great iron teeth: it devoured and brake in pieces, and stamped the residue with the feet of it: and it was diverse from all beasts that were before it; and it had ten horns...') and Revelation 12:3 (And there appeared another wonder in heaven; and behold a great red dragon, having seven heads and ten horns, and seven crowns upon his heads'). Often linked to Leviathan, this Biblical dragon is indeed nightmarish, the archetypal enemy that must be overcome.

Hesiod's *Theogony* offers a similar vision to that of any appearance of a dragon in the Bible, in the form of Typhon: '...there grew a hundred snakes' heads, those of a dragon, and the heads licked with dark tongues...' Zeus battles Typhon and eventually buries the vanquished foe under Mount Etna, though from the beast rises further hellish progeny like Chimera, Ladon (the guardian of the golden apples of immortality later battled by Hercules) and Hydra (another opponent of Hercules that itself offered serpent/dragon heads that were self-regenerating).

The tale of Beowulf offers a shade of Typhon with its '...scaly, malicious Worm which seeks out funeral mounds and flies burning through the night, wrapped about with flame' that the hero battles with and dies alongside, suggesting the place of sacrifice (and therefore resurrection and immortality) within the wider concept of the dragon-beast.

Among religious texts, the *'Rig Veda'* (c. 1000 B.C.E.) tells of Indra overcoming Vitra (the beast that has sealed up all the waters of the earth) not once, but on a cyclical basis which ensures the return of the life-giving water, which includes the sap of vegetable life and the blood of animals and men, to the world of the living. We also see the Babylonian Marduk slaying the dragon Tiamat – symbol of chaos and the primordial waters – that was split to form the heaven and the earth. Though the idea of Tiamat having taken the form of a dragon is now disputed, the correspondence of the story and its meaning with other global examples is compelling.

A converse application of the dragon as chaos is found where it represents the 'status quo', the restrictive and limiting 'norm' which must be overcome to establish a change and then growth / expansion. In this form we find dragons as the 'keeper of the past' that jealously guard and hold on to tradition and accepted truths; the Hero is the individual that has *become*, forging through battle that which is *becoming*. He is the embodiment of actualisation, deconstructing reality in order to re-integrate it and create a new phase of being, or a new 'reality.'

Apollo, Perseus, Siegfried and St. George all represent facets of this at once cosmic and personal battle, where the sword or staff (the active principle or Monad) slays the dragon of Form (Tetrad) to create the Pentad, the unification of the elements and the prominence of spirit over matter. In the parlance of psychoanalysis it takes the Hero to acknowledge the shadow within, which is the darker aspect of the self, and assimilate this into his or her own consciousness – the application of developed ego over regression which forces us to understand all that we are in order to find peace and the means to progress.

St. Margaret of Antioch offers an interesting example of this process, though of course here within a decidedly Christian framework: when she resisted the temptations offered by the Devil he transformed himself into a dragon and swallowed her, only to explode and leave her unscathed, and unshakable in her faith. The serpent of temptation here segues into the consuming beast, which is another common form of adversary that links to other traditional mythologies of 'the dark night of the soul', of which Jonah is a paradigm.

The dragon is therefore the tyrant and hoarder, the consumer (like the basilisk) and egotist, but it also serves as the guardian of arcane and profound knowledge, and regularly features as an image of initiation (potentially due to its being a beast of air, earth and water and so suggestive of a mastery over the elements and, therefore, over the mundane sphere). A dragon is the state of ignorance that guards the Golden Fleece of enlightenment, just as the dragon Fafnir guards the gold of the dwarfs while bearing in his blood miraculous qualities (which results in Siegfried being able to understand the language of birds). One of the grades of Freemasonry requires that the dragon Typhon, of passion and anger, be slain through the wielding of the 'flaming sword' which is 'universal truth'.

For the Chinese the conquered dragon is a mark of imperial

power and, by extension, the male yang principle, fertility, the East and the sunrise. Within feng-shui it offers a form of cosmic energy akin perhaps to Kundalini, where it is understood to represent the flowing energy patters that are the undercurrents of creation (with 'lung mei' or 'dragon lines' noting their network of power) which again can be interpreted or, rather, utilised, in positive and negative forms but which cannot be said to be innately of either nature.

Elsewhere the dragon is linked to Mars due to its perceived aggression and poisonous quality, and Saturn (alongside other creatures including the wolf, mule, toad and of course the serpent) due to its solitary bent and melancholy. However, where the dragon most readily finds symbolic expression is within its form of the beastly adversary or shadow self, with the threat of death or deconstruction ever-present, yet the potential of wisdom, growth, transformation and immortality tantalisingly within the grasp of the brave Hero.

Few symbols epitomise the concept of resurrection and transformation as succinctly as the cross, but there are copious forms of cross and even more applications of them within religious and esoteric doctrine, of which the following are but a choice selection:

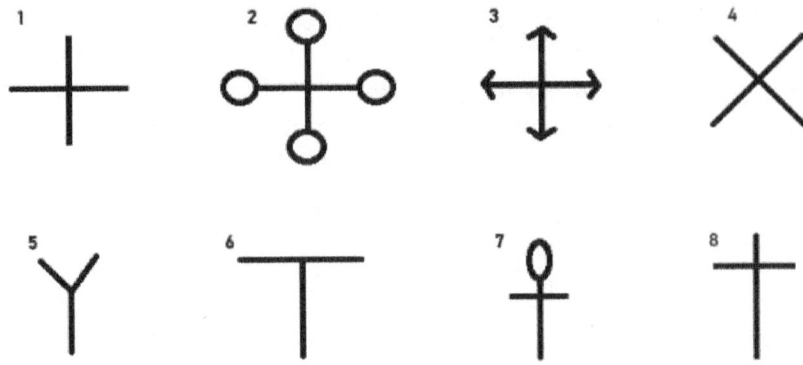

1 Direction: In terms of navigation, the earth and heaven; also time and space. Conjunction and unity, but also antagonism and martyrdom. The path to reunion.

2 Cardinal points.

3 Centrifugal forces.

4 St. Andrew's Cross: The union of upper and lower worlds. Plato's *'Timaeus'* states that this was the form of the sutures that were used to knit the world soul back together. Also 'X' as 10, which was perfection to the Pythagoreans.

5 Of common use within medieval systems, for the division of forms and/or substances. Duality and choice, from one single point of origin.

6 The Tau Cross: The equilibrium of opposites. Used by the American Indians, the Mesoamericans and the Druids, the latter of whom would cut branches from an oak tree and secure one across the trunk of an oak to form the symbol. CHiram Abiff, the legendary architect to the Freemasons, was given a hammer in the form of the Tau, and the T-square commemorates this.

7 The ankh: Represents the composite form of the sun/sky/earth, as well as the head/arms/body. The Ancient Egyptians buried an ankh with deceased kings to depict the energising power of the life essence (as the 'Crux Ansata' or 'Cross of Life'). Images depicting the ankh emerging from mouths of the king are similarly representative of the ' life-bestowing'energy. The form of the ankh was similar to that of the 'hydrometer' that Egyptians used to measure the inundations of the Nile, which also served as a symbol of consciousness, life and growth. The ankh was linked to the water gods of the Babylonians, and to immortality by the Scandinavians.

8 The Christian Cross: A form suggesting the ternary of the higher aspects mastering the quaternary, with the horizontal arms nearer the apex of the cross than to the base.

On a macrocosmic level the cross can represent the cardinal points, the four elements and the directions of space and time, with the essential unifying point of origin at the centre, which is likewise the case where the cross is a representation of the world axis. In a similar vein the cross symbolises a state of embodiment, with its centre serving as the source from which creation springs, or the individual self around which the material form takes shape.

Inherent to this symbol is a certain 'antagonism of being', which is clearly depicted by the four arms of the cross that denote opposing or divergent forces that can certainly be linked to a return to the source but which often suggest an outward expansion (toward a greater distancing of the constituent parts). This antagonism of being lends itself to the cross as a symbol of crucifixion, which itself represents modes of suffering, sacrifice and deliverance that is found within the stories of Prometheus, Apollo, Bacchus, the Buddha, Osiris, Horus, Indra and Quetzalcoatl to name just some instances.

In the state of crucifixion the cross can represent existence and its source, upon which the agony of crucifixion is the state of corporeality; we are presented with a fixed status that can only deliver pain as it is a limited condition. A similar state can be perceived within the symbolic use of 'dismemberment' which also graces numerous myths and faiths, which is ultimately a process of sacrifice, deconstruction and re-birth, seen in the story of Osiris (who was torn into fourteen pieces) as well as Bacchus (who was torn into seven pieces by the Titans).

This is unity become form, and from that a dispersal of the parts so that a refined and purer new form can take its place – as such a dismemberment of the dragon is, within alchemical works, the separation of the elements in an effort to purify and raise their core, divine nature, and the shaman often experiences a form of 'dispersal' of self as the spirits and gods bestow the gifts of true vision and mediumship.

Much of this concern for unity, as well as the symbology of a world tree, returns again and again to meditations on the point of origin, as well as the 'centre', be that in relation to an individual, a tribe, a culture or the microcosm. The centre is the point of reference around which all else revolves, and so we frequently find sets of beliefs and religions that identify their own sacred sites, or significant countries within their faith, as that of the centre-point.

Sacred mountains serve this purpose, so to the ziggurats that replicated the mountain as a man-made ladder to the divine. Babylonians recognised their land as that where the divine had chosen to manifest into the world, while Jerusalem is cited as the centre (with its Temple, as with the ziggurat, held to be the spiritual heart of that centre). China has been afforded similar prestige and importance, and it has been common for Chinese houses to have an opening at their apex to serve as a 'window to heaven', the land being so connected with the celestial.

On a practical level this is perfectly understandable, as humanity builds the world around itself as a model of the universe, in a form suited to a particular context and attitude; it defines reality and offers stability, and where the centre serves as a 'pillar of heaven' that links the world with divinity, that stability is all the more prized. What stands outside of the model is effectively chaos, because it does not complement the pattern within – and where that chaos threatens to permeate the harmony of the created world, whether through migration, conquest or cultural divergence, the chaos takes the role of evil, the dreadful adversary to the established order (glimpsed in countless forms including that of the Egyptians, who identified their Pharaoh as the mighty Re and all enemies as Apophis, the dragon).

On a symbolic level, the search for the centre can be the passage of the initiate through successive grades, just as it can be the journey of the self through the levels of consciousness towards individuation, or the manifested being following a path towards union with a god. The application of labyrinths to suggest this complex process has been a common one, where both internal and external realities are illustrated and the tortuous nature of the quest are perfectly given form.

The labyrinth is often the unconscious, where the careless wanderer can all too easily be fallen upon and devoured by the beast (the Minotaur) that is the base and animal passion. The network of paths can also overwhelm and confuse, to the point that he or she without sufficient understanding will fall by the wayside, exhausted, to waste away and die. By extension the labyrinth can be the illusion of the lower world that beguiles and misleads humanity, guiding it ever further from ultimate truth and that profoundly-desired return to the centre.

To find and protect the centre is to fight and slay the beast, be it the man-bull, the dragon or the atavistic self. The champion is the Hero, who can potentially traverse the labyrinth once more as it dissolves, as a spiral, into unified consciousness or a return to the creative source; the material gives way to the spiritual, dualities are transcended and the final test has been overcome.

Such a process can also be represented in the circular form, which brings us once more to the basic graphic images already noted, so too the symbol of the Ouroboros. Indeed, the circle as unity and completion is as old an association as we might hope to discover, and the archetypal symbolism of the circle or disc unites ancient history with the modern day, linking such disparate ideas as circles of standing stones, the circles of Dante's Inferno, the wedding ring and even the U.F.O.!

Mandalas are a traditional means of exploring the concept of the circle and its symbolism, in forms that include drawing, painting and even dancing, all towards a higher level of consciousness or a process of projection that allows for reflection and meditation toward that same end. Geometric, concentric patterns, they can be constructed as a three-dimensional model but the central idea remains a projection through which a path to ascension can be sought, with Mircea Eliade describing them as '…birth-places, vessels of birth…'

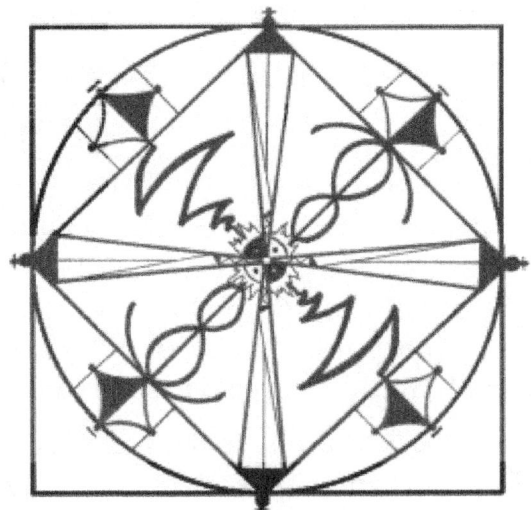

The mandala has been given numerous stylings and can be found in use as a 'psychocomogram' which depicts the cosmic forces, with the addition of the cross in certain Tibetan forms, where demons sit at each of the furthest extremes, and as the standard model of the certain Mesoamerican calendars. Medieval cities were even constructed as mandalas, which were separated into quarters that bore gates at each 'corner' and often had a church at their centre (the point where the 'lines of the cross' would intersect). Washington D.C. in North America is another, more recent example, of this application, and the 'rose window' of many Gothic cathedrals offer a microcosmic counterpart.

At its core the mandala is the recognition and application of order from chaos, as well as the expansion of being from a single point – always with the hope and intent of a return to that point. In many mandalas the actual centre is a void around which all else takes shape, which denotes something of that which is unknown, from which we see but shades in what is known.

Jung applied much thought and teaching to the idea of the mandala, and held that it was an unrivalled expression of self that could be used to both represent any psychological split between primitive instinct and irrational drives and the 'now', and serve as a means for the individual to re-establish sense and order. With the pattern as an externalised representation of the turmoil being experienced within, the means to recognise this, work it into a more stable form and thus reintegrate the chaotic, was beyond parallel – not least because it so prominently utilises forms and symbols that are so inherent within individual and collective consciousness.

As Jung himself stated in his *'Du'* (1955) which would come to be included in *'The Archetypes and the Collective Unconscious'*: 'The squaring of the circle is one of the many archetypal motifs which form the basic patterns of our dreams and fantasies. But it is distinguished by the fact that it is one of the most important of them from the functional point of view. Indeed, it could even be called the archetype of wholeness.'

Moon

Jung, of course, holds a prominent place within the analysis of dreams and their symbols, which seems to have been a source of inspiration and enquiry from the earliest civilizations. Perhaps in part due to the ancient tradition of 'dream work' that has taken various forms, it can be unarguably stated that many people – across continents and centuries – see dreams as being especially meaningful to them and the source of great revelation of self and the wider world, to the extent that dreams can take on a far greater significance than waking life, as though the sleeping self or subconscious is the real sage, and consciousness its blinkered sibling.

The Sumerians were studying dream symbolism with sufficient gravity to offer texts on the subject, and evidence of their efforts date back as far as 3100 B.C.E. Among many other popular types of augury, dreams were believed to be an important tool for divination but were also thought to offer glimpses of other worlds and dimensions, with an aspect of the individual or a part of the soul traversing the various astral plains as the physical body slumbered.

Dreams were interpreted with one central distinction, namely that they were either the product of positive entities or the malicious result of negative ones, thus it was vital that the validity of any symbolic event was first established, before any responding action was taken. Texts suggest that many dreams revolved around commonplace matters like family relationships, sexuality and visits to strange or familiar locations, though battle and conquest were frequent concerns within analysis, with Kings and military commanders often receiving what appeared to be divine communications. The prestige and import afforded to dreams was such that one Assyrian ruler, Ashurnasirpal II (883 – 859 B.C.E.) had a temple constructed to Mamu, considered to be a deity of dreams, to ensure that suitable veneration was made and, it would be likely, in the hope that greater revelatory omina would be divested as a result.

Certain Egyptian priests named 'Masters of the Secret Things' were employed with the specific purpose of divining dreams and hieroglyphics suggest the active use of dream interpretation, while the Greeks had 'Asclepieions' where dreams were utilised as part of the cure for the sick and infirm, alongside the more traditional esoteric practices. Where Aristotle did not attach any great mystical significance to dreams, Plato's understanding that some dreams may well derive from a divine source was a popular one that helped works like the *'Oneirocritica'* or *'The Interpretation of Dreams'* by one Artemidorus of Daldis in the 2nd century C.E. find a keen audience.

The Bible is far from alone as a sacred work that frequently cites dreams as the source of occult wisdom, but it is nonetheless remarkable in this case if only for the number of dreams that are mentioned. Dreams were the stuff of epiphany (as in the case of Ezekiel's vision and Jacob's ladder), just as they exposed those who were unworthy (Zechariah 10:2 'For the idols have spoken vanity, and the diviners have seen a lie, and have told false dreams...') and, in their absence, heralded the forsaken (Samuel 28:15 '...Saul answered, I am sore distressed; for the Philistines make war against me, and God is departed from me, and answereth me no more, neither by prophets nor by dreams...')

Dreams, however, were a primary means of communiqué with God and the heavenly realms, and necessitated care and attention when experienced, lest great truths and dire warnings were being offered (Acts 2:17 'And it shall come to pass in the last days, saith God, I will pour out of my Spirit upon all flesh: and your sons and your daughters shall prophesy, and your young men shall see visions, and your old men shall dream dreams').

As with so much else it was the Islamic influence which continued and disseminated much of the ideas and 'lore' that had been established at that time, and certain Muslim scholars offered their own analyses, including the work of Ibn Sirin (654 – 728 C.E.), Avicenna/Ibn Sina (980 – 1037 C.E.) and Ibn Kaldun's *Muqaddimah* (1377). Though the place of a suitably versed expert or scholar was maintained in these works, the developed theory of analysis here came to include an understanding of the individual that has had a given dream in order for any true meaning behind it to be fully exposed.

Of course, while the study of dream interpretation enjoyed a lofty reputation with only the finest minds of an age applying themselves to its rigours, the popular consensus often remained that where dreams proved revelatory they had been delivered from a divine source, rather than as a process of the human mind and human understanding alone. Dreams for guidance have thus retained their place within spiritual pursuits, whether that is in the form of a shamanic night journey, a church-goer in crisis or even the otherwise 'faithless' struggling with problems, desires or fears and pleading with the universe for direction.

James Frazer wrote that 'dreams are personalized myth', while Friedrich Nietzsche stated that dreams are the 'passage through the thoughts of all history', which together offer dreams the especial power of a timeless and depthless source while remaining specific to the individual dreamer – myth, faith, history and everyday experience combine and issue a response that is perhaps recognisable to all, even those long gone, but is wholly relatable only to the mind and personality of the dreamer in question.

For man or woman to tap any form of collective unconscious, even where this is simply the bouillabaisse of images, stories, ideas and other responses to existence, and to then experience those anew through the prism of their own personal frame of reference (including all of the senses as well as conscious and unconscious drives and desires, as well as memory) is as compelling an experience as most might wish to undergo. The fact that any 'message' to be gleaned from the dream can be held to be intensely personal, either from the depths of the self or imparted for the self by an external force, only adds to the mystery and strange power that dreams hold over many of us.

It is possible, though, for the fruits of dreams to be applied for the greater good, and the betterment of others. The Senoi tribe of the Malay Peninsula have their children 'bring back' information from their dreams that include songs and dances as well as prophesy and means of protection against wayward spirits, all for the tribe to profit. On a more individual basis, dreams have informed the works of Goethe, Baudelaire, Dickens, Poe and Mary Shelley among others, while a dream of the Ouroboros led the German chemist August Kekule (1829 –

1896 C.E.) to identify the chemical structure of benzene!

Freud's *'The Interpretation of Dreams'* (1899) stated that dreams are effectively the wish-fulfilment of a desire that the dreamer keeps suppressed or 'censored in the subconscious: '...the unconscious converts the latent content, which is unacceptable to the conscious self, into an acceptable form.' His later studies came to acknowledge the inclusion of 'day residue' in dreams, whereby the dreamer works through the stimulations experienced the day before.

The main thrust of Freud's theories, however, remained that the subconscious uses dreams to break through the veil of consciousness and present the deepest-seated fears, anxieties and desires to the individual, though in a disguised form so as to find more ready acceptance there, where the unvarnished truth may well be unwelcome, if not abhorrent, to the self. The 'censor' that suppresses these truths is strong enough to ensure that where dreams do occur, they are symbolic for this very reason – it protects the conscious self, even though an awareness and acceptance of the base instincts and drives would ultimately establish a more united and healthy mind.

The successful analysis of dreams would, Freud stated, relieve psychic tension between the subconscious and conscious self, though the problem has since remained exactly how such symbols as appear in dreams might be fully understood. It is an injustice to Freud to overlook his broader and more nuanced approach to this area, though it is true that sex drive and sexual urges are frequently seen to be a fundamental cause; phallic imagery is abundant (the staircase as an erection), drawers, pockets and other 'containers' are representative of female genitalia, and pleasure of any form (such as the euphoria experienced in flying) is synonymous with the sex act, which may suggest a limited scope of enquiry but which, given the human occupation with sex and gender from an early age, cannot be entirely rejected.

For Carl Jung, of course, the focus of dream analysis was somewhat more mystical. Dreams, for Jung, spoke of the individual and collective unconscious, with symbols capable of bearing immense personal meaning while being informed by and further enhancing a timeless, metaphysical human understanding. Here the dream is the effort of one's self to relay what it sees to be essential knowledge and understanding to the ego and, with this in mind, Jung noted that approaches to analysis could be objective (with the individuals in a dream taken to be exactly who they really are in waking life), or subjective (where those individuals are instead seen to represent aspects of the self, potentially revealing thoughts, emotions and knowledge that the dreamer cannot or will not accept as that of their own mind).

Jung noted the importance of each individual's own psychology and context, and though a staircase may well represent an erection to one man (or the descent of a staircase by a woman represent post-coital detumescence, as in Freud's schema), this pattern would not fit all men and women at all times. Indeed the symbols of dreams, being informed by the 'collective unconscious' and utilising images of mythological, esoteric and historic significance, are the result of a much more personal and spiritual vocabulary, at once speaking of temporal and eternal thoughts, desires and responses.

Dreams, then, can offer insight of the hidden man or woman where very practical and 'material' concerns are involved, but they can also offer insight into the 'total being' that is the subconscious and conscious self, with disguised appearances by one's anima, animus or 'shadow', those aspects of self that are integral to any and all dissent and/or ultimate sublimation. A staircase here can be, among other things, a transition or passage from one state to another, flight is a form of transcendence and a death of the Father is a desire for independence and action, rather than an oedipal projection.

Much of these interpretations can be found in the more mainstream works of Ann Faraday and others, though the empirical analysis popularised in the 1970's and thereafter largely avoid the sexual and spiritual extremes of the fathers of psychoanalysis. Much is seen to be a representation of one's recent past, with a dreamer essentially reliving or deconstructing true feelings about events that have happened during the day or two before. There may be instances of spiritual revelation or the sexual energies of an Electra complex, but for most individuals dreams are much more relatable and thus much easier to decipher.

Falling dreams become a fear of loss of control, while flying (and how well we manage it) suggests how confident we are about the control that we might have over a given situation or event; the return to a schoolroom of an unexpected test can represent lessons that need to be learnt, or that have been forgotten, from one's distant past; death in its many forms can be taken as a sign of transition, while houses can signify the unresolved (where the dream is of a childhood home) or the search for something new (where the house is unknown). The discovery of new rooms or secret and concealed spaces in already-known houses and buildings suggests that new aspects of the self/personality are being discovered.

This approach can be readily applied to many types of dream with little obvious difficulty, though when it comes to any dream of a more complex nature, where less relatable symbolism is at play or an apparent importance beyond the mundane is signified, the Jungian approach can certainly offer more elucidation. Such a mystical bent is also beneficial, depending on how we might look at it, where potential revelation and even telepathic vision is concerned, those dream-events which suggest a concatenation of macro- and microcosmic forces.

Easily rejected where faith and spirituality is a less-influential factor, Jungian dream analysis nonetheless holds an appeal for many as it suggests so much that the symbols, and archetypes, themselves, suggest – recurrent cycles, ancient and continuing themes and ideas, and a continuance of an aspect of self that can be interpreted as a form of immortality, which can be identified with the likes of the Akashic records, as well as the existence of the 'soul' and the apparently 'supernatural' abilities of humanity that both imprint knowledge on especial levels of existence and allow dreamers to access those indelible and eternal marks which constitute true wisdom.

Eliphas Levi noted this in his *'Transcendental Magic'* when he said: 'Somnambulism, presentiments and second sight are simply an accidental or induced disposition to dream in a voluntary or awakened sleep – that is, to perceive the analogous reflections of the Astral Light.' Dreams are the point at which the mundane, corporeal self comes closest to its occult counterpart, and so it is unsurprising that abilities such as precognition, regression and telepathy might be experienced.

The fact that symbols serve, as Joseph Campbell put it, as spontaneous products of the psyche bearing the 'germ power of its source' explains the singular relevance of symbols within dreams as well as myth, and all other esoteric thought and reflection. They impart a dynamic response and with that a message to the self without preamble or dogmatism, and so are as evocative as they are meaningful without any apparent limit to their meaning, while also being imbued with a rare power exactly because they are timeless and ubiquitous to the human condition.

As Jung wrote: '...who speaks in primordial images speaks as with a thousand tongues', and it is easy to understand why dreams have frequently been the focus of some of the most compelling and effective examples of revelation, issuing as they do from the threshold of the unconscious and in terms that are often beyond our means to understand – the very substance of revelation and spiritual wisdom.

Magician

When it comes to the practical application of symbols, little segues from the area of dreams as perfectly as the hermetic arts and alchemy. Few pursuits are as imbued with the use of symbols, with which it is fair to say that alchemy is synonymous, and this study can give but a cursory glimpse of what is an immense and complex relationship.

Should we think of alchemy as a form of pre-chemistry where much of today's scientific knowledge of certain substances and processes were initially observed, the interpenetration of 'known' and 'unknown', exoteric and esoteric can perhaps be better understood. Through that, we might also better appreciate the hermetic texts that are replete with symbols which in some cases are immediately identifiable, in others somewhat disguised and in still others downright fantastic or apparently nonsensical. Alchemy is, fittingly, a work that is in continual flux, where knowledge crystallizes and finds acceptance while invisible depths continue to forge new patterns of thought below the surface of consciousness, and common knowledge.

Much relies on core substances that are often depicted without abstraction, such as when the four classical elements are noted:

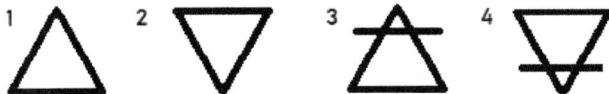

1: Fire (Father, linked to the tarot suit of wands).

2: Water (Mother, linked to the suit of cups).

3: Air (Son, linked to the suit of swords).

4: Earth (Daughter, linked to the suit of pentacles).

Similar can be said of the 'tria prima' that recur within the hermetic work and were central to the theories of matter and medicine expounded by the likes of Paracelsus (**1**Sulphur **2** Mercury **3** Salt):

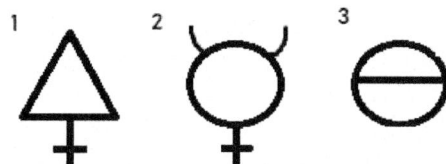

The metals, being associated with the then-known seven planets, most commonly bore the symbols utilised within Western astrology, while the individual alchemical processes were linked to a sign of the zodiac: Calcination – Aries; Congelation – Taurus; Fixation – Gemini; Dissolution – Cancer; Digestion – Leo; Distillation – Virgo; Sublimation – Libra; Separation – Scorpio; Ceration/Incineration – Sagittarius; Fermentation – Capricorn; Multiplication – Aquarius; Projection – Pisces.

Of course alchemy is renowned for its esoteric nature, which was applied in order to withhold wisdom from the ignorant, but can also be said to have propagated a desirable sense of mystery and obscured truths for the very good reason that the 'truth' was not always definable, if it was any kind of truth at all. As Geber (Jabir Ibn Hayyan) wrote: 'Wheresoever we have spoken plainly, there we have spoken nothing, but where we have used riddles and figures, there we have hidden the truth'; we are certainly reminded of the symbolic labyrinth, where lost souls would perish in confusion on their search for an incomparable yet elusive goal.

The language of alchemy, which inherently utilises symbols, is similar to the written form of many tantras (the 'sandhyabasa' or 'twilight language'), where the image and/or any specific meaning is impenetrable to the uninitiated. As alchemy is the search to realise the spiritual aspect within the physical, such a 'bridge' or conduit as symbolism is not only logical, it is unavoidable – images of human, animal and fantastic form appear alongside 'universal' metaphors and mythical aspects because the knowledge being shared and the ideals driving the search is a combination of being and not-being, matter and spirit, consciousness and sub-consciousness.

As such we see Mercurius (quicksilver and the world-creating spirit) represented in such manifold and diverse forms as the dragon, the serpent, the bee, the lion, also as a priest, a whore, a virgin, a mermaid and as tears, rain, the philosophical tree and more. Mercurius is an especially malleable form because of its innate volatility, and so an image that perfectly represents it at one stage of the process would in no way suit its character at another, but the range of applied symbols is suggestive of the intricate and often overwhelming language at play.

Similar can be seen in depictions of the Philosopher's Stone, where a logic reveals itself to he or she with sufficient knowledge but remains impenetrable to the ignorant, such as when it is symbolised by the mythical Basilisk or Cockatrice, the reptile hatched by a serpent from a cock's egg that can kill with a single glance – this is the alchemical elixir which 'kills' base metals and turns them into gold. There are always, it seems, many possibilities or aspects within one substance or idea, thus the symbolism can and does shift dramatically:

Adam: Represents the 'prima material', primal matter, that from which all of creation emanated, as well as the state of gradual transmutation and transcendence. Adam can appear as a hermaphrodite, when we consider the creation of Eve from his rib, and the prior state of bisexuality/union of opposites that pre-existed her 'birth' – where the androgynous has been parted into the dual sexes, it is the 'Chemical Wedding' that reunites them in the original, Adamic state.

Chemical Wedding: The entire cycle of the Great Work through the repeated process of 'solve et coagula' (the three repetitions being represented by the three circles formed by the entwined serpents of a caduceus). Union on all levels – male and female; sulphur and mercury; hot and cold; spirit and body. The Wedding is depicted at points as incest, the winged and wingless dragon, as hen and cock, sol and luna, and king and queen.

Dismemberment or beheading: Division (a sacrifice) toward the higher stage, illustrated with birds, dragons, king or a tree.

Cross: A form of dismemberment is glimpsed within the cross, where the four arms are the elements that are united at their meeting point, the centre. Here lies the element of Quintessence that binds, and the state of unity. Nicholas Flamel stated that the serpent nailed to the cross illustrates the point of completion. The cross is knowledge moving towards wisdom and the mastery of spirit over matter.

Death: The process of refinement often appears in forms of death, such as a couple entwined on or in a (glass) coffin. This is the release of 'spirit' or a higher form of being within the vessel, as well as the attainment of a higher level of consciousness.

Labyrinth: The journey through the Great Work, including the challenge of confusion, misdirection and the loss of self. Elias Ashmole stated that alchemical books themselves were as a labyrinth, leading the uninitiated and ignorant astray.

Ouroboros: In the *'Book of Lambspring'* it states that 'His venom becomes the great medicine. He quickly consumes his venom, for he devours his poisonous tail. And this is perfected in his own body, from which flows forth glorious balm, with all its miraculous virtues. Here do all the sages rejoice loudly.' The self-devouring serpent is Mercury dissolved and coagulated, which is the dragon killed.

Serpent: Another form of the prima materia and Mercurius. The initial serpent/dragon of the process is the chthonic force which kills corruption (and in George Ripley's *'Compound of Alchymy'* the corrupt metal is dissolved by the mercurial serpent).

Dragon: The winged dragon is a volatile substance, while the un-winged dragon is a fixed substance. Dragons fighting can represent the stage of 'putrefaction' which is the disintegration of matter/substance/psychic being.

Philosopher's Tree: This depicts the entire process, as well as the revelation and transformation of both self and psyche. It suggests at once the prima materia and the ultimate goal, the Philosopher's Stone. As such the tree appears in many forms, including that of a small plant. A tree of moons can represent the lesser work and a tree of suns the greater work, while a tree bearing the planets or metals suggests the emergence of the different forms from root that is the prima materia.

The idea of inversion is one we have seen before in the application of the world tree, with roots in heaven and limbs serving the role of matter and creation; in alchemy it is also a potent symbol as a form of the Philosopher's Tree, as well as a model of the entire magnum opus. Maria Prophetissa, a renowned alchemist who lived between the 1st and 3rd centuries C.E. and invented, among other apparatus, the Bain-Marie, stated: 'Invert nature and you will find that which you seek' and it might be said that the same principle might be applied to some of the more fantastic of the hermetic texts – a truth lies within them, but one must be well-versed with the language of symbolism to consider following the trail laid down by those who have passed before.

Unity and a divine purity of being remains the core focus of the work, whether in the form of the Philosopher's Stone that turns base metals to gold, the elixir of life that grants immortality or the transcendence of spirit over matter which joins the pneuma within the individual and rejoins it with the creative source. Unity and the return to the 'centre' is the recurrent symbol applied in so many forms, and however exalted or material the seeker's aim, the route is, suitably, one and the same, as noted by Gerhard Dorn in 1661: '...You will never make oneness out of otherness until you have yourself become oneness.'

The idea of individuation within psychoanalysis may be the ultimate goal here, or that may simply stand as a newer understanding of a greater aim that has been sought throughout history. However we define it, it is the 'squaring of the circle' that is the overcoming of apparent limitation and converse states, toward a new form that is a state of cohesion, balance and oneness:

Such an image applies itself well to the magical tradition, which utilises the 'thousand tongues' noted by Jung, including mythology, history, philosophy, psychology, alchemy and the scientific arts, while striving to encapsulate these within succinct symbols – in word, image and action – so as to direct an individual will and cause a desired change.

Symbolism is inherent to magic, where it is immediately recognisable in the wand, pentacle, chalice and dagger that are frequently employed within ritual and of course in the divinatory processes of the tarot. Human aspects of will, force, emotion and spirituality are thus embodied within a form or an object, so too the fundamental active and passive, male and female principles, in such a manner as to tap the magician's subconscious as well as his or her knowledge, without the need for direct effort or concentration of the mind; the symbol is known and understood, and so its energy is automatically present and the imaginative faculty of the magician can begin to exert its influence.

The aforementioned ritual use of the circle as a form of protection (the created world establishing the magician's sense of order and control) and the triangle as the 'art' (where the magician, as creator, controls the form within) certainly apply to the same principle, with a deeply-rooted 'knowledge' of those shapes and their associations serving as an unspoken but imperative part of the work being performed.

The use of the symbol is an instinctive act that relies on that knowledge, which has been compounded by a collective wisdom passed through all manner of pursuits from the earliest of humanity's responses. As much can be said of the potential recipient of any magical work, such as the intended focus of an effigy, poppet or wax doll – the beliefs and fears that are an integral aspect of the symbolic act are sufficient to inflict damage upon a victim, regardless the ability of any magician.

Symbolism for magical purposes has an ancient pedigree, and can be found in various forms (and to various ends) in the runes of the Germanic peoples and, to an extent, in the veves of Voodoo. The veve is a geometrical drawing that represents the loa or iwa of a given spirit, the use of which has been noted in a number of West- and Central African locations as well as by the South American Arawak people, the Taino of the Caribbean and in the Umbanda religion of Brazil.

The veve can take an elaborate or simple form, and are usually drawn by one with sufficient wisdom and power to perform such an act, which within Voodoo is namely a 'mambo' or priestess, or an 'oungan' or priest, with flour, coffee, herbs, cornmeal and ashes being used among other potential materials to create the image. A learned individual is best placed to create the veve as it is a material representation of the loa being called, effectively serving as a focus for the spirit, and the result of improper procedure and lack of due reverence would be severe punishment.

Some of the most widely-known veves are really quite recognisable due to the images used within them which characterise their respective loa – for instance, Ezili Freda (love and luxury) has a veve with a heart as its prominent image, while Dambala Wedo and his wife Ayida Wedo (the serpents that were the first created from which all else was formed) have twin snakes within their veve, and Papa Legba (life and death, the transition between worlds) has a cross as a central point of his veve.

Strictly speaking, the veves represent an alphabet more than they serve as symbols but the potency of their forms which is instantly recognisable to adherents, along with their application as a focus of intent and imagination towards a spiritual materialisation, most certainly suggests their relevance to a study such as this.

Aleister Crowley stated that symbols are either an occult force within the human subject, or a principle that obtains an 'intelligent moving force', and we see an application of this in the Enochian alphabet of John Dee and Edward Kelley, with each individual symbol representing something of the Adamic knowledge as well as a sound that, correctly uttered, resonates such that a specific aspect of the subconscious is stimulated. The alphabet thus serves as a means of unlocking the self, as much as it touches on the further reaches of creation:

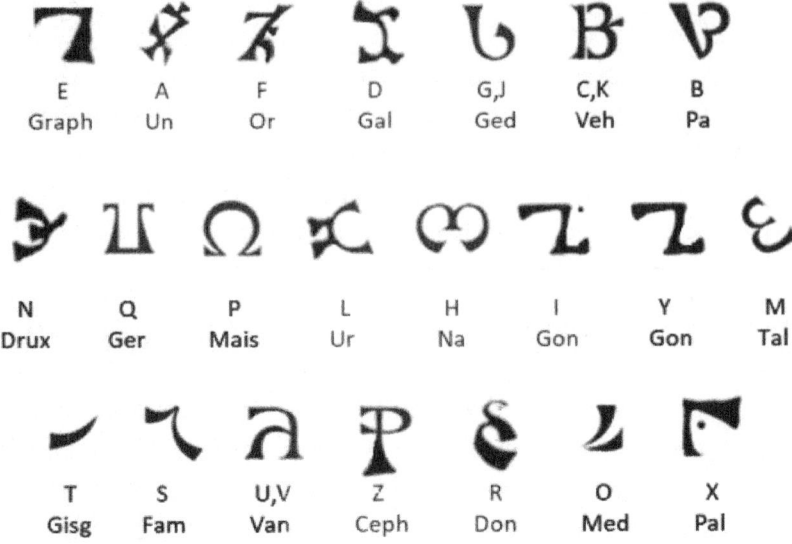

Crowley's Thelema used the unicursal hexagram (drawn with one continuous line), which can be placed within a circle or with the hexagram's lines passing each other in such a way as to form a knot.

This image has been linked to the ankh and other similar symbols whereby the interlinking of macrocosmic and microcosmic forces is achieved. The magician is thereby offered knowledge and power that combines the corporeal and the spiritual, at once mastering the earthly elements while piercing the cosmic veil and tapping the celestial energies.

Within the rites of Thelema the symbol often had a lotus at its centre, the petals of which signify the five points of the pentacle (Babalon) in relation to the six points of the hexagram itself, which represents the divine (Beast); together, these forms equate to the eleven-fold union of human and divine consciousness, as well as the art of magic. There is also thought that for Crowley the five points signified man in relation to the six that was God, thus a union was being sought that would raise man's capacity and ken to a divine level.

Much of the symbolism that is most actively used in the act of magical ritual is in the form of the sigil, (a term deriving from the Latin 'sigillum' that means 'seal'). Typically found in medieval grimoires, sigils serve as representations of angels, demons and other spiritual entities that a magician may wish to invoke; more than that, however, these sigils were believed to equate to the true and hidden name of the entity in question, the knowledge and use of which would of course afford a magician the necessary power to control what might otherwise prove to be a dangerous, if not lethal being.

As we have seen, magic squares were sometimes used to decipher the name of an entity, and the result was the abstract symbolic form of the sigil. Such an approach was endemic to the magical tradition some time before even the earliest of the grimoires and has retained popularity through the likes of the Golden Dawn and Chaos magic, into the movements and practices of the 21st century.

A formative magician in this field was Austin Osman Spare who, similar to Aleister Crowley, believed that the entities like those of the goetic demons found in Solomonic grimoires were in reality aspects or complexes that were formed in and projected from the human subconscious. On one level this might suggest a rejection of the entire 'sigilization' process, but in effect it was a liberation of the sigil and its use from the restrictions of history – if the entities being communicated with were of the human mind then an appropriate sigil, forged and directed by the accomplished man or woman, could *create* rather than evoke. Man is, then, God in this instance, and the extent of man's creative power is potentially limitless.

The common means of creating a sigil within Chaos magic derives from the work of Spare, with a statement of intention being written down and then reduced and incorporated into an abstract form which represents that intention. Desire is thus externalised in the form of a glyph, and that glyph is given an active, 'living' energy through meditation and the focusing of one's will. Spare, however, made clear that the ultimate efficacy of a glyph or sigil created in this manner was achieved through the magician's active forgetting of it, essentially meaning that the image should become such a reality for the creator that it resides beyond his or her limit of consciousness, replacing the intent so that it essentially takes on an existence of its own.

Where such energy, emotion and will are invested to a sigil it can indeed, it has been suggested, take on that life of its own, working the intent autonomously on behalf of its creator. In the case of an individual magician, the result is known as a 'servitor', while the product of a group is called an 'egregore'. These creations exist to fulfil a specific task, thus their role is their very essence – but they can become of such dynamic a force that they exceed this vocation and exhibit a degree of thought and deed that belies the original intent and demarcates an independent existence altogether.

The possibility of such an event is recognised by many within the sphere of magic, as it in essence underlines the fundamental belief that magic exists to prove – the realisation of change through the application of the will. As Eliphas Levi put it in his

'*History of Magic*': 'The natural function of imagination is to evoke images and forms, but in a condition of abnormal exaltation it can also exteriorise forms...'

It is also a potential hazard resulting from the use of 'thought-forms' like tulpas, which are essentially phantoms generated and given a degree of existence through a mixture of imagination and will – not wholly unlike servitors and egregores. Made of a plastic substance, thought-forms often decay quickly, but this is not always the case and widely-spread cases of more permanent and, it would seem more concrete, beings establishing themselves have been long told.

The thought-form is noted in Buddhist texts including the '*Samaññaphala Sutta*' where the capability of giving form to a 'man-made body' is one of the gifts of the sufficiently contemplative life, and the philosopher-monk Vasubandhu (c. 4th - 5th century B.E.) named 'nirmita', the ability to create an illusion of form with no material reality, as a siddhi or esoteric power. Even where the thought-form is thus at its most 'ethereal' and 'unreal', the skill of manifesting such an entity is a superlative one, not least when we consider that for Buddhists matter itself is unreal!

The tulpa as a thought-form is linked to Tibetan Buddhism, and gained prominence in writings from Theosophist Annie Besant and Spiritualist Alexandra David-Neel (1868 – 1969 C.E.) among others. Besant suggested that such thought-forms can be generated purposefully by a sensitive individual, but also that emanations of emotion from the astral plain could gather and forge a distinct entity; further still, she stated that elemental spirits and other lesser beings might take hold of what is effectively a shell and seek to claim it as a body – all of which raises clear links with instances of hauntings, poltergeist phenomena and even possession (the latter of which, in turn, can be seen to bear a link of sorts to the tantric 'kriya shakti' or 'creative power' that utilises potent sexual energies toward spiritual manifestation).

David-Neel wrote of having created a 'Friar Tuck' figure through thought alone following observance and practices of esoteric rites in Tibet, a merry entity that eventually seemed to exist outside of her control and even appeared to others, before she undertook the gradual process of 'dismantling' it so as to avoid any further danger. Dion Fortune (1890 – 1946 C.E.) writing in her *'Psychic Self-Defence'* (1930) told of a spectral wolf that she encountered as she fell victim to the psychic attack of another mystic, further suggesting the potential of genuine effects resulting from directed will.

We might reject the validity of these tales for a number of reasons but, as with the use of dolls and effigies in magic, there is no doubt that there can be material results from a shared belief; the efficacy of magic and in this case thought-forms is irrelevant in this case, as the desired goal is achieved even if it is through the manipulation of another's mind in the form of induced hallucination or other psychological means of warfare.

Tulpas and thought-forms are not served in the same manner as servitors when it comes to symbolism, but they are mentioned here because they are a further example of thought, will and imagination being directed to concretise an effect. The potential of psychic forms leading to material events, changes and entities is an integral one to the study of the symbol, as it is this psychic capacity that is being reflected in and tapped by any ritual or mythic use of symbolism.

As has been noted, correspondences can be used to establish a network of associations for the ritualist, but the symbol can be used even without those sensory and intellectual trappings – speaking to the conscious and unconscious at the same instant, the symbol can unite the total mind (and perhaps being) of man and woman, including the rational and irrational facets. Where this is applied to a mindset where all existence is believed to be composed of one substance (regardless how many gradations might exist within it), the forging of concentration into form is not as far-fetched as might be supposed, and the symbol is the perfect bridge that unites the otherwise disparate facets of the human condition.

Chaos magic holds that anything can serve as a symbol, as long as the connection with the person using it is meaningful and significant. This is why symbols like the cross, the tree, the serpent and the labyrinth can maintain a resonance both collectively and for the individual, but where practical magic is concerned the sigil – the articulated desire condensed into a glyph – is of especial power, formed as it is by the very person who seeks to actualise its potential.

World

Apparently timeless symbols certainly feature prominently within the tarot, though within a framework that also relies on personal insight, reflection and the imagination of a given practitioner. The variations of form are now many, but the fundamental symbols and images from which the tarot has been developed remains largely unchanged, and singularly relatable.

Ideas as to the origins of the tarot are suitably manifold, and often rather romantic, including passages from India and China, as a form of wisdom originally maintained by the ancient Celts and as a model of thought reflecting the action and figures of Dante's hell. Papus (Gerard Encausse; 1865 – 1916 C.E) suggested several potential birthplaces for the tarot – among the Gnostics, where it was passed to the Freemasons in a bowdlerised form and then ultimately lost; within the mystical tradition of the Cabbala and then, through the esoteric application of letters and numbers, into Biblical scripture, where it was again lost in obscurity and ignorance; and finally within the gypsy peoples as a 'Bible of Bibles.'

No one theory has been proved, and Papus' own suggestion of a continued knowledge and application of the tarot by the gypsies that was in time passed into wider awareness has been largely rejected as impossible due to historical anachronisms. There is, however, a stronger argument for the dissemination of tarot use and symbolism through the Muslims and into Europe through their Spanish conquests, though the prolific use across Europe of cards similar to the tarot as learning aids does muddy the water somewhat and indicates that the deck now known as the tarot may be but one incarnation of a commonplace past-time.

It should be noted that, among the learning aid-type cards

(consisting of those teaching about social orders within a given society, the Christian virtues, as well as Classical and mythical figures) certain images might be identified that certainly link with the symbolism of the tarot, however these similarities may simply be a reflection of the medieval mindset, where social standing, vices and virtues, reward and punishment were all widely and frequently applied as a result of day-to-day life. What we can, perhaps, take from these possibilities is that by the 15th century C.E. cards that were at the very least a composite of inherent symbols and understandings were being produced, along with a burgeoning application of the ideas and responses that had begun to be built up by the cards themselves.

The Franciscan St Bernardino of Siera was not alone, in 1423, in believing that the tarot was a product of the Devil that promoted idolatry, and he was certainly not the last to state as much, with the likes of John Wesley continuing to warn of dangers resulting from any use of the cards in the 18th century. The cards were compelling enough to garner great acclaim in other quarters, however, not least because their inherent meaning, much like their origin, was compellingly mysterious and abstract. All manner of ideas and associations could be applied to them with no derogation of the cards themselves, which would stand unaffected by even the worst of affiliations!

Antoine Court de Gebelin (1719 – 1784 C.E.), a French Protestant theologian, believed the tarot to be a 'book' of symbols with a lineage stretching back to Ancient Egypt. The language was, alike that of alchemy, suitably that of the symbolic so as to deliver revelation to the initiated while pleasing the ignorant, who would nonetheless remain ignorant in spite of any amount of effort. Such thought passed from de Gebelin to the writer and esotericist Eteilla (Jean-Baptiste Alliette, 1738 – 1791 C.E.) and to Papus, where the profound worth of the cards remained a certainty, no matter the individual theory applied to them.

As is often the case, Eliphas Levi in his *'History of Magic'* neatly summed up the case for the tarot, with these ideas in mind: 'The basis of absolute hieroglyphical science was an alphabet in which deities were represented by letters, letters represented ideas, ideas were converted into numbers, and numbers were perfect signs.' As such the tarot was the 'Book of Thoth', the ancient spiritual wisdom of the Egyptians that served as the 'universal key', preserved in a safely esoteric form that might be abused by some but which offered true insight to the gifted and knowing user.

A disciple of Levi's, Jean-Baptiste Pitois, extended the origin story of his master and suggested that the tarot related to twenty-two paintings that were passed by initiates undergoing ceremonies of the Egyptian Mysteries at the Great Pyramid. Similar thought also influenced Samuel Liddell MacGregor Mathers (1854 – 1918 C.E.) who was one of the founders of the Golden Dawn and wrote extensively on the tarot, while Arthur Edward Waite (1857 – 1942 C.E.), who translated Papus' work into English, rejected much of the theories therein as a 'tissue of errors' – for Waite the appeal of Egypt and ancient wisdom blinded many and led to fallacious theories that only served to detract from the importance of the universal language that the cards represented.

One interesting connection that Papus made was that of the Hebrew term YHVH with ROTA, an anagram of TARO. He applied the form of the cross to the four letters of each and suggested the following affiliations:

King: (the apex of the cross). Yod; Spirit; cards with the values of 1 (Aces), 4 and 7; Sceptres/Wands. The state of creation.

Queen: (left extreme of the cross). He; Vitality; cards with the values of 2, 5 and 8; Cups/Chalices. Preservation and Love.

Knight: (nadir of the cross). Vau; Matter; cards with the values of 3, 6 and 9; Swords. Transformation and Conflict.

Knave: (right extreme of the cross). He; Transition; cards with the value of 10; Pentacles/Coins. Money and Spirituality.

Similar associations were made between YHVH, the Yod of which is the creative force from which all else is derived, and the 22 letters of the Hebrew alphabet, which in turn could be linked to the paths of the Sephirothic Tree of the Cabbalists.

However, contention has long been a part of the interpretation of the tarot and extends to the order and naming of the cards as much as any symbolism identified with them. Questions of where to place 'The Fool' in the deck, dissention over the allocations of the Hebrew letters to the cards and the replacing of the 'Female Pope' with the 'High Priestess' are but a few of the challenges to surmount if we try to unravel any 'original' form and order for the tarot, and this is before we start to broach the subject of interpretation.

Where Papus (in his *'Tarot of the Bohemians'*; 1889 C.E.) does underline the importance of the tarot is not in the endlessly arguable issues of origin, nor among the correspondences or individual truths that we might define within its system, but in the unchanging symbolism that speaks to the human mind (and spirit) outside of the constraints of time and without any necessity of understanding the historical pedigree of the cards or their images: '…our end, not in finding the explanation of the symbols, but in leading us to create them one by one by deducing them from fixed and general principles.'

We return to the idea of images and symbols emanating from a single creative spark, of which we all share substance and potentially knowledge. The cards themselves represent the various emanations of existence, including the cycles of chaos, to form, to dissolution, then back to chaos and re-birth, with appropriate symbolism to fittingly represent those cycles – and the human responses to them:

I Juggler / Magician: Unity and the source of unity. Power and stability; mastery over the elements (suggested by the lemniscate, which can be worn on his hat). With one hand pointing up and one hand pointing down, he characterises the adage 'as above, so below.' The Ouroboros worn as a belt in the Rider-Waite deck signifies eternity and completion, and the lemniscate can also represent the testicles in relation to the phallus that is his wand. The male principle, he reminds us that 'God created the heaven and the earth'. He is will and action, the Microcosm of God (Adam). There are links to Thoth / Hermes Trismegistus, the god of wisdom, and to Mercury, the messenger.

The 'traditional' Marseilles Deck presents the Magician as the everyman, who has dice, coins, cup and a knife before him. It appears that he thus has the potential of greatness, but is either unaware of how to develop himself or does not realise that these tools should be taken seriously. In this latter point we perhaps see a metaphor for the tarot deck in its entirety – is it a frivolity, or does a greater truth pervade it and its use?

The Magician can appear to enjoy great standing and 'presence' but in reality be no more than a charlatan or, at least, a peddler of trickery, though he *could* be a genuine magus if only he can find the means within himself (the lemniscate hat that is the union of opposites alone tells us this, but this on top of the circular upper-form and the cross made by his arms together offer the sign of mercury – the vital, and ever-malleable, element).

Divinatory meaning: Dexterity. Skill and confidence – excelling outside of what would be termed 'normal' boundaries of thought and action.

II The High Priestess / The Female Pope: Speech and erudition. Natura. The hidden, veiled knowledge (with a link to Isis). She is intuition over experience, but signifies also the potential pitfalls of this. She therefore embodies progress, yet possibly at a cost. To pierce or remove the veil is to cross a threshold. She is the feminine principle, the spirit, passive and responsive to the male influence, though with a striking effect upon it (sometimes in the form of the medieval virgin who tames the unicorn, which places its horn in her lap. She is the Middle Pillar on the Tree of Life (Shekinah), the Anima Mundi and Gnosis. The Anima of Jung.

The Marseilles 'Popess' is passivity (the blue cloak) that is only dormant and quite open to development (the bright red clothing revealed by the cleft in her cloak, which suggests the female sex organ).

Divinatory meaning: The female element, in opposition to the patriarchal faith and its overbearing dogma. Mystery and tenacity.

III Empress: Embodiment and generation. Transition; the result of the first two cards. The Great Mother, curing and yielding. As Demeter she is fertility and fecundity, though perhaps to the point of abandon and excess. Links to Ishtar, Artemis, Isis and Minerva. The Empress sits within the lost paradise, potentially that of Eden.

The Marseilles image offers us the direct product of the first two cards, where the receptive quality of the Female Pope/High Priestess has overcome the passive element of femininity through union with the active male presence of the Magician and become a state of utter fecundity (a point which is reflected in the image of the card where the head, spread arms and lap form a diamond-shape that is itself a broader and more welcoming 'opening' to transformation).

Divinatory meaning: Home, or the land of one's origin. Protection; initiative.

IV Emperor: Entity, abundance and form. The universe. The Father and protector, who wields temporal power. Dionysus, as the god who dies to be reborn. He is the Breath of God, and through that action, dynamism and actualised potential. A modern form shows him making a triangle with the form of his head and shoulders, while his legs are crossed – representing the symbol of Mercury. Thus the Emperor is the 'fiery principle'. Links with Osiris. The Animus of Jung.

The Marseilles Emperor offers the crossed legs and suggestion of Jupiter, with a reclining torso suggesting that the spirit (a crescent shape) is being 'lifted' by the material element. This is the state of form from the initial triad, though further refinement is required – complimentary influences are necessary in any further stage of unification.

Divinatory meaning: Material authority. Aid and protection on a temporal level.

V The Hierophant / The Pope: The reunion of opposites. Animation, and the breath of life. The Hierophant as the high priest of the Eleusinian Mysteries. He is analytical intelligence and perspicuity, holder of the Keys of Knowledge. He is the adviser, the keeper of wisdom, though perhaps can be rigid in his understanding. Also a spiritual authority. His hand in modern decks makes the sign of benediction and blessing which resembles Taurus, the trinity – though its shadow is alike the Devil's head, with horns.

The Marseilles deck offers twin pillars behind the Pope that are phallic in nature, and a triple cross on a staff that has been associated with the lingam. This is active knowledge, and generative power, but as the composition of the image offers the Pope himself as an upward-reaching triangle above the square of materiality where adherents watch, the direction of movement is a positive one.

Divinatory meaning: Orthodoxy. A focus of respect, though caution is necessary. Inspiration, but also potential servitude.

VI Lovers: The eye. Light. Communication between the Self and the World. Bond. A choice, with the associated commitment thereafter. Also the choice between vice and virtue is apparent; prelude to the Fall. The Golden Dawn suggested that this is inspiration overcoming empty and redundant habits. The risk of a poor decision is seen with the 'threatening' presence of Cupid's arrow. The arrow and bow also serve as a representation of sexual union. Links to Gemini and Janus.

The Marseilles Lovers give us a male in striped garb that further enforces the position of choice – the possibilities are being considered, and as yet undecided. He is flanked by an older and a younger woman, and appears to be more closely allied to the younger (who may well represent the sweetheart as opposed to the mother-figure, as well as the solar aspect of femininity as opposed to the lunar). There is a salient psychological aspect to this card, where the male is required to know his whole self in order to make the correct choice and make that choice a successful one.

Divinatory meaning: Combined energies. Attraction overcoming the rational or the norm. Beauty and love.

VII Chariot: The directed arrow. Rule; victory in all worlds / spheres. The action of the conqueror. 'Triumph'; though possibly as a juggernaut, blind destruction and the excess of ego. The Merkabah of Ezekiel – thus potential transcendence alongside the danger of loss of self. Crossing the abyss. Release from bondage. Also, the result of the Fall.

The Merseilles deck shows us the male of the Lovers, following his choice. In movement and enjoying a control over his position, the need for awareness and balance is again made clear in the image – mind (his head), body (the chariot) and emotion/passion (the horses, apparently striving to run in different directions) must be united for the victory to be a sure one.

Divinatory meaning: The heroic. The moral and selfless act. Success. A darker aspect suggests vengeance and war.

VIII Strength: Strain results in balance; imposed equilibrium. Advice carefully weighed, both earthly and oracular. The ability to choose, but excessive focus on intellect over instincts is limiting. Link to Hercules (who wears the skin of the vanquished lion). Strength of purpose and morals. Subjugation of the lower instincts and passions, which is discipline rather than brute force. Crowley saw a descent into perversity given the woman's domination of the lion, which for him represented a reversal of the natural order.

The Marseilles Strength card gives us another lemniscate in the form of the female figure's hat, and here we see the practical and enlightened union of opposites where the spiritual insight of the female masters the raging passions of the solar/male lion. In many ways the focus here is the lion and not the woman, as it is willingly giving itself over to her so that a further 'refinement' of nature can take place; this is the result of self-knowledge, as demanded in the preceding cards.

Divinatory meaning: Fortitude. Focus overcoming distraction. Power, action and courage.

IX Hermit: 'Roof', sanctus. Wisdom begets safety. There is a suggestion of Time (Chronos, the consumer). The Microcosm outside of time, thus denoting a liminal state. He is wisdom, but also avoidance of others and their world, possibly as a form of escape. Elsewhere he is the state of virility in stasis. Links to King Solomon, Christ and Christian Rosenkreutz.

The Marseilles Hermit is moving toward the left, with his lantern lighting up the path before him. However, this suggests that he is looking toward the past, rather than the future, and while there may be value in the lessons that he can learn, the likelihood is that he will be weighed down by memories and old perspectives that will cause him to stagnate. As the body and cloak of the Hermit suggest a rather stocky, square figure, there is a foreboding that unless a new outlook can be obtained, the light will eventually die on his slow journey.

Divinatory meaning: The passage of time. Solitude. Prudence, but possibly also corruption.

X Wheel of Fortune: The cycle of existence and a possible command over it. Time; the spirit in duration. A later form shows ROTA upon the wheel, which carries the figures of the Sphinx, the serpent and Anubis. The four corners house the beasts of Revelation, namely man, eagle, bull and lion, as well as the fundamental substances of alchemy – mercury, sulphur, salt and water. All cycles are represented, not least that of birth, life, death, and rebirth.

This is the point of change, and dealing well with that change – the acceptance that further changes will come and so no situation is final, whether it be seen to be positive or negative. The Wheel of Fortune was a popular medieval symbol which insinuated the lack of one's control over Fate, as well as the natural cycles of ascent and descent.

The Marseilles deck offers two creatures, one being lifted and the other dropped, that will soon undergo quite the opposite experience as the wheel turns. A third, crowned, creature sits above the wheel, quite free of its movement – possibly suggesting a being that has united the opposites, located the centre of the wheel and has thus transcended the otherwise endless cycle of existence.

Divinatory meaning: A sense of helplessness. Recognised limitation. The chasing and pursuit of false idols, or an empty vision of success. Also, however, destiny and felicity.

XI Justice: The hand; clutching. The further emanation of life. Cyrene, as she is linked to Artemis; she who Apollo fell in love with. The Egyptian scene of judgement at death. Dharma and the moral law. Also the joining of the sexes. For Crowley, XI was Lust, the 'divine drunkenness' and 'will of the Aeon.'

The Marseilles Justice offers a downward crescent-form as made by the chair which the figure rests on, while that figure's body is arranged in a circular manner; together these shapes create the sign of Taurus, which is ruled by Venus – the balancer.

Divinatory meaning: Impartiality. Equity. The institution of 'Justice' and imposing of balance.

XII Hanged Man: The arm; reaching. Elevation and extension. Revelation and 'punishment', ergo the cost of that wisdom. Also known as the traitor (Judas with his coins?) Sometimes he is in the form of an inverted '4'. Waite placed him on a Tau cross. This is a state of change, where the change is rapid and at a cost – though the initial sacrifice made may lead to wisdom and transcendence and thus be necessary, if not pre-ordained.

This is the dying and resurrected god – Attis, Odin as well as Jesus Christ. Suggestions link the Hanged Man to the concept of spent passion. A reclamation of what has been lost is notable, if we acknowledge the figure's often serene appearance. The overturning of understanding and order to truly SEE. For Jung, the descent to the unconscious.

The Marseilles Hanged Man is an isolated figure, who smiles in spite of his predicament. This suggests ignorance of his situation, and that of the world around him (with starkly-bare trunks at his sides). The cross-form of the legs above the downward-pointing triangle of torso, arms and head, represents the spirit in chaos (with links to Judas), though the hair which barely touches ground that, nearby, is sprouting new grass offers hope of regeneration from this plight.

Divinatory meaning: Discernment. Prophecy. The state of being accused. The exposing of a moral guilt. Humiliation.

XIII Death: Life, death and life. Passage and transition. Waite's Death appears as a knight in black armour. He wields a scythe, or a strung bow – with the scythe representing Saturn and Time, the devouring beasts. Death also serves as a form of cosmic justice, the great leveller. He is transition and rebirth. Papus linked Death to Shiva as Destroyer.

The Marseilles Death shows a decaying corpse or cadaver cutting a swathe through a field of scattered body-parts, all of which suggests that this is dissolution, rather than outright demise. The Death figure makes a crescent-shape with his body, again noting a spiritual aspect, above hands and arms that make a cross and the scythe which offers a further crescent, together offering the sign of Saturn. This is matter weighed down to its nadir, and though hope is evident there will need to be great transformation in order for any further spiritual growth.

Divinatory meaning: Awareness of fallibility. An end, and a new beginning. Mortality. That where the cycle reaches a nadir and yet is rejuvenated.

XIV Temperance: The condition of corporeality, being a reflection of the life-giver. The result of movement and the interference of forces. Temperance is moderation and equilibrium, with links to the concept of mercy. Continuity. The bridging of conscious and unconscious. Associated with Sagittarius. For Crowley XIV was Art, the fulfilment of the union in the Lovers with an androgynous figure, otherwise the Chemical Marriage.

The Marseilles card offers yet another union of opposites. A blue and red jug are being used to pass the sacred waters, reflecting the natural transfer and flow of passive (blue) and active (red) energies. The colours and form of the image suggest the yin and yang principles and the inherent balance that exists and requires maintaining.

Divinatory meaning: Rising above limitations through the ability to change. Frugality.

XV Devil: Weapon / fatality. The limitation which can be transcended or overcome; the blinkers of the material and the familiar that CAN be broken. Pan. The adversary, both internal and external. Potentially the shadow self, the unconscious. Caution against opposition and such influences that can overwhelm and control. The untamed. For Crowley, the ecstasy in all.

The Marseilles Devil is of both genders and is both human and bestial/birdlike. The blue wings and trousers denote the immovability of the Devil, and serve as his own chains to the material realm. Passion dominates, with the eye-line of the two human figures at the level of the Devil's genitals – which sit at the centre of the entire image.

Divinatory meaning: Sheer passion. Excess and greed. Temptation. Violence and fatality.

XVI Tower: Degeneration. Fall and reconstruction. The Tower of Babel and the lost unified language, to punish the ego and disrespect that built the original (flawed) edifice. Also the destruction of Sodom, and the Temple in Jerusalem which was struck by lightning at the time of the crucifixion. This is the punishment for pride, but also the active power of male sexuality. A true goal, sought with false means, or denial, or ignorance. Destruction is inflicted so that a new and purer foundation can rebuild.

The Marseilles 'House of God' shows a tower that is pink in colour, suggesting that this might be a symbol for man or woman. The tower appears to be of a square construction while the dislocated top storey is circular, which makes clear that the two parts were never truly compatible (much like the higher mind and the uncontrolled passions and emotions). Understanding of self is again required for any sound construction to be raised.

Divinatory meaning: Freedom from desire and temporal wants. Ruin and disgrace. Deception.

XVII Star: Speech. The vision of 'return' following the trial that is life. The guidance of a higher wisdom. The pure waters are potentially those of the unconscious, though with a divine light to guide us by. The Higher Self, and/or the revivification of a tired world. Links to Hebe, giver of nectar to the gods.

The Marseilles deck shows us further red and blue vessels. The blue jug covering the female figure's genitals and her bared breasts suggest nourishment and creation, all through the stimulation of higher thought and inspiration. Trees growing behind her are representative of the same waters feeding life, and promoting growth.

Divinatory meanings: The reconciliation of opposites. The initial stage of a journey, or the glimpse of a greater truth. Potential loss and abandonment.

XVIII Moon: An end. Passion of the body. A reduction to chaos. The shifting of cycles and patterns of thought and action. The course being set on a new, perhaps truer direction. Threat and transition from base instincts and passions, which can be a hazard. We should be weary that the unconscious may mislead, but can nonetheless offer genuine wisdom. The dog bays at the moon as man and woman mourns lost opportunities or strives emptily for impossible ideals and goals. The towers on the horizon of the known world, giving way to another plain of being.

The Marseilles card clearly shows drops of water that are heading up to the Moon, rather than down to the ground. The Moon is thus drawing life from the earth, effectively draining the life-force from it. This is the domination of base instinct and possibly the subconscious, to the point of mania (the baying hounds). This is an unsettling image, which brings to mind the cabbalistic realm of the 'qliphoth' which are but the husks or shells of life, that domain where direct solar influences are absent and shadows lead individuals astray.

Divinatory meanings: Atavistic, Dianic energies. A greater vision of the truth glimpsed with the 'Star', though still obscured. Potential error and danger.

XIX Sun: Materiality. Renewal, and the return to our creator. A state of existence akin to that of a child, with a purity of spirit. Life, warmth, energy; sustenance. There are, however, risks when we believe that we can see all clearly – there can be dangers in plain sight, not least when we take for granted that we are blessed with clarity: there are still shadows, even if they are unseen. Activity and perception. The divine essence.

The Marseilles Sun is of course directly linked to the preceding image, not least as it represents a wholly opposing influence (seen rather starkly in that water droplets are clearly falling from the sky to nourish the earth. There is growth through active energy, though the presence of two young men suggests that the female influence of the moon is required for further generation to occur; even so, where the creatures of the Moon are wild and aloof, there is here contact between the males which gives a more positive impression of this stage in 'process'.

Divinatory meanings: innocence. Perception. Optimism and contentment.

XX Judgement: The head of man. Motion and renewal. A distinctly Christian image, with links to the Archangel Michael. Some portrayals show a child, a man and a woman being raised – they represent the human trinity, at a point of potential punishment and reward. Suffering towards growth and a new phase of being or new level of understanding. Death and New Life, and by that token the condition of aspiration. For Crowley XX was Aeon, the new era, the new spiritual vista following an overdue awakening of human spirit and consciousness. Here the Egyptian Nut serves as an aspect of the heavens, upon the dawning of the new age, which is that of Horus.

The Marseilles Judgement offers an angel in a circular form, above the square forms of matter, which is the division between spirit and corporeality. A male and female may be the sun and moon respectively, while the middle figure could represent their progeny; as such, a further conjunction of opposites has been completed, though the fact that this 'child' is faced away from us might denote a degree of denial or rejection and, therefore, the need for yet further development of substance.

Divinatory meanings: New hope; the state of revitalisation. The overturning of old modes of behaviour.

XXI World : The womb. Reciprocity; the union of elements, and of the trumps. The creative and the created. The four corners of the Earth, the elements (with the human form at the centre potentially serving the role of the quintessence), the apostles. Links to the vision of Ezekiel. This is completion on a material basis, as well as transition from one form to another. Macrocosm and microcosm; harmony and order. Paul Foster Case (1884 – 1954 C.E.) identified this card with the 'cosmic instinct', and a state of being one with nature. Associations with Saturn and the Egyptian Sebek, the devourer.

The Marseilles World returns us to the imagery of the Hanged Man, though here in a reversed and wholly more pleasing composition. The crossed legs of the female and the upward-facing triangle of her arms and head suggests the dominance of spirit over matter; she is the anima mundi/quintessence as surrounded by the balanced elements, and the dense foliage of the garland that encircles her is a stark contrast to the bare trunks of the twelfth card.

Divinatory meanings: The unifying spirit. Connection. Permanence within the impermanent. Voyage; success.

XXII or 0 Fool: Movement; duration; evolution. Fate itself; the end goal. The Fool as a wise man in an idiot's garb – though the card can also represent the individual who is living a fickle life, enjoying wealth and power, that which is only temporal but which is held to be the most important. Humanity being beguiled by materiality and the ephemeral. However, the Fool's 'aloof' mentality can identify him as a divine figure – one with his head in the clouds as he represents spirit over the pointless complexities of the worldly life.

The Fool can also be interpreted as the 'child', which is one example of why many tarot decks place him at the head of the major trumps (the unshaped at the start of the journey, or the wise figure who has passed through the cycles and has gained true insight and a return to the pure spirit of youth).

The Marseilles Fool may well be carrying the tools of the Magician in his bindle, though might be ignorant that he does so; again, the means of deliverance are with him, but he is distracted and looking outside of himself for answers which only the inner-self can deliver. The hound that appears to be biting at the Fool is also compelling him forwards, perhaps blindly, and the man's many-coloured attire denotes a frivolous nature and a distracting array of emotions and responses, without focus.

Divinatory meaning: Nonconformity; insight. Can speak of mania, self-intoxication and vanity. Potentially telling of loss, or disaster.

Of course the beauty of tarot interpretation is that, for all the associations of each individual image (the image itself, the shapes and colours within it, any traditional symbolism and the intuitive response it creates), a typical spread of cards will offer a somewhat unique overall meaning given which cards are drawn, their relationship with each other, the proliferation or absence of major trumps and suits, and reversed cards. A single card can therefore offer a significantly different facet of itself from one instance to another, and the symbolism of the tarot remains to an extent malleable – formed and reformed with each successive spread.

This understanding is perhaps an ideal one for the tarot, which (as we have seen) can also be said to have had no clear 'origin', thus it remains in all regards an enigma. We can reject it as legerdemain and chicanery, but it is nonetheless easy to understand its appeal for so many over such time; with its representations of life and death, moral and spiritual symbolism and compliant form, it certainly presents us with something of a physical embodiment of Jung's 'collective unconscious', or as De Givry put it: '...in which destiny is reflected as in a mirror with multiple facets.'

Judgement

However it is that we are brought into contact with images, symbols and archetypes of the occult, they are not fixed and closed forms. These are images and concepts that may suggest certain traditions or faiths, likewise longstanding myth, moral and belief, but there is always a degree of adaptability within them that ensures endless and often personal reinterpretation; symbols convey an impression and stimulate instinct, imagination and just possibly that unconscious knowledge that links us with our most distant forebears, so their effect is an intense and moving one. Dogma has no place in their presence.

G.I. Gurdjieff suggested that myth (emotion) and symbols (wisdom) both transmitted ideas and responses to the higher centre of the self, beyond the strictures and conditioning of the intellect. He held that a symbol 'discloses its essence', but only with any great success where there is a pre-existent awareness of its form, which might be extended to that of the subconscious; the core significance of a meaningful symbol is its inherent dynamism, the capacity it has to touch deeper levels of awareness and arouse an emotional, and not necessarily an intellectual, response. Symbols, as we have already noted, are thus *experienced* in an immediate sense in a way that other information is not.

Heinrich Zimmer, as others, noted that words are symbols, likewise forms of ritual, manners and customs – symbols, then, surround us and are an integral aspect of our daily, waking life, to the extent that much of the meaning is subliminal.

Our minds therefore being accustomed to the presence of such symbolism, it is not beyond belief that symbols of a more abstract and esoteric nature, particularly those that have passed across the globe for thousands of years, would inform us in a way that most data could not hope to.

Zimmer also stated that symbols, as representations of ideas, were indicators of broader universal truths, which is something that Mircea Eliade wrote very powerfully on across several works. He makes the point that every aspect of existence is but a fragment of the ultimate whole, and thus reflects something of that whole within its nature; as these images recur throughout history they might have new meanings applied to them, potentially to the extent that they are transformed far beyond their earlier form, but the underlying meaning – that glimpse of the great whole – remains present and untouched, waiting to be experienced once again.

Symbols are a means of communicating knowledge, they are not the knowledge in itself. Ultimate truth is in part within them, and to pierce the veil at one point grants a vision, however fleeting, of the unity that links all symbols, and all of creation, to the one source. Beyond context and historicity, they return us to the primordial waters (which can be interpreted as the subconscious mind) and speak to us without words and, indeed, without restriction.

They utilise aspects of our selves that are themselves compelling and mysterious, but more than that they connect us with each other, and the entirety of existence, in a way that itself is overwhelming to the man or woman who feels this revelation. As Jung's Archetypes, so too as the thought-forms of the East and servitors of the modern magician, they also suggest a degree of malleability to this reality that we all exist within and partake of, raising the question of how real we ourselves are, and how we might use our energies to shape the reality around us.

Even if it initially arose through the reflections of humanity, the fact that a symbol might be so concentrated upon for so long that it could become rooted in a collective unconscious is astounding, but not unbelievable. If this is the case, then the symbol has effectively taken on a kind of existence all its own due to this and we can at once perceive the power of symbols upon us, and understand the efforts that have been made to 'activate' them or to create new life from specially-generated symbols, all with an intent to make changes, direct will and satisfy the imagination.

In this understanding we must realise that we hold within us the wisdom of the ages, also perhaps the great truths of existence – and we find ourselves at the ever-present brink of greatness, epiphany and transcendence. We have, in fact, not fallen so far after all, nor have we become as estranged from our full beings or our creator as we might often feel is the case…we simply require the correct vision and a suitable approach and we can confront the primordial abyss with confidence, and through that the return that appears to be so very fundamental to our core.

VI: ABYSS

Symbols, then, hold an elemental function within a complex system of relationships not just with one another, but also with the human mind, intuition, imagination and, it has been said, the human spirit. A dominant aspect of symbols is their ability to link polarities, not least of which being the corporeal and spiritual worlds, or the conscious and the unconscious – they bridge the otherwise insurmountable gaps of what we know and what we believe; what we see and what we intuit; what we are in a physical condition, and what we may be beyond it.

Symbols offer the essence or 'experience' of an answer where the questions are of a decidedly metaphysical nature, notably those relating to creation, existence, death, soul and god; where no empirical evidence can allow for a firm conclusion, they represent the closest that we can come to a satisfying denouement because symbols are, ultimately, as nebulous as the subjects being considered!

This is certainly the case when we consider the ultimate paradox, the idea of 'non-being'. Alike any attempt to grasp the immensity and (on one level of thought, at least) emptiness of space, studies and reflections of the 'abyss' are largely beyond the ken of humanity because it is so contrary to our living experience of a tangible and temporal world – how does a thing of such definite *being* begin to comprehend the *absence* of being, the vast and formless abyss that is so very outside our understanding and so very alien by definition?

The answer to that is one that speaks directly to the heart of all spirituality, mysticism, religion and even magic, in that it begins and ends with both awe and fear, the 'Mysterium Tremendum' of Rudolf Otto that we will return to throughout this last study. The abyss, like any god or creative force, has to be wholly 'other' or it is, like us, limited and definable, and it that same ineffability that draws us to it in wonder while also striking the most primitive dread in us, forcing us to question ourselves, our sense of reality, and our limited grasp of what this life actually is.

So evocative is the concept of the abyss that even approaching its bailiwick presents us with a multitude of emotions, reactions and philosophies; this is the concept of the threshold, which is always heavily-loaded with meaning (as we have seen with the noted rites and stories associated with blood, sex and death) and we see its application in the guardians and grotesques that greet us at medieval Cathedral doors, with representations of dragons in Oriental architecture and of course the disorientating practises that historically began stages of initiation in the Mystery schools.

The threshold is the barrier and/or gateway to a new state, condition or environment, at once the place where opposing forces are at their closest and yet the very point where their separation is made manifest, or as Mircea Eliade put it, the '...frontier that distinguishes and opposes two worlds, where passage from profane to sacred worlds becomes possible.'

In the realm of spirituality the idea of the threshold is a fundamental one, as it serves as a representation of *passage*, the transition of one level of consciousness or form of life to another. It also reinforces the vital sense of order in that the threshold is a clear point of demarcation between the known and the unknown, or 'us' and 'them', with 'our world' that associated with right, reality and the sacred as opposed to those who dwell beyond the border who are questionable at best, otherwise those with distorted beliefs and attitudes, the profane and the evil.

The immediate world of any group is, as James Frazer stated in *'The Golden Bough'*, personalised, and the inhabitants enjoy a sense of mastery and influence over their domain through that personalisation – where there is an encroachment it is an attack from the 'outsider', which is so often mythologized as the marauding dragon which descends to sow discord and chaos, and many ancient and 'primitive' rituals have been practised to cyclically ward off that attack, and maintain the status quo at all costs.

The threat of the other and the significance of the threshold are even more prominent when the menace is vast and faceless, thus we have the recurrence of imagery relating to deep waters, dense forests, bottomless pits and the nightmares of the deepest subconscious. No danger is more alluring or overwhelming to the senses than that which is instinctively felt but not seen, and so the idea of the primordial abyss is for many a terrifying one exactly because there is no name, face or intent to associate with it; this is the 'other' *par excellence*, where all our preconceptions of existence are proved fallible and our sense of order, stability and reality are dissolved, and there is little more terrifying to the human mind than the recognition of its ignorance and, therefore, its apparent vulnerability.

Chaos, the very stuff of the abyss, is often the root of our fear – though as we will see it has often been chaos that creation was said to have risen from, thus we have a contradiction that must be overcome: if the faceless chaos contains, somewhat like the tao, all potentiality and indeed did and will again contain all that we are, why should chaos fuel such fear in our deepest selves, and why should a return to the state of primordial chaos serve as the very apogee of horror?

Chaos

The term 'chaos' has its root with the Greek 'kháos' that was applied to a situation of great emptiness, such as a chasm or abyss. Hesiod's *'Theogony'* stated that chaos was the initial substance to exist, from which creation emerged in the form of Gaia, Tartarus and Eros, though it is not made clear where the chaos itself emanated from, if it was created (which would suggest an intelligent force pre-existing chaos), or if chaos simply existed, perhaps as the most basic and fundamental state of all.

As in many other mythologies, the Greek use of the concept of chaos was most apparent in stories of cosmogony, that point where sky and earth or sky and waters are separated and life begins to form within them, and it is this understanding of the idea that has remained the most prominent – here chaos is the changing, dynamic 'thing' from which all else emanates in one manner or another, something of a terrifying ocean of potency that is nonetheless enrapturing in a spiritual or mystical sense as it suggests the primal, primordial unity of all that we have since strained to rediscover.

Heraclitus (c.535 – 475 B.C.E.), for one, held that chaos was indeed the fount from which all came into being, and that Primal Chaos was the true reality; by extension he also believed that the conjunction of opposites was the key to harmony on a personal and cosmic scale, and that 'becoming', the philosophical condition of constant change, re-organisation and flux, was the foremost attribute of the created world – one belief that would align him with a number of Eastern faiths, esoteric philosophies and $20^{th} - 21^{st}$ century Western magicians, among others.

Plato's *'Timaeus'* holds chaos to be shapeless and malleable space ('chôra') which contains the component elements of life but in a disorganized and unstructured state; he also notes that this chôra is '...a receptacle of all becoming...' which again brings to mind the Chinese concept of the tao and offers a somewhat affirming understanding of the nature of chaos, without the added complexity of stating how the becoming eventually began to take place!

Ovid did not stray far from this understanding in his *'Metamorphoses'* where he described chaos as the 'shapeless heap' of disordered elements, that containing every possibility of life and form but which has not yet been activated or forged. Similar may well be implied with Genesis (1:2) where we find '...the earth was without form, and void; and darkness was upon the face of the deep'; the abyss that is here termed 'tohu wa-bohu' is, again, formlessness that is awaiting some kind of seed to be planted so that the organisation of composite form can commence.

Of course, we cannot easily move beyond the mental stumbling block of imagining or describing 'non-being' and are only truly on safe ground when we can focus on the creation that emerges from that state. Genesis goes on to offer us one of the most common visualisations of this nothingness when 'the Spirit of God moved upon the waters', and it is often water which is used to represent the abyss and the abysmal depths not just because of its life-sustaining properties and/or unseen extremities, but also because it is an elastic and ever-adaptable substance, that which can seep, flow or deluge and assume the shape of any given 'container.'

The idea of an immense depth of the abyss – a vast expanse of formless chaos – easily applies itself when we also attempt to define and chart the lower reaches of the human mind in the form of dreams, atavisms and instincts that are termed 'subconscious.' Human beings cannot help but see themselves as the 'centre of all', if only in terms of their own lives, and with that understanding comes the belief (or at least the hope) that we are much more than we appear to be, potentially glimpsed in intuitive insight, imagination, the ability we have to foresee and grapple with our own mortality and, certainly, the very fact that we dream and seem to have a nocturnal existence that is quite beyond our waking, conscious limitations.

However, though this 'hidden realm' or abyss offers us the potential for all manner of greatness if we can but perceive and work towards it, its very nature as the hidden world (night/waters) where no clear light shines by which we can orientate (forest/cavern) and no recognisable order exists (wasteland/desert) frequently stirs contrary responses that may in fact represent the fears that we have of ourselves, but which most often take the form of fears of any other being or beings that can become the scapegoat (old and vengeful spirits/demons/monsters).

The problem is that we so depend on a sense of order for our own sanity and social cohesion that *any* lack of order is anathema to us, as noted by Boethius (c.477 – 524 C.E.) in his '*Consolation of Philosophy*' when he states: 'it is not surprising...if ignorance of its order makes people think a thing is unplanned or chaotic.' That which is outside of our frame of reference is by definition alien, and so the concept of a primordial chaos or abyss is certainly an affront to what we hold most dear, namely our grasp of reality and self.

This returns us to Rudolf Otto (1869 – 1937 C.E.) and the 'Mysterium Tremendum' which is the unreasoning awe and fear felt when an individual experiences the truly unknown, and never more so than when that unknown is the 'numinous' or holy. It is true that what is being sought when a god or creator is worshipped must be so very 'other' to be able to perform the acts and enjoy the supernatural wisdom that are attributed to him/her/them/it, but it is that stark 'otherness' that is ultimately the most terrifying, so much beyond our capacity to comprehend that we can only experience the briefest and most cursory glimpses.

The Ultimate, whether in the form of a being, an intelligence, an energy or a state more subtle than any of these, cannot be cognised by the human mind, or it could not be the Ultimate. This is reflected by the Sanskrit term 'upādhi' which signifies 'attribute' yet also 'disguise', a dual-meaning that indicates something which is all and yet nothing, everywhere and nowhere, a truth and yet a lie. This is chaos and the abyss, which mythology and symbolism have perhaps best attempted to define through analogy and archetypal imagery precisely because no means of fully describing it, its aims, abilities and foci is possible, with it, after all, not really being any kind of 'it' at all...

Void

A typically philosophical understanding of the abyss can be found within Hindu mythology, which accepts the cosmic cycles of existence that again and again see creation give way to gradual decay and eventual dissolution, before the next emergence of form can take place. The Yugas or eras begin with a point of absolute perfection, when the creation is essentially new-born, but immediately a form of decomposition is inherent within creation that will grow and, in time, reach critical mass.

'Dharma' which is effectively cosmic order or the 'correct' way of living is that which fades with time, and the only means of its renewal – and that state of perfection being rediscovered – is through the necessary reaching of a nadir; as such, though there may be little comfort for those of us existing in this 'Kali Yuga', the last of the great epochs of Hinduism, the dissolution that is taking place is a natural one that has existed long before our time and will occur again, perhaps many times, before any kind of final end is achieved.

The abyss, then, is the universal or cosmic womb, from which all in existence finds form but into which all duly returns – nought is able to avert the return of its tide, and all will be reclaimed by the Great Mother in a relentless cycle of birth, mortal life, annihilation and re-incubation, a pattern that does not only encompass humanity but all of creation. That which nourishes also destroys, which is a fundamental understanding within the Indian religions which is profoundly explored through the various forms of the goddess, she who is protector and marauder, mother and murderer.

We once more find that the energy of Maya – the stuff of life such as blood, sap, rain and milk – is closely aligned with the image of water and fluidity, as Maya is that which is constantly changing, the life-giving essence for corporeal forms that is, in the absolute realm of the spirit, 'unreal'. It is said that to dive into Maya is to seek the very secret of life, as it is imperishable and limitless, at one and the same time the source and the grave of all.

The threat of chaos, and the abysmal waters, is elsewhere a much more active ingredient in myths of creation and cosmology. The Sumerians, for example, believed that the great cosmic mountain which was split in two to create the heavens and the earth had risen from the primordial waters, but those same waters contained cosmic peril and must be cyclically quelled to ensure stability and order (mythologizing the challenge that the Sumerians had in taming and controlling the rivers that they so desperately depended upon for subsistence).

Zu was the Sumerian dragon which so many others appear to have descended from, rising from the watery depths to steal the tablets that the great god Enlil (himself a river god before his instatement as one of the land) wore. The laws of the entire universe were inscribed on these tablets, thus their reclamation was of paramount importance, and it is said that Zu was subsequently vanquished by the sun god Ninnurta in a prototypical example of the sun falling upon the dragon of chaos and driving it into its chthonic pit before rising again, in still greater glory.

A similar tale was central to the Babylonian religion in the creation story of the *'Enuma eilish'*, which was composed no later than the end of the 2nd millennium B.C.E. Here, before the sky and earth were made manifest, there was the male Apsu (fresh water) and the female Tiamat (salt water) who conjoined to produce the gods; when the gods became noisy and disruptive, Apsu became greatly angered and considered how he might bring an end to them and their troublesome ways.

Before any action could be taken Ea, the god of magic, enchanted Apsu into a deep sleep and killed him, which of course led to Tiamat seeking vengeance – she thus created monsters to attack and slay the gods, who were sufficiently frightened to beseech the mighty Marduk as their hero. Marduk, a huge figure who breathed fire and had two faces, battled the monsters and won and ultimately tore Tiamat's body asunder to make the universe; he also instituted the cycles of the year, the stars and the paths of the sun and moon, before finally creating humankind as a servant for the gods.

Many inferences can be made from this story, though we again find most prominently the image of the saviour/sun god destroying the female personification of the original abyssal state. The mother of gods becomes a raging, destructive force that has to be obliterated and scattered to ensure that the established order can be maintained, though from her component parts new life is sowed in the cosmos, thus a form of re-birth takes effect (and the Great Mother takes her place as the root and end of all life).

The Ancient Greeks held a number of creation beliefs, including one whereby it was Darkness that bore Chaos, and from those two sprang night, day, Erebus (the personification of darkness, the shadow) and air, and another where the God of All, appearing in the midst of Chaos, split the earth from the heavens, then the water from the earth, with level upon level of creation culminating with humanity, each member of which housed a spark of the divine element that was First Creation, in the form of the soul.

The symbols of the abyss are apparent, too, with the 'Daughters of Water' such as the Sirens who lure men into the chaotic depths, the dreadful Gorgons who repel men away from it and the rather neutral Graeae who sit at the threshold (sometimes depicted as swans to suggest their graceful appearance on one side of the 'pit' while the unseen half works away, unrecognised by the limited perception of humanity).

However it is the myth of Typhon that is most notable in this study, given its close parallel with the aforementioned stories of Zu and Tiamat. Hesiod's *Theogony* states that Typhon was the son of Gaia and Tartarus, while elsewhere we are told that he was born of Gaia (Earth) alone or the goddess Hera. In the latter example Hera, who was enraged at Zeus for having produced the fair Athena without her, prayed for a son that could challenge and better Zeus – and Gaia and the Titans, those prayed to, were apparently happy to oblige.

Typhon was a giant whose head, according to Apollodorus, touched the stars, with serpentine attributes (most prominently the one hundred snake heads that sat upon his shoulders spewing deafening bestial sounds and fire in Hesiod's account). A beast of immense strength and prodigious appetite, he was also at points described as having many hands, wings and snake tails, though his eyes of fire, wild hair and matching demeanour are recurring aspects of this hulking beast that was neither man nor god.

It is said that Hera left Typhon in his infancy, placing him under the care of Python, and that her son grew to be a terror to all humanity, not least as he reached manhood and coupled with Echidna who herself was half-woman and half-snake; their progeny included Cerberus (the hound with many heads that served as the guardian of Hades), Hydra (the serpent with many heads that only grew more if any were cut from her body) and Chimera (the composite lion/goat/snake monster that, like its father, breathed fire). In some accounts, the children of Typhon include the Harpies and Gorgon, the mother of Medusa.

In time, Typhon fulfilled the destiny set for him by his mother and laid down a challenge to Zeus, and the battle which resulted is at points described in a suitably apocalyptic tone. Hesiod describes a sea raging from the heat of thunderbolts, Olympus and Hades quaking at the mighty tumult occurring betwixt them, which wrought havoc on the earth. Eventually of course Zeus smites his foe with a thunderbolt and dashes him to the ground, where he leaves a scorched crater that in one account was linked to the volcanic plain of Catacecaumene or 'Burnt Land' on the Gadiz River, in modern-day Turkey, and elsewhere beneath Mount Etna in Sicily and the island of Ischia off the coast of Naples.

We have noted that the stories of Typhon and Python are linked, which is no less apparent than in the story of Python's own demise at the hands of Apollo, following a failed uprising (elsewhere the serpent-being killed by Apollo is a female named Delphyne, who was named as the female guardian of Typhon when he was delivered to Python, thus the links are rather profuse and complex). Nonetheless we see an epic retelling of what appears to be an archetypal myth, which for the Babylonians was that of Marduk and Tiamat and for the Sumerians that of Zu and Ninnurta, among others.

Further to this, Typhon is at points identified with the great opponent of Egyptian myth, Set/Seth, with the murdered, dismembered and scattered Osiris linked to Dionysus and the avenging son Horus linked to Apollo. There may be no clearly demarcated pathways between these ancient cultures and their mythology, but such central figures, events and symbols pervade them that it is difficult to disregard that those pathways must have existed. However we judge, it is clear that the chaotic abyss was perceived as the giver of life that then sought to reclaim what it had borne, and the great serpent of the depths, then the dragon, came to personify that threat of chaos to order, stability and to life itself.

Other familiar symbolism is inherent within the creation story of the Orphics, who relied on the written works of the mythical poet and philosopher Orpheus. Here, at the beginning of all, was the Absolute (which can be understood as a form of stasis or suspended time). Once activated, time was Wholeness, that which encompassed all manifestations and forms of creation and was divided into two distinct aspects – Ether or 'the Bound' which serves as a symbol of primordial activity, limited to place and duration, and Chaos or 'Infinity' which is totally unlimited, unorganised and sometimes linked to a first, creative deity.

Existence as we understand it occurred when Ether touched upon the great Chaos in the manner of a whirlwind (a spiral) which led to the formation of an ovoid, later known as the 'Cosmic Egg'. The image of the egg as the birthplace of 'life' is common to many mythologies, no doubt for its simple analogy that makes immediate sense to the human mind, based on direct experience, and we see eggs hatching to give form to the world or, instead, revealing the deity that will make such a creation their magnum opus.

An Egyptian myth sees the supreme sun god appearing from an egg that was formed by the union of eight deities who were the various forces of chaos, while China's creative god Pangu was gestated inside an egg held in the great void; when he burst from its confines some 18,000 years later, the denser matter was scattered to form the earth, and the airier matter took its place as the heavens.

The significance afforded to the egg in connection with the process of divine creation was such that creatures that laid eggs were especially venerated by many cultures; thus we see the Iban of Borneo offering obeisance to the first two beings, the birds Ara and Irik, that waited patiently over the abysmal waters before taking from it the two eggs that gave forth the earth and the sky, and the Egyptian Apep who is a more familiar image of chaos itself, given his embodiment as a serpent.

Just as the symbolism often returned to the snake and dragon, so too the concept of creation repeatedly brought peoples into contact with the abyss and its chaotic horror, which may be in itself dormant and neutral, but which required divine or positive activation for it to allow any product to be ordered from its mass. The 'fons et origo' or 'source and origin' is the original state from which creation takes shape, but it is more often the case that creation is a gift by a divine entity and an improvement on the original, disordered matter of the cosmos (in spite of the apparent limitations that the created form endures, not least of which is its eventual demise).

The abyss is a tool in the process of life-giving, not often the director of that process, and it reclaims what was taken of it whenever the opportunity arises. No malefic agenda lies behind this reclamation, it is simply an inevitable stage in the arc of life, but in many ways such a stoic and detached menace is more terrifying to the mind of men and women than any gurning monster wielding a bloody sword, hence why the idea of the abyss has frequently remained a decidedly troubling one, and why beliefs have often relied on myths of 'Creatio ex nihilo' or the creation of matter by a god, rather than the seemingly paradoxical 'Ex nihilo nihil fit', where matter simply 'was' before the first creations emerged. We cannot comprehend the nature of the abyss, thus we choose to depict its use by a more relatable, albeit divine, figure.

As has been noted already, the threat perceived by 'chaos' and the 'abyss' is hardly removed once the contentious subject of creation has been dealt with; the abyssal water gave vent to life but usually not often of its own doing, and awaits every individual and indeed the universe as a whole with unending patience, for it exists outside the paradigm that is time. It is true that, symbolically, the return to water can be held to have the very holiest and most positive of outcomes, but even here the dangers and potential horrors of sacrifice and re-birth are the more prominent aspects of the tale.

Thus, where Tertullian (155 – 220 C.E.) can describe water as the 'seat of the divine spirit' and baptism be regarded as a return to an original, pure and unstained condition, the same purification by water can take the form of the cataclysmic deluge (overcoming Atlantis and sparing none bar Noah and his Ark) or the potentially fatal 'Night-Sea Crossing' where the Hero is swallowed by a beast of the depths (Jonah) or travels the Underworld (Osiris, Orpheus, etc.) in order to overcome the great opponent and – hopefully – rise triumphant, often through a sacred point such as the 'world navel'. We see the same application of symbol with Christ at the point of his crucifixion – the abyss must be confronted, entered and crossed for any higher state of being to be achieved, and this by its nature cannot be an easy or risk-free journey. The abyss appears to be anathema.

Of course, this is not universally the case, and it might be argued that most of the fears about chaos and the abyss result from the lack of meaningful interaction that the human mind has with them as concepts, let alone as potential realities, for darkness will always remain dark unless we choose to shine a light toward it. An example of a more positive and certainly more intimate relationship with the abyss can be found within

Voodoo, where veves are man-made links to the abyss and serve as opened gateways to any loa that is sought and sufficiently venerated.

Veves are drawn to effectively create a meeting-point (or crossroads) between the created world and the abyss, and offerings are made to appease a loa and invite its attendance at a moment of ritual; the abyss is thus an omnipresent and imminent quantity that is actively tapped to commune with a deity. Water is held to be the source of all life, and so the abyssal waters are where loa emerge from and return to, should they wish it, including those who serve an individual throughout their lives, the so-called 'master of the head'.

Rites (Dessounin) are carefully performed upon a person's death to ensure that the gros-bon-ange (self/soul) departs the body, so too the divine loa connected to it, and that both are duly freed to journey to their next destination, but the fact remains that the abyss is, here, a means of potentiality, akin to many of the earliest creation myths – it is the dwelling-place of the 'other', namely the various deities of the religion, which allows them to travel to the human realm at will and even nurtures those human souls that require a period of time before taking their place back in the company of their loved ones.

In this case the abyss remains the 'fons et origo', just as the swallowing of Jonah by a whale, the archetypal passage through an underworld or even the sacrifice of one's life in a spiritual context can be devastating and terrifying, the very definition of an ordeal, but ultimately serve as the means of dissolution towards a re-birth. Like the path of the shaman or sages throughout history, communion with the abyss is the greatest challenge and certainly the most threatening to the self – but little else, if anything, can offer the rewards that are possible by that return to our primordial source.

As in Voodoo, the abyss is frequently considered to be imminent and all manner of cracks and breaks in the ground, any chasm or void, is seen to be an entrance/exit to it; for the Celts the abyss was believed to reside within mountains (suggesting a certain 'welling-up' of energies that have strived to break through into the created world), while various Mediterranean peoples have held that it resided at the point of the horizon, where it forever waited on the threshold of perception (and consciousness), unwavering in its gaze.

So often the further manifestations of the abyss, that is to say that which has followed our world and humanity itself, are of a negative variety. As we have seen, the dragon or serpent that can offer wisdom, knowledge and insight nonetheless commonly serves as the destroyer or marauder, seeking to overturn established order; likewise the beast of the sea, in its many guises, can be the means of a great passage towards a higher state of consciousness or being, but is frequently more foe than friend.

With the seas and other open stretches of water so closely aligned with the idea of the abyss, and personified by chaos, it is interesting that so many malign yet intelligent forces have been said to have arisen from it with a reason d'etre of total destruction in one form or another. Hence the great sea serpent Leviathan spoken of in Job, Isaiah, Psalms and the apocryphal Enoch; also Behemoth in Job which has been depicted as a fish or serpent but may well have been considered to be in the form of a hippopotamus, and the gigantic cephalopod Kraken from Scandinavian folklore, which was said to be up to 1.5 miles in circumference and thus all too easily mistaken for an island.

Even when they have been successfully charted, the vast waters of our planet remain enigmatic, alien and forbidding, as not only do they represent awesome powers of destruction but they conceal depths that boggle the mind and thus remain unconquered and to an extent unknown to us. In this manner the waters are the perfect symbol for the abyss and indeed for any god, in that we can never fully understand them and run an immense risk when we attempt to do so.

We can see, then, why the beasts of chaos often rise from the watery depths and why, for instance, the whale's mouth has at points been equated with the gaping mouth of Hell. Like the Kraken tempting the sea-wary to land that is not land but death, the mouth of the whale is the snare of man that may result in epiphany for the Hero, but will mean certain death for many others who enter the belly of the beast without sufficient wisdom to burn or burrow their way back out.

The great battle between Ahab and his nemesis in Henry Melville's *'Moby Dick'* (1851) is a fascinating exploration of the theme of humanity seeking and confronting the chaos and/or the shadow within, not least because it is left to the reader to conclude which of the two protagonists is the true monster. Why are the concepts of chaos and the abyss such terrifying commodities unless they are representative of a part of ourselves that we would rather overcome, tame or destroy – much as we perceive that the actually neutral 'chaos' wishes to do to us? Ahab battles himself in the novel and, as his fear of losing himself becomes increasingly desperate, his attempts to strike down the monster intensify and make that loss of self become inevitable.

Indeed, some of the most pertinent and sophisticated explorations of chaos come from the understanding that it lies within us, very much a part of us, and we deny its presence or attempt to quell it only at a dire cost to ourselves. Kali, for one, is a goddess of chaos, coloured black (which her name itself denotes) as a symbol of the depths and primordial energy; she is thus mystery itself, though also represents the dynamism of chaos through her role as marauder – with bulging eyes, fangs, a necklace of skulls and carrying the head of another, she is associated with rage, war, illness and sacrifice.

Kali is the dark side of Nature, and can take the form of the suffocating womb of the earth which claims life, but she also serves as 'Kali Ma' or 'Mother Kali', the protector who guards her own as only the great primordial female force could. She is the shadow side of the psyche, where we meet the threat of the wilderness and the aspects of self that we largely avoid acknowledging, but she is not a force of evil; the only evil that she brings is when she is rejected and ignored, lambasted as a demon and barred from entry to our consciousness and our lives.

Dionysus is another such figure, whose story tells us all that we need to know of the nature and place of chaos and its place in human existence, and the cosmos. He is a god of the wilds, but is much more closely linked to the wild that lies within humanity than in nature and is, like the abyss, barely perceptible as a being because he is always so very close to us – he is glimpsed, perhaps in the corner of the mind if not the eye, but disappears from our 'vision' before we can fully witness him, and with good reason.

It is said that Dionysus ran roughshod in life and later joined the Olympians, rather tellingly claiming the seat of Hestia (the goddess of hearth, home and domestication). He had at one point been torn apart and devoured by the Titans, but was fashioned back together and returned to life, before being driven mad by Hera and wandering the countryside with one Silenus and various bacchantes, leaving a trail of madness, extreme violence and bloodshed in his wake.

Order was of prominent concern to the Ancient Greeks, whose understanding of creation depended intensely on the maintenance of the order that had been divinely established, thus 'letting go' of oneself was a form of madness that was not tolerated, least of all from women who were expected to ensure harmony above all others; to turn away from the typical duties and role of womanhood was nigh on a sin.

The '*Bacchae*' of Euripides (c.480 – 406 B.C.E.) tells of Dionysus returning to Thebes, which was said to have been his place of birth. When his Mother's sisters refuse to acknowledge his divinity, he delivers madness unto them and they wonder the country much as Dionysus was said to have done; eventually confronted on a hill-top by a group of herdsmen who wish to stop their carnage, they tear the cattle apart and devour the raw flesh, before pillaging the village and stealing its children. They later return to their senses and are overcome with horror and remorse at their actions and are duly exiled.

A clear moral to the story is to acknowledge the godhood of Dionysus, but this in reality means that we cannot reject the Dionysian aspect that is inherent to us and to Nature as a whole. Dionysus, like Kali and like Melville's whale represent a shifting of order, but not incidents or modes of being that are intrinsically malignant or wrong – certainly, bliss can be experienced by embracing the Dionysian madness, spiritual epiphany can be obtained, and the greatest products of faith, art and philosophy can be formed (also seen in the 'creative derangement' associated with Pan).

The Fool of the Tarot is stepping into a void but is blissfully ignorant or unaware of his situation. He may just as well be venturing into the mouth of the sea beast or communing with his Dionysian aspect, but this is not necessarily the action of a madman or an idiot (though history suggests that this, too, is possible!) One must be aware of the risks of pushing beyond the threshold and of tapping the abyss or engaging with one of its manifestations, but the rewards that can be found, for some, outweigh those risks and one can only truly hope to transcend present limitations by undertaking the Night-Sea voyage, or accepting the shadow self as a valid aspect of who and what we are.

It is possible, of course, for us to encounter the wisdom and creativity that is potential within the abyss without too active a relationship being developed – though again, the importance of accepting what is found in its truest sense is key to a healthy mind and life, let alone any spiritual wellbeing. To sleep is often seen to be a descent into the abyss of the mind, (hence the Buddhist AUM as it relates to sleep with A = Waking Consciousness, U = Dream Consciousness and M = Deep Sleep), with the dreamer hovering over the primordial waters where being dissolves into non-being.

Of course dreams can only offer the briefest of communiqués with the shadow self and the primordial element, with visions and ideas all too often disappearing beneath the surface of the water each morning much as the sword Excalibur was withdrawn down in to the depths of Avalon's lake, and there is a risk that such glories as are encountered cannot be found again upon any return, as Heraclitus suggested with his famous: 'You cannot step twice into the same river; for fresh waters are ever flowing in upon you.'

That said, there is a reason for the mind's compartmentalisation of the dream and the dream-state in waking life. It is hardly conducive to everyday existence to be in thrall to one's experiences and visions in sleep but, perhaps more importantly, only glimpses can be had or else we again find ourselves at risk. The full journey is a dangerous one that requires sound understanding and approach, lest we lose ourselves – it being said that the silence which surrounds the AUM is the great unknown, where manifestation and non-manifestation meet.

Not for the last time we are reminded of the 'Mysterium Tremendum', which applies just as closely to our efforts to integrate our full personality. For Jung, symbols were used as the mode of communication to offer a glimpse or the experience of a Truth (in Jung's example 'a direct experience of God') without overwhelming us with its totality, and the same can be said for our brief interactions with the abyss, for if we should '...gaze too deeply into the dark mirror, then the awful event of the meeting may befall.'

The Middle Pillar

Cabbalism offers a means of gradually ascending the Tree of Life which can lead an adept towards the great creative force, most directly in the form of the 'Middle Pillar'. The risks of course remain, but a full understanding of the Sephirothic Tree and the manifestations of God that exist upon it allows for a steady journey through the central stations of the Tree towards the perceivable abyss, which is in fact as high as even the most engaged and spiritually-adept practitioners could hope to venture.

Beyond any means of perception is Ain Soph, the creative force in a state of non-creation or the 'incomprehensible Abyss of Divine Majesty' in the words of Manly P. Hall (1901 – 1990 C.E.) Below Ain Soph is Kether, the crown of the tree from which the dual aspects of Chokmah and Binah spring. Together, these first three Sephirah are the Supernals, which are said to give to and inform all other manifestations of life without diminution of themselves, existing as they do on an entirely other plain of being.

The abyss sits between the Supernal Sephiroth and the seven emanations that descend from them, and no living being can traverse this threshold due to the insurmountable difference in states that they exist within – below is the perceivable, where the relationship of subject and object is made manifest and limited, while above there is no such thing as a 'concept' or an 'entity' of any sort. It is said that will, intuition and spirit all occur among the Supernals, but in an unlimited form that offers but their reflection to the lower Tree, and indeed to humanity.

The vast desert of the abyss, as it is often considered within Cabbalism, thus separates the ideal from the actual and the infinite from the finite, thus that which lies on its furthest shore remains totally outside of any frame of reference that we have or might hope, even in our loftiest dreams, to attain. The numinous must remain numinous, and we must learn what we can from the perceivable Sephiroth that constitute the human soul or Ruach (intellect borne of reason, will, imagination, memory and emotion).

It is a fitting point that much of what can be said about the abyss is linked to a Sephira that in most regards is not a Sephira at all. Daath is often absent from depictions of the Tree. It has been stated that it is not in itself a manifestation of God alike the other ten stations but is rather a host to all of those other aspects; it has also been suggested that Daath is a functional aspect of the Tree in place of Kether, as Daath is the perceivable reflection of the first station. Daath, then, is the image of God as opposed to the godhead that we cannot comprehend.

This eleventh station of the Tree unifies Chokmah (Wisdom) and Binah (Understanding), and as such is often associated with the Tree of Knowledge of Good and Evil that grew in Eden; it is itself 'knowledge', the state of realisation and consciousness that is the key to both generation and regeneration that feeds from the abyss and down through to Tiphareth, the central station that is linked to the sun and the Biblical idea that God said 'Let there be light', and there was light.

Tiphareth, in turn, is the station of messiahs and saviours, the assorted spiritual 'light-bearers' who bring with them the fire from heaven and as recompense suffer a sacrificial death, as the sun itself rises and falls. Of course the death is a symbolic one and does not mean an end but a necessary translation from one form to another – but the wisdom passed on from the children of Tiphareth was carried through the abyss and then Daath before being disseminated to humanity, and the ability to make the passage was that which signified their pre-eminence among humankind.

The potential of expansion and, perhaps, glory are therefore integral to Daath, and by that token it is also known to be the place where lesser beings have fallen in their attempts to achieve clarity, transcendence and at times greatness. In some accounts it is akin to the desert of the abyss, as we are told that it is the eternal abode of the failure, likewise of the empirical egos of men and also the previous creations of God.

In many ways it is a Purgatory, where wasted or unworthy material is passed from the world of creation and husks of beings take on nightmarish form, garbed in this cast-off emotion, desire and energy. We might also say there lies a counterpart of Daath within each of ourselves, where we find the shortcomings, excesses and failures of our current and any previous incarnations. The keyhole to the Supernal thus also serves as a vacuum, and will cut a deadly swathe through most who attempt to rend the veil and glimpse what lies beyond it.

That vacuum can also draw us through Daath and into the realm of the Qliphoth, the realm of husks that is a mirror-image – or, rather, parody – of the true Tree, with the various stations serving as obstacles rather than gateways. It is true that in their way the Qliphoth aid the Sephiroth, surrounding them in a form of sheath or shell which can mislead the uninitiated who believe they have reached God when they are instead in a sphere of lies and legerdemain, but which nonetheless shield the core emanation that is the Sephiroth from any outside influences or disintegration.

The realm of the shadow-tree is alike the desert of the abyss in that it is a land of the soulless, those that either lost life and were trapped within its confines, the elemental forms which crave life but have never experienced it, and the excessive and wasted energies and thoughts of humanity. It is the astral graveyard, the void, where unbalanced forces roam and demons stir the forces of dissention, more recognisable as a Hell than a Purgatory.

There is a belief that it is often this sphere that is tapped during séances and where those on a spiritual journey stray or are misled, though it can result in the creative works of the visionary. William Blake (1757 – 1827 C.E.) for one practised sciomancy and regularly joined séances and as a result filled sketchbooks with all manner of 'apparitions' – like *The Ghost of a Flea*' – that bear the mark of the lower astral world and elemental, but which certainly gave vent to some of the poet-mystic's finest creations.

Where the interaction is not quite so casual, however, and the seeker is actively engaging their 'Higher Self' or 'Holy Guardian Angel' but is beguiled and drawn away from the true path, the price paid is irreversibly damaging, more so as the individual embraces what is believed to be ultimate truth and divine light and is instead claimed by the forces of chaos, which Dion Fortune stated was one of the kingdoms of the Qliphoth.

Through Daath and the Qliphoth we also enter the domain/dimension of Lilith, Adam's first wife. We are told that she was greatly attracted to the sparks of light that she could perceive (angels in one form) and attempted herself to rise up to the heavens in pursuit, only to be cast down and sent to Eden by her creator; she was then drawn to Adam but was rejected by him in favour of the more beautiful Eve, and finally made one further attempt to enter Heaven but was sent down into the seas.

Elsewhere, it is said that Lilith was created from dust, as Adam was, and sought equality with him, including in sexual matters. Of course this was anathema (chaos) and suggested a wayward female principle, wishing to consume rather than create, and so Lilith was again cast out as an embodiment of earth without spirit, serving as the epitome of passion, matter and the grossest of all corporeality.

Either way, Lilith continued to be attracted to the sparks of godhead that she saw in others and had a particular obsession with young children and babies who bore the clearest signs of this pneuma, making it her mission to find minors in need of punishment and striking them down with the burning sword of Genesis 3:24. From this aspect of Lilith we see the future striges and night-hags that terrified children for centuries thereafter, so too we can appreciate her connection with incubi, succubi and the other assorted shells of existence that desperately seek any experience of life, often at the cost of the living.

Lilith copulated by the great seas and produced giant demon spawn; she bore monsters and grotesques that wreaked havoc on humanity; she lay with Cain, who had also initially spurned her, and the malignant spirits of earth and air were subsequently released – Lilith *is* chaos and unleashes it in a variety of hellish forms. Through Daath she rules over the domain of the failures and takes possession of the addicts, the obsessives, the base, the weak and the egotists.

The British Jewish artist Fay Pomerance (1912 – 2001 C.E.) offered a perfect illustration of this Lilith in her '*The Sixth Palace of Hell*', where we see a man in his last moments, lying in his deathbed. As he passes, he begins to see beyond the earthly veil and perceives that which has always been around him, but was heretofore invisible – the eternal temptress Lilith, riding on the archangel Samael (the seducer and destroyer). To the dying man she is beautiful and voluptuous, while her shadow-side, still obscured from his view, is corrupt and rancorous. Lilith is seeking one final sin from the man so that she can claim his last breath and house him within her realm of shells, and her lies are so convincing that she may well succeed.

As in the '*Zohar*' Lilith is often described but not named, so as to keep her partly obscured and in the shadows where she is forced to reside. Indeed, she is the shadow, and the stuff of the threshold that beguiles and confuses the wanderer and the pathetic. However, as we recognised in Kali and Dionysus,

Lilith too is already part of what we are and can offer genuine wisdom; she is the shadow of ourselves, the aspects that we choose to ignore or that we are simply and naively unaware of, often only seeing it in others around us.

Weakness, submission, decadence, passion, lust, and egotism are certainly no strangers to most individuals, though we hide from those impulses or repress them in most cases – or indulge in them fully at the expense of all else. Neither extreme is healthy, and neither offers the equilibrium of a good, happy and enlightened life. Lilith is another archetypal warning of what we risk by not daring to view ourselves and know ourselves as a total being, as well as a warning of what we will have to face if we wish to have that understanding; the most feared demon of all, which bears our own face and lies in waiting within our own created abyss.

Self And Shadow

Magicians, too, venture on this dangerous path towards then great oblivion, and though their reasons for embarkation may in some respects parallel those of the mystic, the end goal can differ in the extreme. Personal spiritual development remains the primary objective, but success here means that the individual obtains more than the fleeting understanding that magic (or magick) gives of the incommunicable essence of all that lies beyond the abyss, and returns a changed person who has indeed 'stolen the fire from heaven.'

Further to this, the very nature of the Supernal Sephiroth make them an ultimate aim of the magician, as experiencing them means tapping the sphere of 'potential'. Any who accomplish (or believe that they have accomplished) even the barest contact with this higher, noumenal plain have dipped their proverbial toe in the eternal waters of the divine – but first they must pass fully through the murkier and treacherous waters of the abyss.

Various rituals guide a magician on this path, including the 'Oath /Crossing of the Abyss' and the 'Night of Pan' though the preparedness of the individual is of paramount importance and other abilities must be nurtured and mastered before any attempt is made, lest insanity or death be the only sure outcome; 'The Sacred Rites of Abramelin the Mage' are possibly the most widely-known of this type, having been a staple part of (and challenge to) the magickal career of Aleister Crowley.

These 'initiatory' rites are themselves exhaustive and necessarily difficult, as they seek to foster an inherent self-discipline within the magician, unite his or her psyche and attain a meaningful communiqué with his or her 'Augoeides' which is elsewhere called the 'Higher Self' and the 'Holy Guardian Angel'. The Augoeides is the real, permanent and bountiful aspect of the consciousness from which inspiration and spiritual insight is sustained, and its usual abode is the Sephira of Tiphareth (the sun that all else revolves around).

Daath is a focal-point of many studies in this light, as it sits in the Middle Pillar between the station of the Tiphareth and the abyss, beyond which the Supernals emanations await. It has been described as a loophole through which the human will might be directed, a 'sphere-shaped hole in the fabric of the universe' (Regardie) and the rent in space through which 'non-being seeped...to become conceptual thought' (Fortune). The ego of each individual has its roots on the far side of the abyss, and it is the puncture in space that is Daath through which those roots reach down to all of them.

One who has sufficient ability and spiritual fortitude to even approach this passage is utilising a level of consciousness that is currently unknown to humanity as a whole. He or she who crosses the abyss in any of its forms is the conquering Hero who has overcome the beast – be it serpent, sea devil or Red Dragon – and partaken of the divine light, one who has reached within the self and achieved a balance between ego and instinct such as that equated with the great Taoist work of meditation and 'Inner Alchemy', the 'Golden Flower.'

Following this train of thought, it should be noted that the microcosmic Daath is said to reside at the nape of the neck, where it serves as the symbolic link between the higher genius and the ego. The Middle Pillar exercises used to approach this great reservoir of potential include, for the 'Order of the Golden Dawn', the 'Path of the Arrow' which utilises the pillar and Sephiroth in forms of either a lightning strike or the 'flaming sword', and while no archangel is linked to Daath in the manner that all other Sephiroth have associated angelic guardians, Regardie notes names that John Dee and Edward Kelley applied and which apparently resonated with the eleventh station: 'Elexarpeh', 'Cornananu' and 'Tabiton'.

Kenneth Grant (1924 – 2011 C.E.) makes the point that Daath is associated with the image of the 'mouth' (Hebrew 'Pe') which has a Cabbalistic value of 85; that same number is the value of the term 'endeka' which means 'eleven', which of course denotes Daath's position on the Sephirothic Tree. The mouth is, then, the means of speaking the Word which creates and destroys or, as may be the case, remains silent and maintains cosmic chaos, and the passage or orifice through which matter emerges to take form, or return to its primordial state.

Grant wrote extensively on the subject of the abyss, and described at length the 'Mauve Zone' which surrounds it, the substance of which is the 'marsh effluvium' where the Qliphoth are reflected. He notes that one who goes astray in 'Desert of Set' is to become a 'Black Brother', and going astray is likely for most given the stripping away of self that is required, the deconstruction of the shaman that reduces an individual to his or her innermost state and confronts that individual with the truth of what they are – the result will be a form of madness, whether borne of total breakdown or, in the case of one who wrongly believes that he/she has been granted divine vision, the self-destruction of the messiah complex.

But, again, this is the realm where the Word is unuttered or withdrawn – the primordial waters of chaos – and what finer substance could a magician wish to work with? What greater capacity could be hoped for than where one is harnessing boundless potential in its purest, most malleable condition? The allure is great, and the potential wisdom (and power) beyond normal human means, even if one may lose him- or herself in the process.

The essential point that we keep returning to is that the abyss is not malignant, even if it is wholly alien to us, we who associate chaos and deconstruction only with loss. However the abyss is not the enemy, and the divine source that we seek will only be mistaken as a horror unless we understand the true nature of All, as Grant points out in his *'Nightside of Eden'* (1977): 'The noumenal source alone IS, because it is NOT. Once this truth is grasped it becomes evident that the ancient myths of evil, with their demonic and terrifying paraphernalia of death, hell and the Devil, are distorted shadows of the Great Void (the Ain) which persistently haunt the human mind.'

As has been apparent throughout this present study, any work with the abyss is a work of psyche and psychology as much as, if not more than, the work of spirit and spirituality. Crowley applied this understanding to the tarot, where The Empress and other cards represent the plight of the individual stranded in the abyss, effectively lost within egotism, while The Lovers illustrates the choice between obedience and disobedience to the highest law and The Chariot is the victorious crossing of the abyss, and the piercing of veils to a higher level of being/consciousness (as in Ezekiel's vision).

The Lovers are the key, and Crowley states that the individual must be willing to be destroyed (in a form of self-annihilation) and the true self be united with the universe as a whole, for the passage through Daath and the Mauve Zone of Grant to be successful. Loss of self is not a risk, then – it is a necessity.

The 'opponent' that will inevitably be met has been given various names, though one which gained popularity through application in the Theosophical Society and remains familiar today is that of the 'Dweller' or 'Guardian of the Threshold', actually a literary invention of the occultist and mystic Edward Bulwer-Lytton from his novel *'Zanoni'*. In this guise it is a shadow figure that is the sum of an individual's good and bad actions, a belief echoed by the Theosophists who saw it as the raw karmic energies of all one's incarnations that would be met at the point of initiation, or death.

The appearance of the Guardian is said to be different each time it is encountered, due to the malleable and shifting nature of the abyss, the ever-developing karmic state of the seeker and the fact that the Guardian is itself a shadow. This does not stop its being associated with the archetypal guardians such as Cerberus or the primordial dragon, and certainly does not temper the fear that the frequent aim of the Dweller is to block any passage through its domain, and given that every individual on such a path must meet their Guardian to move beyond the threshold, there is a definite miasma of dread about its inevitable presence.

Aleister Crowley and many others have identified the Guardian as 'Choronzon' (also 'Chozzar' and 'Choronzain', the latter of which unites the concepts of 'chronos' – time and 'zain' – the sword which cleaves the temporal state, including time, in two). First noted in the Enochian works of the Elizabethan mage Dr. John Dee (1527 – 1608 C.E.) and his equally-fascinating partner of one time, Sir Edward Kelley (1555 – 1597 C.E.) where it was described as 'that mighty devil', the role of Choronzon was epitomised by Crowley within his Thelemic system of magick and has since been the epitome of 'dispersion and confusion', the very essence of the abyss, for many mystics and magicians alike.

Kenneth Grant describes this entity as the 'perichoresis of two distinct dimensions' and, in his *'Hecate's Fountain'*, states that: 'the hierophant Choronzon stands between those universes as a point (bindi) at the centre of the twin loops of infinity.' Elsewhere it has been termed the 'functional aspect of the negating factor' and, by Crowley, as the contrary of the process of Magick. Choronzon thus unites the noumenal and the mundane, and actualises through an absence of being – a suitably abstract description for a complex metaphysical idea!

In more relatable terms (though, perhaps, too relatable to aid a sound understanding), Choronzon is linked to the great opponents of religious and spiritual history, most notably of course with the Devil but also Set and Typhon. There is a Cabbalistic basis to this identification of the Guardian of the Abyss, as the Dragon/Beast of Revelation who is said to hold presence in Daath has a numerical value of 666, from which the male Shugal ('the howler of the desert') is 333 and corresponds with what is understood to be the female Choronzon, also with a value of 333.

Nietzsche famously stated that 'If you gaze in the abyss, then the abyss will gaze into you', and this is precisely what occurs when an individual enters the domain of Choronzon; the known self meets the hidden self, with a view to the destruction of the ego so that further spiritual progress can be made. The Thelemic 'Night of Pan' is one ritual with this unification of the All as its focus, but it should be noted how few might actively attempt this – or at least how few should attempt it; indeed, the Guardian is only ever given form in this way and evoked with the belief and intent of restraining and controlling it.

This is not always possible of course, even where it is an adept that is piercing the veil. Though there are inconsistencies in the accounts recorded and there can therefore be some doubt as to the details of the event, Aleister Crowley himself gazed into the abyss and tangled with Choronzon during his work with the Aethyrs in Algiers, in 1909 as he travelled with Victor Neuberg. The tenth Aethyr equates with Choronzon, and with the words of invocation uttered ("Zazas, Zazas, Nasatanada Zazas", which, it is said, Adam used to open the abyss) an ill-fated, and nearly fatal, encounter began.

A magic circle was drawn in the sand, and the Triangle of Solomon outside of it. 'Choronzon' was written in one triangle and three pigeons with their throats cut were placed at each point. The collected blood was poured onto the sand, and Crowley called for the Guardian to take possession of him.

In the most well-known account, Neuberg at one point saw Crowley as a woman who tried to seduce him into breaking the lines of protection, before praising him and offering to worship him. Crowley then reappeared, naked and begging for water. Following further talk, as Neuberg scribbled notes to document the event, sand was thrown onto the marked lines of the triangle, obscuring them and breaking down the barrier of protection – Crowley fell on Neuberg and the two wrestled, with Neuberg close to being strangled, before he managed to utter sufficient names of God to force Choronzon/Crowley back to his original mark, and fresh blood was poured to activate the barriers once more.

With the store of blood depleted and Choronzon apparently exhausted from the commotion, it disappeared. Crowley went on to describe the demon as being the 'black of night' and 'of many things', supporting the earlier point made in the records that there is 'no being in the outermost Abyss, but constant forms from the nothingness of it.' As Choronzon, Crowley said that 'I am I' and declared himself as the 'master of forms; from me all forms proceed.'

No face, feature or trait is therefore a dependable description of this being, which is not a being, and it seems that the sheer overwhelming nothingness, from which the potential of all might emanate, was simply too much for Crowley. This point is clear, whether we accept that a form of intelligence was indeed inducted into the triangle, or should we choose to believe that this was an aspect of Crowley's intense psyche – after all, the latter is exactly what Choronzon is believed to be!

There is an unsettling nature to this figure, as it is the embodiment of chaos in its most unbridled state. Choronzon is shade, shadow and dispersion – constantly changing, there is no fixed being or form to perceive from which one might begin to understand. There is, apparently, no intent, aim or direction, only a profound 'now' that most certainly 'gazes back into' the seeker. It is said that Choronzon hates silence (a vacuum) and that it gains power over an individual through their talking, for in this manner the known self over-exposes itself while the shadow-side remains obscured in the shadows.

Austin Osman Spare rather succinctly acknowledged this weakness in humanity to fill the silence, staunch the vacuum and deplete the self when he wrote in his '*Micrologus*': 'We are overstuffed with words.' Even when the initiate has completed the appropriate trials and enters the arena of the abyss with due understanding of what will be met and how he or she will be confronted and opposed, the human panic at chaos – and its terrible silence – still overpowers and allows the balance of power to shift against them as they attempt to define the formless, and describe the indescribable.

It seems that we are simply too rigid in our thinking and our perceptions to find it within ourselves to remove all blinkers and conditions and allow the chaos of the abyss to wash over us – but can our ways of thinking, perceiving and responding be overhauled, then reconstructed towards a more suitably mercurial and unfixed state? This would certainly allow for a more evenly-matched meeting when we call upon Choronzon, with whatever face or guise our own Dweller of the Threshold might appear to us with.

Embracing chaos and achieving this more plastic form is certainly one aim of Chaos Magic, which makes its ethos the rejection of dogmatism, the 'deconditioning' of the self, the relevance and importance of personal experience and direct personal gnosis. Genuine skill and technical prowess of the magical art is no less a part of the magician's make-up, but within Chaos it is the individual's created mythology that is key rather than the restrictions of those that have gone before, and the individual's connection with a given ritual in whatever form chosen, rather than exhaustive rules and instructions laid down by practitioners of the past.

The aim is to foster a greater degree of power and ability by fully-investing the self within a framework that has especial meaning to that person; music, suffumigation, meditation, daggers, wands, hallucinogens – all can be utilised, or just those that most resonate with the psyche of the magician, or of course none at all, if these accoutrements are seen as trappings rather than the means to a ritual end. In this manner, Chaos Magic does not propagate chaos at all, simply the right of the individual to his or her own method and framework of belief with the allowance that these may well change over time, if not from one ritual or cogitation to another, and while this lack of structure may appear to be chaotic, it is for many modern-day practitioners a much-needed liberation.

Something of this philosophy is represented in the 'Symbol of Chaos' (also known as the 'Chaos Star', 'Symbol of Eight', 'Star of Discord' and more) that was originated by the fantasy author Michael Moorcock in relation to one of his novels, though similar symbols have roots in ancient and eastern religions and Aleister Crowley's Eight of Wands in his Thoth Tarot depicts a similar form, said to be a representation of scattered energies, travelling at great speed:

Where we find the outright adoption of chaos is in the beliefs and practices of the 'Discordian Society' who follow the example of the Greek goddess of chaos, Eris. The progeny of Nox (night) and the wife of Chronos, Eris herself gave birth to children that included Disease, Hunger, Lies, Murder and Sorrow – all 'discord' is thus linked to her, and any misrule or breaking down of order or stability.

Eris was one of the Titan goddesses, who was not invited to the wedding of the human male Peleus and the sea goddess Thetis and as revenge threw a golden apple into the congregation of the Olympians, bearing the mark 'To the prettiest one'. This of course caused havoc, with Aphrodite, Hera and Athene all claiming the apple as theirs, and Hermes asked that Paris judge the true winner to settle the argument.

At first wisely refusing to make a decision, Paris was forced to relent at the insistence of Hermes and the goddesses all disrobed before him so that he could make an informed decision; each of them was truly lovely, but sought to ensure his favour with bribes nonetheless, and it was ultimately Aphrodite (not least due to her sheer loveliness) who was named victor when she promised Paris that he would receive the favour of Helen of Sparta, another of unparalleled beauty.

Of course Hera and Athene were far from pleased with this outcome, and they planned vengeance against Paris for this sleight and began a series of events that would eventually lead to the Trojan War! Aside from teaching us the importance of never angering a goddess, this story perfectly exemplifies the nature of Eris and her brand of chaos – playful (if sometimes spiteful), the prodding at and exposure of ego and the breaking down of order which are the games of a child, a 'happy anarchy' as Phil Hine puts it…though with potentially serious and long-standing effects.

The central tenets of Discordianism are that 'Everyone is a Pope', every individual has the same access to power and knowledge, and that every stimulus is relevant and informative to the magical frame of reference of the magician in question. We might once more echo Crowley and say that 'Every man and woman is a star', though here we are accepting that we are ever-changing, and so our beliefs – and the symbols, images and stimulants that resound with us the most – will also shift and change.

Habit and long-held belief is a form of decay, and there should be no fear in accepting new forms of the 'old' self; far from it, as the latter maintains a vibrancy, immediacy and personal investment that is otherwise lost with any repetition of incantations or the adoption of strictly archetypal imagery that may have no genuine impact on the psyche. Further still, if (as Discordianism holds) there is no true reality, only plastic illusion, then works of fiction are as believable and valid as any myth and any faith, as well as any scientific 'fact' or empirical observation of life.

Discordian mythology states that Eris was the sister of Aneris, both of whom were the daughters of 'Void', and where Eris was the goddess of disorder and being, Aneris was the goddess of order and non-being. Aneris was bitterly jealous that her sister was born in a state of pregnancy as she herself was sterile, and so began to redact existent things into a state of non-existence. This of course suggests the reason for birth, the great coming into being, and subsequent death where that being appears to dissolve, though the truth lies beyond Eris and Aneris as they were simply creations, just as 'order' and 'disorder' are the creations of humanity. Chaos is the eternal form, and the human habit of defining everything including existence in limited ways only limits existence and denies the ultimate nature of All.

With this in mind, Phil Hine suggested that the Holy Guardian Angel is simply a 'Mask of the Void', a temporary and fleeting face that can serve as a gateway to inspiration but cannot be fixed and the connection between conscious self and the Higher Self maintained indefinitely. The point is made, not for the first time or the last, that the belief that something noumenal and divine has been touched may well be true, but only in as far as the divine spark within us can allow – a link it may be to the great Chaos, but not a means of communing with it and/or being invested with its primordial energies and abilities.

Indeed, the ego all too often is what we *believe* or see ourselves as being, not our actual state of existence. Where we are misled by epiphanies to think that we have been lifted above others, chosen from the many and invested with godhood or the role and powers of the Prophet, we are simply being beguiled and imbalanced by the inflated opinion that we have of ourselves. This kind of 'genius' therefore sets in motion an inevitable disaster, with that genius destroyed either by sheer egotism or the crushing realisation of the error made.

Effectively we journey within ourselves to find our reflection, and where we find 'greatness' it is the echo of our own professions of worth, and when Choronzon takes on its most horrific and powerful of guises it is simply the counter-action of our own misguided beliefs and attitudes. Crowley made the salient point that the foolish and deceived make a 'false crown of the Horror of the Abyss' and 'clothe themselves in the poisoned robes of Form.'

Man sees God and survives, but only because he has in truth

only seen an aspect of himself – and the resulting inward spiral of narcissism, obsession and madness are his eventual payment for such heresy. The angels that communicated with Dee and Kelley supposedly said something that applies here to humanity, and the various thresholds within and without it: '...in use we are perfect; misused, we are monsters.'

Austin Osman Spare stated that the augoeides is the most perfect vehicle of kia in the plain of duality. With will, knowledge, one's frame of reference and reality itself an illusion and the Holy Guardian Angel a changing face of the divine within us, a prism emitting different light in different forms at different times, seeing the augoeides as an 'avatar of kia' is the soundest means of contacting divinity without being engulfed by it.

The kia, like chaos and the primordial waters, is what it touches – filling a vessel and apparently becoming it, only to move on when the form breaks down and effortlessly taking on new form elsewhere. To believe that it can be grasped is a nonsense, and the numinous can only be known through an individual's own response to it, thus we must accept the limitations of our relationship with the 'other'. As Spare puts it, we are 'dimensionally chained' regardless our own level of ability or insight, and understanding that is the gateway to a more balanced and meaningful relationship with the numinous.

Spare's methods of reaching higher states of consciousness and the Guardian of the Abyss included the 'Death Posture', staring into a mirror until vacuity takes over, holding one's breath until unconsciousness beckons, engaging in sexual acts so as to reach a state of blissful exhaustion – the resultant state is the closest that we can come to the threshold without slipping through it entirely, and irreversibly. Nietzsche's abyss most certainly gazes back at the gazer because the abyss *is* that of the individual looking inward, ever inward, to look outward.

In addition to the playful disorder of Discordianism, the works of H. P. Lovecraft (1890 – 1937 C.E.) have been enormously influential on certain modern forms of magic. His 'Cthulhu Mythos' as it was later called by readers and other writers perfectly encapsulated the new magical view of understanding and embracing chaos within a new-framework-which-is-not-a-framework, as Lovecraft created profoundly moving and unsettling images of gods and other beings that were ever-present and imminent to humanity, but largely invisible to the eye and thus indefinable.

More powerful still was the overall philosophy that Lovecraft appeared to have, with humans being relatively – if not completely – irrelevant to the wider cosmic story of which the 'Great Old Ones' and others are a part. They are unconcerned by us and our lives and so, like chaos, appear grotesque and uncaring to mortal perception though in truth they simply do not recognise us as a notable form of life. Humanity is growing within and contained by the maelstrom they represent, but in itself has no bearing on the greater picture.

It's also notable that a number of Lovecraft's 'heroes' who narrate their stories are descending, or have descended into, madness due to their albeit sparing glimpse of a god; for the final time we tip our hat to Rudolf Otto and remember the unavoidable outcome of experiencing the numinous, and the works of the Cthulhu Mythos serve as delicious yet troubling accounts of just that kind of fatal interaction between two opposed levels of being.

The Old Ones walk between the known realms; they are of another dimension or another planet entirely and lurk within any and all shadows, including those of the deepest chasms, waters and the dreams of men and women. They exist between the cracks of perceived reality and occasionally slip through as a result of cosmic chance, but wreak havoc and horror without intent, response or care – they are the faceless demon of chaos in its most unadulterated form.

The assorted entities of course includes the great Cthulhu

(not living yet not dead; shape without matter) that resides beneath the Pacific Ocean, but also the likes of Ghatanothoa (first-born of Cthulhu, an amorphous mass that turns any who gaze on it into a living mummy), Juk-Shabb (a giant ball of sentient energy, able to communicate telepathically and a knower of magic), Shu-Niggurath (an Outer God appearing as an evil cloud-like mass with black tentacles that drip slime and the legs of a goat) and Tawil at'Umr (a gate-keeper wrapped in a cloak which suggests a humanoid form but conceals nought but protoplasm).

There is sufficient description to offer a dream-like representation in the mind, but no more, and Lovecraft ensured that his entire 'mythos' remained at best a rough sketch of what it might be, allowing readers to fill in the blanks as they saw fit and discover their own personal face of horror. This served him well as an author of uncanny and eldritch tales, but also as the fount of a magical mythology for the age of the Chaos magician.

The 'Necronomicon', which is perhaps the best known component of Lovecraft's legacy, also serves as a springboard for imagination and rumination. Lovecraft refers to it several times as a legendary grimoire, the work of the 'Mad Arab' Abdul Allhazred, which charts the personages and histories of the Old Ones and offers the means of invocation for them, though the book remains as much of an enigma as those it is said to chronicle – ever just out of reach or sight of those most seeking it.

Numerous books have been published under the name 'Necronomicon' but few follow the mythos of Lovecraft to an appreciable degree, and none truly match the import of the legendary, fictional tome (but, of course, how could they?) The mythos thus remains, as Lovecraft intended, intensely personal for readers and ever-expanding both in the minds of individuals and in the works of new writers, but never to be exhausted or fully defined. These gods truly are the epitome of 'otherness' and, to our eyes, chaos, and can never be tamed or controlled.

Threshold

All of this more recently-developed theory, including Aleister Crowley, A.O. Spare, the Chaos magicians, Discordians and indeed the followers of Lovecraft, suggest an antinomianism that is decidedly at home within 20th and 21st century thinking and culture, even if those traits, ideas and similar movements have existed for some thousands of years previous to the current era. Overturning dogma and restrictions in favour of personal spirituality and the exercising of the individual will is in many ways the zeitgeist, and so finding mystical or magical meaning through the application of fictional entities (and non-entities) is entirely appropriate.

The recent search for the numinous has seen old rules and traditions obliterated in favour of wholly unique efforts, and our understanding of the abyss is the epitome of that development; casting off the shackles of any overarching religion or belief and accepting that *all* forms of thought and *all* forms of ritual can serve a meaningful role is a great liberation that prepares the seeker, at least in some small degree, to better appreciate what they will find should they reach the abyss, as the abyss is *all* potential – dynamic, plastic, unending, other, it is many faces to many different people, at one and the same time.

This concept is hardly new; Hinduism tells of the original androgynous figure becoming self-divided at the point of uttering 'aham' or 'I', and it is that sense of 'I' and what it means that is fundamental in the spheres of mysticism, faith and magic. We must first accept our limitations before we can understand something of the immense potential of the abyss, and from that the 'non-being' that is seemingly alien to us and yet is actually the natural, primordial state.

The Egyptian Book of the Dead as translated by Normandi Ellis makes this point beautifully, summing up our relationship with existence, spiritual belief and magical practise in terms no less relatable or applicable some 3,500 years after its probable composition: 'In seafoam, in swirling and imaginings...I am an urge, an idea, a portent of impossible dreams...I am possibility...Who you are is limited only by who you think you are. I am the word before its utterance...I am a child in the throat of God...I am the name of everything.'

To confront the abyss is to accept death and insignificance – but by encountering the primordial chaos from which we and all around us emerged and will in course return to, we tap endless potential and achieve the closest thing to godhood attainable by humanity, with its blinkered perceptions and responses: an experience with a 'fecund emptiness' that cannot be defined or known, only experienced, and a moment of clarity wherein we clearly understand that we are what we make of ourselves. Truly, 'Know thyself' and know God.

BIBLIOGRAPHY

Abraham, L. *A Dictionary of Alchemical Imagery, 1998, 2010,* Cambridge University Press

Agrippa, H.C. (et al) *The Fourth Book of Occult Philosophy, 1554, 2005,* Ibis Press

Agrippa, H.C. *Three Books of Occult Philosophy, 1531, 1993,* Llewellyn

Ahmed, R. *The Black Art, 1936, 1994,* Senate

Avalon, A. *The Serpent Power, 1918,* The Lost Library

Barrett, F. *The Magus or Celestial Intelligencer, 1801, 2007,* Nonsuch Publishing

Berg, Rav P. S. *The Essential Zohar, 2002,* Three Rivers Press

Besant, A. *The Ancient Wisdom, 1897,* The Lost Library

Besant, A. *Theosophy, 1912,* London, T.C. & E.C. Jack

Black, J. & Green, A. *Gods, Demons and Symbols of Ancient Mesopotamia, 1992, 2004,* The British Museum Press

Boethius, *The Consolation of Philosophy, 1969,* Penguin Books Ltd.

Budge, E.A. Wallis *Egyptian Magic, 1901, 1971,* Dover Publications

Budge, E.A Wallis *Egyptian Religion: Egyptian Ideas of the Future Life, 1899, 1987,* Arkana

Burland, C.A. *The Arts of the Alchemists,1967,* Weidenfeld and

Nicolson

Butler, W.E. *Magic: Its Ritual, Power and Purpose*, 2001, Thoth Publications

Campbell, J. *The Hero With A Thousand Faces*, 1949, 2008, New World Library

Campbell, J. *The Masks of God volume 1: Primitive Mythology*, 1959, 2020, New World Library

Carroll, P.J. *Liber Null & Psychonaut*, 1987, Red Wheel/Weiser

Carroll, R & Prickett, S. *The Bible: Authorized King James Version with Apocrypha*, 1997, Oxford University Press

Cavendish, R. *A History of Magic*, 1977, 1978, Sphere Books

Cavendish, R. *The Black Arts*, 1967, 1977, Pan Books Ltd

Cavendish, R. *The Powers of Evil in Western Religion, Magic and Folk Belief*, 1975, Routledge & Kegan Paul

Cavendish, R. *The Tarot*, 1975, 1986, Chancellor Press

Chireau, Y. *Black Magic: religion and the African American conjuring tradition*, 2003, 2005, University of California Press

Cirlot, J.E. *A Dictionary of Symbols*, 1962, 1976, Routledge and Keegan Paul

Crowley, A. *The Book of the Law*, 1904, 2004, Red Wheel/Weiser

Crowley, A. (ed.) *The Goetia: the lesser key of Solomon the King*, Red Wheel/Weiser

Crowley, A. *Magick in Theory and Practise*, 1929, 2011, Pober Publishing

Crowley, A. *777 and other Qabalistic Writings of Aleister Crowley*, 1973, 1986, Red Wheel/Weiser

Crowley, A. *The Vision & The Voice*, 1972, Sangreal Foundation, Inc, Texas

Davies, O. *Grimoires: A History of Magic Books*, 2009, Oxford Uni-

versity Press

De Givry, E. G. *Illustrated Anthology of Sorcery, Magic and Alchemy*, 1929, 1991, Zachary Kwintner Books Ltd.

Deren, M. *The Voodoo Gods*, 1953, 1975, Thames & Hudson

Drury, N. *The History of Magic in the Modern Age*, 2000, Carroll & Graf Publishers, Inc.

DuQuette, L.M. *The Magick of Aleister Crowley: a handbook of Rituals of Thelema*, 1993, 2003, Red Wheel/Weiser

Eckhart, M. *Selected Writings*, 1994, Penguin Books

Eliade, M. *Images and Symbols: Studies on Religious Symbolism*, 1952, 1991, Princeton University Press

Eliade, M. *Occultism, Witchcraft and Cultural Fashions*, 1976, The University of Chicago Press

Eliade, M. *The Sacred & The Profane: the nature of religion*, 1957, 1987, Harcourt Brace Jovanovich, Inc.

Ellis, N. *Awakening Osiris*, 1988, Red Wheel/Weiser

Fortune, D. *The Mystical Qabalah*, 1935, 1976, Ernest Benn Limited

Fortune, D. *Psychic Self-Defence*, 2006, Glastonbury Books

Frazer, Sir J.G. *The Golden Bough*, 1890, 1994, Chancellor Press

Gettings, F. *The Hidden Art*, 1978, Cassell Ltd.

Gettings, F. *Tarot: How To Read The Future*, 1973, 1993, Chancellor Press

Grant, K. *Beyond the Mauve Zone*, 1999, 2016, Starfire Publishing

Grant, K. *Hecate's Fountain*, 1992, 2014, Starfire Publishing

Grant, K. *Nightside of Eden*, 1971, 2014, Starfire Publishing

Grant, K. *Outer Gateways*, 1994, 2015, Starfire Publishing

Guazzo, F. M. *Compendium Maleficarum*, 1608, 1929, Dover

Hall, M.P. *The Secret Teachings of All Ages*, 1928, 2003, Tarcher/Penguin

Hawkes, J. *Man and the Sun*, 1962, Cresset Press

Hine, P. *Condensed Chaos*, 1995, 2010, The Original Falcon Press

Hine, P. *Prime Chaos*, 1993, 2009, The Original Falcon Press

Jahoda, G. *The Psychology of Superstition*, 1969, 1971, Penguin

Jung, C.G. *Aion: Researches into the Phenomonology of the Self*, 1959, 1978, Princeton University Press

Jung, C.G. *The Archetypes and the Collective Unconscious*, 1959, 1990, Princeton University Press

Jung, C.G. (ed.) *Man And His Symbols*, 1964, 1978, Pan Books Ltd

Jung, C.G. *Psychology and Alchemy*, 1944, 2008, Routledge

Jung, C.G. *Symbols of Transformation*, 1956, 1990, Princeton University Press

Kramer, H. & Sprenger, J. *The Malleus Maleficarum*, 1484, 1928, Dover

Levi, E. *The History of Magic*, 1860, 2011, The Lost Library

Levi, E. *Transcendental Magic: its doctrine and ritual*, 1855, 1955, Senate

Metraux, A. *Voodoo*, 1959, 1974, Sphere Books Ltd.

Miller, M. & Taube, K. *An Illustrated Dictionary of the Gods and Symbols of Ancient Mexico and the Maya*, 1993, Thames & Hudson

Muldoon, S. & Carrington, H. *Projection of the Astral Body*, 1929, The Lost Library

Otto, R. *The Idea of the Holy*, 1923, 2010, Martino Publishing

Ouspensky, P.D. *In Search of the Miraculous: fragments of an unknown teaching*, 1950, 1987, Routledge & Kegan Paul Ltd

Papus, *The Qabalah: Secret Tradition of the West*, 1977, 2000, Samuel Weiser

Papus, *The Tarot of the Bohemians*, 1896, 1994, Senate

Peterson, J.H. *John Dee's Five Books of Mystery*, 2003, Weiser

Peterson, J.H. (ed.) *The Lesser Key of Solomon*, 2001, Weiser

Plotinus, *The Enneads*, 1991, Penguin Books

Reade, W.W. *The Mysteries of the Druids*, 1861, The Lost Library

Redford, D.B. (ed.) *The Oxford Essential Guide to Egyptian Mythology*, 2003, Berkley Books

Regardie, I. *A Garden of Pomegranates*, 1932, 2005, Llewellyn Publications

Regardie, I. *The Eye in the Triangle: an interpretation of Aleister Crowley*, 1970, 1996, New Falcon Publications

Regardie, I. *The Middle Pillar*, 1938, 2007, Llewellyn Publications

Regardie, I. *The Philosopher's Stone*, 2013, Llewellyn Publications

Regardie, I. *The Tree of Life: An Illustrated Study in Magic*, 1932, 2006, Llewellyn Publications

Robbins, R. H. *The Encyclopedia of Witchcraft and Demonology*, 1959 1984, Newnes Books

Roberts, G. *The Mirror of Alchemy: alchemical ideas and images in manuscripts and books*, 1994, British Library

Scot, R. *The Discoverie of Witchcraft*, 1584, 1930, Dover

Seabrook, W. *Witchcraft: Its Power in the World Today*, 1942, 1970, Sphere Books

Spare, A.O. *Ethos*, 2001, I-H-O Books, England

Stavish, M. *Egregores*, 2018, Inner Traditions

Summers, M. *The History of Witchcraft*, 1926, 1994, Senate

Summers, M. *Witchcraft and Black Magic*, 1946, 2000, Dover

Publications

Tedlock, D (transl.) *Popul Vuh*, 1985, 1996, Touchstone

Waite, A.E. *The Book of Black Magic*, 1911, 1989, Weiser

Waite, A.E. *The Pictorial Key to the Tarot*, 1911, 1971, U.S. Games Systems Ltd.

Waterfield, R. (transl.) *Plato's Timaeus and Critias*, 2008, Oxford University Press

Wilhelm, R. *I Ching or Book of Changes*, 1951, 2003, Penguin

Wilson, C. *Mysteries*, 1978, 1979, Granada Publishing Limited

Zimmer, H. *Myths and Symbols in Indian Art and Civilization*, 1946, 2017, Princeton University Press

Material excerpted from **Awakening Osiris** © 1988 by Normandi Ellis used with permission from Red Wheel/Weiser, LLC, Newburyport, MA www.redwheelweiser.com

Thanks to Michael Staley for his permission to reproduce the words of Kenneth Grant.

BOOKS BY THIS AUTHOR

Magic, The Esoteric & The Occult

Sacred Sites...
Bizarre Rituals...
Deities, Demons, and Man as a God...

This book charts the history of magic, mysticism and occultism from their earliest tribal roots, through Mesopotamia, the Mystery schools of Egypt and Greece, the spread of Christianity, the occult philosophers of the Renaissance, the exotic new faiths of the Enlightenment and increased secularisation, to today.

This is a story of revelation, obsession, divinity and deviance, always fuelled by the inherent human need to understand its self, its place and purpose, speaking to the innermost part of us no matter our own faith or philosophy.

BOOKS BY THIS AUTHOR

Black Arts: Journeys On The Left-Hand Path

Witch…Sorcerer…
Vampire…Werewolf…Demon…
The Black Magicians…

Evil, the chaos it is believed to worship and the darkness it is believed to venerate are all terrifying and fascinating in equal measure, affecting countless minds, defining cultures and forging entire histories.

Herein lies the story of evil, and of those said to have worshipped in its name; all manner of night-hags, beasts and orgiasts are to be found in an enthralling story of faith, fear and wholly human division.

Tribal curses – Zombies – Necromancers – Blood Rites – Black Mass…

All are Journeys on the Left-Hand Path, from which few have returned unchanged.

Printed in Great Britain
by Amazon